D1453383

THE COLOR OF
SUNDAYS

Andrew Conte

Blue River Press
Indianapolis, IN

Cover photo by AP/Worldwide Photography
Cover design by Phil Velikan
Packaged by Wish Publishing

Printed in the United States of America
10 9 8 7 6 5 4 3 2

Published by Blue River Press
www.brpressbooks.com

Distributed by Cardinal Publishers Group
Tom Doherty Company, Inc.
www.cardinalpub.com

This book is dedicated to anyone who has ever been told, "No."

Bill Nunn Jr. never wanted me to write a book about him. He challenged me, instead, to learn about pioneering black athletes and the obstacles they overcame. Only then, when I knew the full story, did he give me his blessing. I am grateful that he pushed me to rediscover so many great moments fading into history.

I have strived to recreate every moment of this book as close to reality as possible. Nunn died while I was working on this project, but we had talked many times and he had shared a lot of stories, including some even his family and friends did not know. Every direct quote, fact and anecdote comes from an interview, a news article or another primary source.

By this retelling, I hope that Nunn's legacy will, in the words of Steelers' Coach Mike Tomlin, "live on in the stories told, lessons taught and wisdom shared with those of us who remain."

Photo by Charles "Teenie" Harris, American, 1908–1998. Portrait of Bill Nunn Jr. wearing polka dot necktie, sweater vest, and light colored jacket, posed in interior with two tone walls, c. 1945-1955. Black and white: Kodak Safety Film, H: 4 in. x W: 5 in. (10.20 x 12.70 cm), Carnegie Museum of Art, Pittsburgh: Heinz Family Fund, 2001.35.40758

4

Table of Contents

INTRODUCTION 9

CHAPTER ONE 13

CHAPTER TWO 39

CHAPTER THREE 65

CHAPTER FOUR 85

CHAPTER FIVE 113

CHAPTER SIX 141

CHAPTER SEVEN 171

CHAPTER EIGHT 205

EPILOGUE 237

ACKNOWLEDGEMENTS 249

ENDNOTES 253

ADVANCE PRAISE FOR *THE COLOR OF SUNDAYS*

"*The Color of Sundays* reveals that sports was not separate from the struggle for equal rights. Nunn was a victim of racism and a triumph for humanity. ... His quiet journalism and eye on society helped to integrate much of professional sports and paved the way for open opportunities for players, coaches, and front office staff."

> — *Samuel W. Black, Director of African American Programs, Senator John Heinz History Center in association with the Smithsonian Institution*

"There are countless untold stories tracing back through the history of racially segregated sports. Conte tells the Bill Nunn, Jr. story in a way that will leave you inspired, but also angered at the injustice that he and millions of others had to endure. This biography will leave you with a desire to learn more about this aspect of football's past."

> — *Kent Stephens, Historian & Curator, College Football Hall of Fame*

"By challenging convention and going where other scouts wouldn't, Bill Nunn Jr. forever changed Pittsburgh's Steelers *and* the National Football League. But author Andrew Conte expertly examines issues that remain relevant – specifically race relations and cultural divisions – while telling the story of Nunn, whose impact transcended a franchise, a sport and even a period of time."

> —*Rob Rossi*, Pittsburgh Tribune-Review *sports columnist*

"As a young reporter, I learned a lot of football from Bill Nunn Jr. His story, *The Color of Sundays*, is a must-read history lesson on how sports can overcome racism. Bill was ahead of his time in getting great players of color into the NFL."

> — *John Clayton, ESPN*

"It would be hard to put into words what Bill Nunn meant to so many players, coaches, scouts and other members of the Steelers organization. Having known Bill Nunn, Jr. for literally decades, I was blessed that he shared many stories about his remarkable life experience. I am extremely pleased that Andrew Conte has captured some of the stores about Bill Nunn, as well as stories that Bill himself was fond of sharing with others."

—*Art Rooney II*

"Bill Nunn is one of the most integral, and yet, one of the most anonymous figures in Steelers' history. A work such as this, chronicling who he was, what he stood for and all that he achieved, is a must-read for any fans wanting to truly understand and appreciate where the Steelers came from and what they ultimately became."

—*Mike Prisuta, sports director, WDVE-FM, Pittsburgh*

"A fantastic read on Bill Nunn Jr., a Steelers' legend, whose contributions to six Super Bowl championships are secondary only to his contributions to the Civil Rights movement."

—*Jay K. Reisinger, Esquire, Farrell & Reisinger, LLC, Pittsburgh*

John Stallworth, drafted out of Alabama A&M in 1974, played a hall-of-fame career as a receiver for the Pittsburgh Steelers for 14 seasons. Photo courtesy of the Pittsburgh Steelers.

Introduction

Walking across the football field at Alabama Agricultural & Mechanical University, John Stallworth felt droplets of water from the grass seeping into his cleats, and he shivered at the late-fall chill in the air.[1] One of his football coaches stood with a couple of other players already warming up, but Stallworth hardly noticed them. He knew that the National Football League scouts waiting on the cinder track surrounding the field had come mainly to see him. This would be his only gauge for measuring himself: Run fast enough – covering 40 yards in 4.6 seconds or less – and he might have a chance to play as a professional; run even a tenth of a second slower, and he might not.

The scouts represented professional teams such as the Chicago Bears, Detroit Lions, Pittsburgh Steelers and others. They were among the only white men on the campus of the small black college in Normal, Alabama. By late 1973, the nation's historically black schools no longer remained a secret: NFL insiders knew at least a few of the athletes could play at the next level, as professionals. The challenge was finding the right ones. Stallworth glanced over at the men long enough to see only one black scout, tall and lean with his hair in a thick afro. Stallworth didn't know the man but guessed he must be Bill Nunn Jr.

Alabama A&M's coaches seemed to know Nunn well. He had been coming to the campus for years. Recently, he had been scouting for the Steelers, but before that he had worked as a sports writer at the *Pittsburgh Courier*, a black weekly newspaper with more than a dozen editions across the country – in Seattle and Los Angeles, Miami and New York. Even then, after joining the Steelers, Nunn still picked the nation's 22 best black college football players for the newspaper's All-America team. When the NFL purged all of its black players in the 1930s, young men at black schools still could dream of having their name appear in the *Courier*. Then after the war, even after teams added blacks back to their rosters, one and two at a time, the *Courier*'s All-America team offered the best chance to be noticed. At small schools like Alabama A&M – not known for producing NFL players – Nunn represented a lifeline.

Stretching out his legs in the end zone, Stallworth felt goose bumps break out across his skin as he took off his sweatshirt. The air felt cold for the South, in the upper 40s. He thought about everything that had led to this moment. Growing up two hours away in the former state capital of Tuscaloosa, Stallworth had imagined playing football at the highest levels. He spent Saturday afternoons watching the hometown team at the University of Alabama, dreaming of catching perfect spirals from Crimson Tide quarterbacks Joe Namath and Kenny Stabler.

In reality, Stallworth knew it could not happen. The United State Supreme Court had ruled against segregation when he was a child, and Congress outlawed discrimination based on skin color just days before his 12th birthday. But Alabama football remained all-white throughout his high school days.

Stallworth first attended all-black Druid High School, but the football coach said he was too skinny to play. So when a court order freed up students to choose where they attended, Stallworth transferred across town to the mostly white Tuscaloosa High School as a sophomore. The seniors that year included the school's first black graduates. On Friday nights, Stallworth looked into the stands to see fans waving Confederate flags and he listened to the marching band playing "Dixie." Stallworth had some close friends among the white students, so he figured people waved the rebel flag because they always had, and not because they really wanted the South to rise up and reclaim slavery.

Even if the University of Alabama had been fully integrated, Stallworth would have had a hard time making the team. Tuscaloosa High School won just one game in each of his final two seasons. Stallworth saw himself as a wide receiver, but Tuscaloosa did not have a strong quarterback. The coach convinced him that it made no sense to try catching balls if no one could throw them. Instead, Stallworth played as a tall, lanky running back. It was not a good fit and he had been lucky to find a college looking his way at all. The father of a teammate had attended Alabama A&M, and Stallworth used the connection to introduce himself to the football coaches and ultimately to win an athletic scholarship. Alabama A&M's coaches said they had expected other schools to recruit Stallworth, but he knew he had been lucky to end up in Normal. Like many other athletes, he had little other chance of attending college.[2]

Standing on the field at Alabama A&M's stadium with the scouts watching, Stallworth wondered whether he would have an opportunity to move up in the sport again. Everything hinged on that one-tenth of a second, the difference between winning the scouts' attention or not.[3]

At the goal line, Stallworth crouched into a sprinter's start and looked down the field where the scouts stood waiting with notebooks and stopwatches in hand. Running on the damp turf would not be ideal for a fast time, but going on the cinder track would have been worse. At the signal to start, Stallworth broke out of his stance and covered the grass as quickly as he could, his entire future hanging in the balance of those 40 yards.

As he crossed the finish, Stallworth didn't even look up. He could tell from the men's reactions – their disappointed sighs – that he hadn't been fast enough. He could feel it. Bent over and still breathing hard, the college senior lacked the confidence even to walk over to the men to ask them about his time, to talk about his chances of being drafted or to ask for a second chance. He stood up, grabbed his sweatshirt and pants from the sideline and quietly started walking back to the dormitory. His moment had ended almost as soon as it had started.

At the other end of the field, the scouts felt the window closing too. They stayed around to see the few other athletes run the 40 yards, but without enthusiasm. The man they had come to see had been a step too slow, barely worth the trip to Normal. Certainly a few black college athletes could play in the NFL, but they had to be better. Stallworth had shown average speed and little charm.

The men folded up their notebooks and put away their stopwatches. Moving as a group, they turned away from the field and walked back toward the parking lot with the cinders of the running track crunching beneath their dress shoes.

Nunn, the newspaper man and Steelers scout, walked with them. Life on the road could be exhausting, traveling across the country, stopping at several college campuses a day. The men around him knew it didn't take much to feel sick, especially in this cool, damp weather.

Nunn started coughing. He wasn't feeling well, he told the men. He must be coming down with something. It would be his loss, but he would have to stay behind in Normal. He would have to catch up with the other scouts down the road.

Nunn stood alone, coughing in the parking lot, until the last car pulled away. He watched the men pulling out of Normal, and then turned. Without waiting any longer, he started sprinting – back across the cinder track, in the direction of Alabama A&M's dormitory buildings.

Chapter 1. Black and White

Finding a quiet corner to hear the fight would be easy for an only child. His father would be ringside in New York City, leaving just his mother and grandmother at home in their yellow-brick house on Monticello Street. Summer had arrived early that June with temperatures spiking into the 80s even before the longest day of the year, and the front porch offered the best chance of a breeze. Bill Nunn Jr. grabbed the family's portable radio, took it outside and plugged it in to the wall socket. Even there, the dense city streets would not cool off much in the long twilight after sunset. With canvas awnings up in the summer, porches became gathering places for families from down the block and close friends to meet over a game of bridge or, on a night like this, to listen to a radio broadcast. Few people had cars and many families stayed close, with older relatives living in the home and even aunts, uncles and cousins living nearby. Nunn's family had a car but no close relatives in the neighborhood.[4]

Only a narrow walkway ran between the Nunns' three-story home and the wood-frame house next door. But as blacks on a mostly-white street, the family felt a larger gulf than that between them and their closest neighbors. Irish ward chair Tommy Kirk lived across the street with his wife, Sarah. He often boasted that he had single-handedly turned Homewood to the Democrats over the previous decade as the country struggled through the Great Depression. Republican politics ran thin when mill workers no longer had enough to eat. And Tommy helped tip the balance by going district-to-district with rented buses, driving voters to the election office so they could change their party affiliation. Now, if anyone needed a city job, a street repaired, bail money or even a bucket of coal when they couldn't afford heat, the ward chair could more often than not find a way to help.[5] And yet, even here, the Nunns had the unusual distinction of having a more prominent house than the others. On the street, theirs was not larger than the neighbors' houses but it had flourishes that set it apart, such as the stained-glass panels at the top of a bay window in the second-floor master bedroom where Bill's parents slept.

The house near Pittsburgh's eastern suburbs also had the odd habit of drawing out-of-the-ordinary guests. Many of the nation's best-known black entertainers made a point of stopping by whenever they came through the city, making their visits so frequently that by age 16, Bill thought little of finding a famous movie star, an athlete or musicians sitting in the family's parlor room talking with his father. Stepin Fetchit, the first truly famous black Hollywood star, had been to the home many times. He had become a millionaire with an act that, like his stage name, could be seen as reinforcing the worst white stereotypes of blacks – or mocking them in a way that was ultimately subversive. Big band leaders Count Basic and Jimmy Lunceford had been to the home too, along with Negro baseball stars such as Josh Gibson of the nearby Homestead Grays.[6]

Bill Nunn Sr. had moved his family into the house owned by his boss, Robert L. Vann, four years earlier in 1937[7] when Vann abandoned the city for a larger home in the wealthier suburbs.[8] Vann had come to Pittsburgh from rural North Carolina to attend Western Pennsylvania University[9], where he edited the school newspaper[10] and then became the first black to graduate from its law school in 1909. Working in his own law office a year later, Vann joined the *Pittsburgh Courier* and then started growing it into the nation's largest black weekly newspaper by writing about issues not being covered in the white newspapers, such as mob lynchings of blacks across the South and simple acts of discrimination. When nine teenage boys were accused of raping two white women on a freight train from Tennessee to Alabama in the 1931 Scottsboro Boys case, the *Courier* sent its reporters, along with NAACP President Walter White, to cover the trial. And while the Kirks on Monticello Street turned their white Irish neighbors toward the Democrats, Vann counseled blacks[11] that they, too, should be "turning the pictures of Abraham Lincoln to the wall" and voting for Franklin Delano Roosevelt to be president. [12] The newspaper stressed the need for blacks to get involved in politics and to join groups such as the National Urban League and the National Association for the Advancement of Colored People. Vann wrote a front-page column called "The Camera" that talked about economics and politics while counseling

Photo by Charles "Teenie" Harris, American, 1908–1998, Bill Nunn Sr. wearing flecked three piece suit and jacquard necktie, seated at desk with newspaper, in interior with chair rail, possibly Courier office, c. 1940-1960. Black and white: Kodak Safety Film, H: 4 in. x W: 5 in. (10.20 x 12.70 cm). Carnegie Museum of Art, Pittsburgh: Heinz Family Fund, 2001.35.36647

Charles "Teenie" Harris, American, 1908–1998. Interior of Pittsburgh Courier newsroom, with men, including Bill Nunn Sr. on left, and women seated before desks and tables piled with newspapers, and 1960 North Carolina Mutual Insurance Company calendar on wall, c. 1960. Black and white: Kodak Safety Film. H: 4 in. x W: 5 in. (10.20 x 12.70 cm), Carnegie Museum of Art, Pittsburgh: Heinz Family Fund, 2001.35.25931

blacks on personal finances.[13] Another column called "Your History" educated blacks about their buried or forgotten past. The paper published editorials by early civil rights activists Marcus Garvey and W.E.B DuBois, and it led a nationwide protest against the Amos 'n Andy radio show because it caricatured black stereotypes. By the summer of 1941, Vann had been dead six months, but his legacy continued to live.[14]

Bill Sr. had left a "secure" job in the Pittsburgh Post Office to join the *Courier* staff more than 20 years earlier,[15] working first as a reporter, then as an editor and ultimately as the managing editor, running the newsroom and choreographing the weekly production of more than a dozen editions that served black communities across the country. The paper went to all the major cities. And for many of the rural towns in between, it was the only reliable source of outside news for black readers. Each Sunday afternoon, editors and reporters turned up at the Pittsburgh Courier Publishing Company's offices[16], with the newspaper's banner logo painted onto the sheet-glass window facing the street in the heart of the Hill District neighborhood, just east of Downtown. They would gather stories from reporters across the country, edit the articles and lay out pages. The men wore white shirts, narrow ties and often a sports coat. They sat on wooden, armless chairs and pored over copies of stories that rested in uneven stacks on big oval tables. Women sat among the men in pretty summer dresses, making copy changes on typewriters and throwing out discarded sheets of paper into the metal waste bins by their feet. Fans sitting on filing cabinets beneath rows of fluorescent lights stirred the air, lifting the corners of papers and wafting the hazy cigarette smoke. A map showing Pittsburgh's city neighborhoods hung on a wall nearest to the editors.[17]

The Courier put out 14 editions across the country, and editors started each week by working on the ones farthest away – in Seattle, Los Angeles and Miami – working their way back to closer cities such as Chicago, Detroit and New York, and finally all the way back to the Pittsburgh city edition that came out on Thursdays. By the late 1930s, the newspaper was printing off as many as 250,000[18] copies a week, with only

20,000 of them staying in Western Pennsylvania. The rest worked their way out of Pittsburgh's Hill District first by truck and then by Pullman railcar with conductors who were willing to carry editions of the paper to distant outposts. Especially throughout the Deep South, black ministers and community leaders would wait eagerly each week by designated railroad crossings, watching for the delivery of a stack of newspapers as the train pulled through town. In areas where racial tensions were hottest, drop-offs had to be done in secret to evade whites who wanted to keep out news of black uprisings and successes in other parts of the country.

Bill Jr. worked at the newspaper too, delivering copies of the weekly city edition to his neighbors in Homewood. Wearing a white shirt and long pants, he carried a canvas newspaper bag, imprinted with the words, "Read the Pittsburgh Courier," slung across his shoulders. He had just started a job as a fly boy too, the lowliest role at any publication, pulling newspapers off the printing press so they could be stacked and loaded onto trucks. Then after each press run, he would climb down into the pits below the presses to muck out the ink and clean up the gears so they would run smoothly the next time. Few people in the business could claim to be closer to the actual printed word. When he wasn't working at the *Courier*, Bill made a little extra money at the local corner market, sweeping up for the owner's wife and handing out advertisements about that week's specials.

Pittsburgh's daily newspapers that evening, on June 18, 1941, had been filled like the days before with news of the war playing out across Europe: British Royal Air Force bombers had started their assault on the ports of Nazi-occupied France, while Axis forces posted victories across North Africa. Hitler's top generals nervously chattered too, if unnamed sources could be believed, that Germany might take its battles to five continents – but it could not possibly hope to win: "…informed Germans fear that Britain cannot be knocked out before the American armaments production, now choking along in a halting fashion, suddenly begins to flow in a formidable and unmatchable torrent."[19] From the industrial river valleys of

Western Pennsylvania, the fighting seemed like little more than the distant flash of heat lightning on a cloudless evening. If anything, the news of war meant factory workers could count on steady orders for steel to make bullet casings and battleships.

Americans still felt free that summer to indulge themselves in entertainment. The country had celebrated two weeks earlier when Whirlaway won the Triple Crown of horse racing in Belmont, New York.[20] The Boston Red Sox's Ted Williams seemed to be hitting every other pitch that summer, tormenting American League pitchers with a .424 batting average[21], and the New York Yankees' Joe DiMaggio had gotten a hit in every game for more than a month.[22]

But in Pittsburgh on that evening, only one piece of breaking news had been bigger even than the Nazi advances, topping the front page in bold type: "Louis Weighs In At 199½; Conn at 174."

No bit of information had been more closely guarded in the previous weeks. Loose lips sink ships, and the actual weight of the two boxers facing off for the heavyweight boxing crown might give one side an advantage over the other – or at least tip off bettors.

Known as the "Brown Bomber" – or more poetically as the "Negro Monarch … with dynamite in his lethal fists" – Joe Louis already had defended his heavyweight title 17 times in four years, and only two challengers had even gone the distance. But word out of his camp suggested that the champ, at 27, already had become the old man of boxing "tripping over his whiskers."[23] Rumors said that Louis had let himself slide, putting on weight as he quarreled with his manager, Jack Blackburn, over tactics. Some "smart money boys" even had suggested that Louis planned to lie down in the ring and throw the fight.[24]

But Louis, alone, did not make the fight captivating for Pittsburghers. Many were more interested in his challenger, Billy Conn, the son of Irish immigrants who was better known as the "Pittsburgh Kid." A local boy, he already had made enough fight money to buy his parents a house in one of the city's nicer neighborhoods. Conn had a championship belt of his own, the light-heavyweight 175-pound title. But at 23, the

Irish challenger "blessed with a choirboy face, blinding speed and a heart bigger than his boxing gloves"[25] had given up his title to pursue the much larger purses of boxing's top tier. If the night went as planned and fans packed into the Polo Grounds – the baseball home of the Giants in New York's Upper Manhattan – a gate reaching a half-million dollars would bring even the challenger more money in a single night than any working man could hope to make in 30 years at current wages.

Conn had personal reasons for needing money. He had his heart set on his teenage sweetheart, a beautiful girl named Mary Louise Smith, from Pittsburgh's working-class Greenfield neighborhood. His attempts to win over her father had captivated the nation in the days before the boxing match. "Greenfield Jimmy" had been a major league baseball player and he had no desire for his daughter to date an athlete, and certainly not a boxer. Against his wishes, the couple had applied for a license to be married the day after Conn fought Louis in New York. "Champion or no champion, I'll punch the hell out of that fellow, and he'd probably be the first one to say I could do it," the girl's father told reporters on the eve of the fight.[26] His boast appeared in newspapers across the country. Back home, only one photo appeared on the front page of the evening paper, showing a smiling Mary Louise with a curl in her hair and wearing a sleeveless top, under the headline: "Conn Battles Louis, Cupid and Irate Father of Girl, 18."[27]

With the fight taking place on a Wednesday night, Nunn Sr. put each of the *Courier*'s editions to bed a little early so he could catch a plane[28] to New York City. Nunn made the trip with the newspaper's city editor, Wendell Smith, who had spent the previous year working with photographer Charles "Teenie" Harris to expose the poor training conditions for black troops at Fort Bragg, N.C. The reporters had found the black soldiers carrying sticks rather than rifles, apparently because white officers had been afraid of arming them. Smith also had trained his attention on baseball's Negro league teams and the inequality players faced there too. In 1927, he covered the "world series" between two Negro teams – Chicago's

American Giants and the Atlantic City Bacharachs. The widely heralded feat of the Yankees' Babe Ruth hitting 60 home runs in all-white baseball went unmentioned in the *Courier*.[29]

Chester Washington, the *Courier*'s sports editor, had planned out other arrangements for the trip by train. He already had traveled the country over the previous six years with Louis to write a biography about the black boxer. By following Louis so closely for years, Washington had gained his own loyal followers. For the fight, he had organized a train expedition called the Brown Bomber Special to take 300 boxing fans from Pittsburgh to Manhattan.[30]

Blacks had been excluded from virtually every organized team sport. Baseball never had allowed black players, giving rise to the various Negro leagues. No black player ever had stood on the grass at the All England Club in London for the Wimbledon Championships, skated on the ice for a National Hockey League game or bowled in a professional match.[31]

Football had started out with blacks – playing the strongest and fastest men, regardless of color or ethnicity. But that was before the National Football League stopped signing blacks eight years earlier.

Blacks actually had played prominent roles in founding the game. William Henry Lewis became the first black college player and first black All-American in the 1890s when he played center at Amherst College and Harvard University. He later coached defense at Harvard for 12 seasons before serving as U.S. Attorney in Boston and Assistant Attorney General in the Taft administration, the highest executive branch position ever held by a black at the time. He wrote one of the first books on the game, *A Primer of College Football* in 1896.[32]

Charles "The Black Cyclone" Follis became the first black professional football player in 1904 when he signed a contract with the Shelby Blues south of Cleveland in the Ohio League, a precursor to the NFL. He played on the team with a white man named Branch Rickey, who would go on in later life to integrate Major League Baseball by signing Jackie Robinson to play for the Brooklyn Dodgers.[33]

Even the NFL had started out with prominent blacks. The league formed when managers of 11 professional clubs met in the showroom of Ralph Hay's Hupmobile car dealership in Canton, Ohio, to form the American Professional Football Association on September 17, 1920. They elected Jim Thorpe, the American Indian all-star athlete, to serve as the league's first commissioner.[34] Frederick Douglass "Fritz" Pollard, a black man, played running back that first season and his team won the league's first championship.[35] The next year, he became the league's first black coach.[36]

Despite those successes, no NFL team ever had played more than a couple blacks at any time. By 1933, the entire league had just two black players. And when they were gone at the end of the season, no team owner had signed another.[37]

That, of course, did not mean that blacks stopped playing football. College football remained more popular than the pros anyway, and many of the big schools throughout the North had at least one or two black players. The black colleges, too, had developed their own rich traditions around the game. The *Courier* sent its columnist, Washington, around the country each fall – logging up to 10,000 miles by plane, train, car and bus, he claimed – to watch as many games as possible and then name the best players to the *Courier*'s black college All-America team.[38] The first black college All-Americans in 1925 came from across the country – Lincoln University in Philadelphia and Howard University in Washington, but also Wiley College in Texas, Tuskegee Institute in Alabama and the Hampton Normal and Agricultural Institute in Virginia. Among the players, none generated more attention than Harry "Wu Fang" Ward of Wilberforce University in Ohio, who drew his name either from having a Chinese relative, as the papers reported, or from a popular comic book character at the time.[39]

For the sports writer Washington, who had grown up in Pittsburgh and started working at the newspaper when he was still in high school, picking the nation's best black college players conferred national fame, at least among black readers.

Boxing and track, then, were the only integrated major sports. Blacks had competed at the highest levels of track at the 1936 Olympics in Berlin, and Vann, the *Courier*'s publisher, had traveled there to cover them himself. When he ended up sitting several rows behind Adolph Hitler, in his third year of power, Vann marveled at both the Germans' slavish, methodical support of the *fuhrer* – and the fact that black athletes could successfully compete with the world's best. "It's the greatest thing of its kind I've ever seen," Vann wrote in the *Courier* under his own byline. "Sunday, I witnessed 110,000 people cheer two Negro athletes, because they were supreme in their field."[40]

But the fight ring was the only place in America where a black man could knock down a white without worrying that he might get lynched for it. Jack Johnson had been the first black to win the world heavyweight boxing championship in 1908, inducing the call from many white Americans for a "Great White Hope" to win back the title.[41] Unlike Johnson, however, Louis represented a narrative that connected with the *Courier*'s readers even before he became the boxing champ. He had been born into the family of a poor Alabama sharecropper, and when his father disappeared, his mother had moved north with her children to Detroit. At 17, Louis went to work on the Ford assembly line and spent all of his free time learning to box. He turned pro in 1934 and won 12 straight bouts. When the *Courier*'s Washington and Nunn Sr. met him late that year, they decided immediately to chronicle his experience. The paper started telling Louis's life story in February of the next year. When he knocked out former heavyweight champion Primo Carnera of Italy in June 1935, the *Courier* gave Louis its biggest headline of the year, above a story that reflected the exuberant joy of blacks everywhere – but especially in New York: "Harlem is hilarious with joy. The huge and colorful crowds, reminiscent of Marcus Garvey's best days, caused old-timers to scratch their heads and marvel at the interest aroused through the upward climb and victory of this stolid but handsome youth."[42]

Bill Sr., writing in the *Courier*, had seen a larger meaning in the success of Louis from the start. The boxer not only gave blacks an opportunity to cheer a sporting figure that could compete with the world's best, regardless of color, but he also represented the potential for blacks to succeed wherever they were given a chance on equal footing. Nunn had articulated the arrival of Louis as "the answer to our prayers, the prayers of a race of people who are struggling to break through dense clouds of prejudice and ... misunderstanding, a race of people who, though bowed by oppression, will never be broken in spirit."[43] [44]

The two narratives – of Louis's boxing success and the drive for racial equality among blacks – became so entwined that each time Louis recorded one of his 27 straight victories to start his boxing career, it elicited celebrations among blacks throughout the country, from Harlem and Chicago's South Side to Pittsburgh's Hill District and Detroit. And when he entered the ring in 1936 to take on the Nazi favorite Max Schmeling, Louis stood to win the adoration of even many white Americans who put national pride – stoked by fears of rising German fascism and the Great Depression – above even racial discrimination. But when Schmeling knocked out the "Brown Bomber" in the 11th round, the disappointment among blacks was felt even deeper. Bill Sr. had been there to capture that feeling too: "You could have thrown a stone from 155th Street to Central Park and not hit a soul, Harlem was that quiet."[45]

When the two men had met for a rematch two years later, the fight drew 70,000 fans to Yankee Stadium for what was billed as a conflict of ideals more than just a boxing match between two men. Louis won this time, with a barrage of punches in just two minutes and four seconds of the first round. Schmeling suffered a serious beating that left him with cracked vertebrae in his back. The *Courier*, again, measured up the fight's outsized meaning: "It was as if each (black) had been in that ring himself, as if every man, woman and child of them had dealt destruction with his fists upon the Nordic face of Schmeling and the whole Nazi system he symbolized. It was more than the victory of one athlete over another; it was the triumph of a repressed people against the evil forces of racial oppression and discrimination condensed – by chance – into the shape of Max Schmeling."[46]

Nunn Jr., although a teenager, had not been invited to attend the fight between Louis and Conn. Children rarely traveled in those days, and as his father and his friends headed for New York City and the revelry that awaited them, no one had thought much of bringing extra baggage. So instead, Bill sat down on the concrete porch at the top of a dozen steep steps and turned on the radio. As he always did for a major fight or sporting match, the boy shunned friends and family to find a quiet place. Inevitably when he tried to listen to the radio with anyone else, they started talking and that drowned out the words describing the action. Bill Jr. wanted to hear the broadcast without listening to anyone else. He scrolled through the static to tune in Pittsburgh's WCAE and he heard the sonorous but unfamiliar voice of Don Dunphy, an announcer making his first major broadcast and not yet known as the "Voice of Boxing."

Across the city, another group of boys sat around a kitchen table listening to the same broadcast. The Rooney boys had gathered as they often did with their neighborhood friends from Pittsburgh's North Side at the family's red-brick home. Grass never grew in the backyard where frequent games of football and baseball kept the lot bare. The boys' father, Arthur J. Rooney Sr., had invested heavily in his own passions for sport, starting the city's first professional football team and promoting boxing matches with his mostly silent partner, Barney McGinley, a white-haired saloon owner from the Monongahela River valley steel town of Braddock. Pittsburgh had earned a reputation as the "cradle of ring champions" with a string of blue-collar fighters – white immigrants and blacks. Most fights took place at indoor venues such as the Duquesne Gardens, a drafty former trolley barn not far from the University of Pittsburgh's Cathedral of Learning skyscraper, or in nearby East Liberty at a former car showroom known as Motor Square Gardens. Because Rooney had outsized ambitions, he also had promoted major fights at Forbes Field, the wood and steel home of the Pirates baseball team.

On this night, the Rooney brothers chattered noisily with the friends over whether their father's good friend might pull off the greatest upset in boxing history by taking down Louis at the Polo Grounds. The Rooneys, too, had grown up in the city as the descendants of Irish immigrants, people who had worked hard at bottom-rung mill jobs, on the railroads and in stock rooms to make a place in America while remaining fiercely loyal to their own native tribes. The boys knew Conn personally. He had been to their home many times, and they looked up to him. Their father had helped Conn make a name for himself, rising up through light-heavyweight matches until he wore a championship crown. When Conn moved up in class, Rooney Sr. had helped him there too. He staged Conn's most recent tune-up weeks earlier, when he had knocked out Buddy Knox before 27,000 fighting fans at Forbes Field.

Rooney Sr., of course, also had traveled to see Conn challenge Louis in person. Now his boys sat at home with their friends. Most of them, white and Irish like the Rooneys argued noisily with excitement. Two black brothers, Joey and Clarence White, from down the street, remained mostly quiet as the first words from Dunphy's voice carried across the airwaves.[47]

Inside an orange-brick, three-story home along Fifth Avenue – among the city's most prominent streets in its toniest neighborhood, Shadyside – 17 Conn family members and friends gathered around three radios set up in the house.[48]

Conn's father, known as "Wild" Bill even in the newspapers, and the fighter's brothers, Frank and Jackie, had gone to New York for the fight. Engaged in Army training at Indiantown Gap in central Pennsylvania, Frank received a furlough to attend the fight and showed up in uniform.

Back home, Billy's sisters, Mary Jane, 20, in high heels and a light summer dress belted at the waist, and Peggy Jean, 11, a redhead in a printed skirt, white bobby socks and black-and-white saddle shoes, sat on the front porch of the home with their girlfriends.[49] The boys and men had gathered in the parlor room near a radio built into a phonograph record player.

Billy's Aunt Mary Herr worked the stairs, carrying messages about the fight preparations up to the second floor where Billy's mother, Margaret, an Irish-born woman known to her friends as Maggie, lie in bed. Fighting uterine cancer for two years already at age 41, she was too sick, doctors said, for her to listen to the broadcast of her son's fight. Visitors downstairs had been constrained to silence or whispered urgings because anything louder would disturb Mrs. Conn. She rested quietly in the dark, praying for Billy to survive the beating he would surely take, and telling her sister to share one message with the people downstairs: "Keep praying."

Ringside in New York, 54,487 people turned out to the Polo Grounds – the stadium that stretched from 157th Street to 159th Street between Eighth Avenue and the Harlem River. The heavyweight championship would be the single largest sporting spectacle of the day, topping interest in baseball's World Series, the Army-Navy college football game, the Kentucky Derby horse race, the annual Penn Relays track-and-field competition in Philadelphia and college swimming.[50] Louis, the champ, stood to make the most from the fight at 42½ percent of the gate, or about $180,000. But even Conn, the challenger, would clear $60,000 – more than enough to buy a house for him and his teenaged sweetheart.[51]

For the "sportsmen's special" of $23.75, Pittsburgh fight fans could purchase a roundtrip train ticket to New York, a ticket to the upper or lower tier of the Polo Grounds, a hotel room with a private bath, breakfast at the hotel, and dinner at Eddie's Famous New York Night Club.[52] The Hotel Paris advertised itself as the "nearest modern hotel" to the Polo Grounds and offered a private room with bath for $2.[53] For many visitors from Western Pennsylvania, the stakes of getting to the Polo Grounds seemed high, the local newspaper said: "The thing becomes all the more attractive – and the pulse more quickened – when the challenger is a native son seeking the highest and most valuable bauble in sports history."[54] Irish Pittsburghers had been arriving at Grand Central Terminal for days, many wearing leprechaun hats, waving paper shamrocks and sucking on clay pipes. Hundreds arrived on special train cars arranged for the fight with the Shamrock Special carrying 300 Western Pennsylvania fans, and another called McManus's Ham and Cabbage Special bringing 400.[55] With the mills booming in the buildup to war, many of the visitors arrived with rolls of money that brought to mind the "unfounded traditions that everyone in Pittsburgh is a Mellon or a Schwab or a Westinghouse."[56] Boxing promoter Mike Jacobs, between bites of stuffed crab and herring at Lindy's restaurant in Manhattan, lamented the trouble of trying to keep up with the demand: "I've got trouble enough of my own. Them Pittsburgh people. They write in for seats, like that steel fellow today: he wants 30 seats and he wants 'em all in the first row or he don't want none at all. Them Pittsburgh people – they think they got the champion's win already."[57] Pittsburgh Mayor Cornelius Scully attended along with Democratic kingmaker David L. Lawrence. White celebrities in attendance included comedian Bob Hope and actors Robert Taylor, Barbara Stanwyck and Burgess Meredith.[58] Grantland Rice, the dean of American sportswriters, sat in the second row.[59]

Prominent blacks had come too from major northern cities such as Chicago, Detroit and Cleveland, but also from Charlotte, Norfolk and even Daytona Beach in the Deep South. Lena Horne, the pretty jazz singer who had grown up in Pittsburgh's Hill District neighborhood, sat in the front row with her father, Teddy. William "Woogie" Harris, the brother of the *Courier's* photographer and the father of Pittsburgh's illegal numbers gambling racket, sat nearby.[60] By then the illegal but widely accepted daily lottery brought in more than $3,000 a day with Pittsburghers of every class and color wagering as little as a penny on the daily outcome of three numbers based on the stock indexes and race track finishes: A $1 wager paid out $500 to $700 in winnings – but meant an even more lucrative trade for bankers such as Harris. The money he made had been spread around, in turn, to help local black entrepreneurs' startup businesses, and it also paid for Harris to take his family on regular trips to Europe and South Florida.[61] His daughter, Marian, was famous for driving about town in a Duesenberg, an American-made luxury convertible with so many stretched out curves that it gave rise to the saying, "That's a doozy," for anything extra nice and out-of-the-ordinary.[62] Running the numbers from his Crystal Barber Shop on Wylie Avenue in the Hill District, Harris developed a close friendship with another prominent black, W.A. "Gus" Greenlee over cards, billiards and business. Greenlee had opened the Paramount Inn in the Hill District at the height of the Roaring Twenties, making his own fortune from running a jazz club that doubled as a speakeasy and gambling den. Then going legit, he had parlayed that wealth into opening a classier jazz club called the Crawford Grill and taking ownership of the Pittsburgh Crawfords Negro baseball team. Greenlee had assembled the greatest talents in black baseball – pitcher Satchel Paige, catcher Josh Gibson and centerfielder "Cool Papa" Bell among them – and built his team a $75,000 stadium on Bedford Avenue in the Hill District.[63]

Yet, despite their prominent wealth, Harris and Greenlee had to go through a white broker when they wanted to buy neighboring houses in a mostly white area at the edge of Homewood.[64] After they moved in next door to each other, the men set up a boxing ring in their adjoining backyards and started training a stable of black fighters.

Pittsburgh fight fans who could not make the trip to New York still could get a feel for a major fight night. As the day turned to a long twilight, thousands who wanted the camaraderie of sports turned out to Forbes Field. That night the Bucs would be playing the New York Giants, who by coincidence made their home at the Polo Grounds. The Pirates had been promoting the game for weeks as a chance to see some baseball – and experience the fight: When the boxing started in New York, the game would be halted, the floodlights dimmed and the radio broadcast played from the public address system, despite the infamous ballpark echo. [6566]

The teams had only white players, appearing in front of a mostly white audience. Most men wore a summer weight suit and tie, and many had a felt or straw hat. The few women sitting among them wore dresses.[67] The game drew 24,738 fans – or about four times the season average – and started at 9:15 p.m., the first home night game of the season played late under the prevalent theory that the lights worked better in total darkness than at dusk. By itself the game would "not be a three-star special,"[68] the papers said, despite featuring some of the biggest names in the game: The Pirates' former shortstop Honus Wagner sat in one dugout as a coach, and the Giants' manager Bill Terry in the other. Four future hall-of-famers played in the game: Al Lopez and Arky Vaughan for the Pirates, and Carl Hubbell and Mel Ott for the Giants.[69]

In other places throughout the city, life went on as normal but accommodations had been made so people would not miss out. At the Hill City Auditorium at 2012 Wylie Avenue in the Hill District, the ladies of the Harriett Tubman Guild gathered for one of their regular cards and games nights. Downtown stores and "prominent colored business places" had donated prizes for the winners. Concerned that too many women would rather stay home to hear the boxing match, organizers wired the room with two radio hookups for the broadcast.[70]

Even without the fight anticipation, Pittsburgh, like the country, split along color lines. Public swimming pools were not divided by law but often were separated in practice. Whites at the large public pool in the leafy Highland Park neighborhood stood watch at the entrance to keep blacks away, beating up any who dared to enter until the message was clear.[71] At the Highland and Belmont theaters, blacks sat on one side and whites on the other. At Kennywood, an amusement park up the Monongahela River, blacks could not go in the pool, and they knew better than to go near the park's dance hall.[72] Athletic clubs did not have black members. Many schools had no black teachers, and the white ones often did not encourage black students to pursue college-preparatory classes.[73]

Nunn Jr. had experienced the discrimination himself, like other blacks, but also as a talented athlete. Despite playing basketball well enough on the playground to beat many kids his age, he had been frustrated to not be invited to try out for the official team at Baxter Junior High School. The team did have a couple of black players – but school officials felt they could not take too many, and certainly not one with Nunn's bad attitude.

It was only when the blacks who had been left out formed their own intramural team that an administrator discovered how well they played and asked the coach to make an exception. They went on to win a city title and lead the city in scoring.[74]

The fight, however, had made the city's racial lines even brighter.

Betting wagers favored the bigger, more experienced Louis with 13-5 odds in favor of a win and 3-2 odds on a knockout. But Pittsburgh's white Irish fight fans believed that Conn would overcome a 25-pound weight deficit by being faster and smarter. Pittsburgh's evening newspaper showed a cartoon of a trim Conn landing a left hook to Louis depicted with a soft, oversized face surrounded by powder puffs.[75]

Hometown boosterism had a lot to do with the support for Conn: Mayor C.D. Scully issued a statement that clarified the city's official position on the outcome: "I know that I express the wishes and desires of every resident of the city when I say – from the standpoint of civic pride – that we hope Billy can bring home the title." But racial and ethnic pride played a big part in the prognosticating too. "Why, Billy has so much speed he'll make Louis think there are two men against him," Walter Monaghan, the city's inspector of detectives, boasted. Fire Chief Nick Phelan agreed with the common wisdom: "Billy will make him look bad, then cut him up, then make a monkey out of him in the late rounds." At the mere suggestion by a white bartender that the champ might have the edge, white-haired Tom Flaherty of Beltzhoover jumped out of his seat to yell across the counter. Asked about the fight, John J. Reilly, a traffic cop supporting his fellow Irishman, stood on a street corner south of the city wearing his black-and-white cap, a white shirt and black bow tie, with his right fist raised to show how he believed Conn would win. "Conn will show everyone that brains still mean something in the sports business," Dick Cooley, a sandlot umpire, said. "He's too smart for Louis and figures to box him until he thinks he is on a merry-go-round."[76]

Not every Pittsburgher favored the Irish challenger. In the *Courier* that week, Nunn Sr. took exception to all the support for Conn. "Just what weapons does the Irisher possess which would warrant anyone believing he can beat the champ?" he asked in a column that covered the front of the sports section. The newspaper had polled 23 boxing experts nationwide and found just two who favored an upset. Because Conn had never lost to a black man, Nunn wrote, he must believe that none could beat him even with Louis's experience and size. He gave

Conn a one-in-ten chance of winning – and even then "the Gods of Chance, the Goddess of Fate, the referee, the judges AND Lady Luck must be riding in his corner on that eventful night."[77]

Even Conn's backers agreed that he might need a little help at least getting into the heavyweight bout at the Polo Grounds. Fast and strong, Conn also had a habit of starting slowly. His handlers had toyed with various ways of warming him up before the heavyweight challenge and keeping him that way. Johnny Ray, his manager, had tried winning a concession for Conn to enter the ring hot, without sitting through the usual prefight festivities and instructions. But Louis's camp, of course, rejected that proposal.

Then a New York company had proposed another solution: an electric blanket that could be plugged into an outlet in Conn's corner. Reporters pounced on the idea, suggesting that Conn could "squat on his stool and be simmered or done medium rare." But when the proposal was revealed as a ruse anyway – concocted by a former reporter hired by promoter Mike Jacobs to build interest in the fight – a compromise was offered for both fighters to enter wrapped in conventional blankets. [78] Conn's handlers still planned to put him through eight rounds of sparring before he entered the ring.

By 10 p.m. in Pittsburgh, the Giants had finished batting in the top of the third inning when the game at Forbes Field was stopped for the fight broadcast. The Pirates were leading 2-1. As the ballpark's floodlights dimmed, many of the baseball players headed for the clubhouses to listen to the game, while a few lingered out with the fans to hear the echo of Dunphy's voice.

Pitcher Cliff Melton, figuring the fight experts were right about Louis defending his title, got up to start warming up for the game to resume quickly.[7980]

Sitting at the top of the dozen concrete steps leading from the street to his home on Monticello Street, Nunn Jr. expected a short evening too. Even when Louis fought John Henry Lewis, a black light-heavyweight champ who had trained in the backyard ring behind the houses that Harris and Greenlee owned, Nunn had rooted for the champ. At a time when black athletes were shut out of most sports, Louis had been given a chance to stand toe-to-toe with whites – and he had won. Lewis, the first light-heavyweight champion to move up in class to challenge the champ, was knocked out in the first round. Nunn, like many fight fans, expected Conn to face a similar fate.

Ring announcer Hank Balough stepped to the center of the boxing ring at the Polo Grounds wearing a white jacket and black bow tie, barking loudly over the roaring crowd to introduce first the champion: "From Detroit, Michigan, weighing 199-and-a-half, he's wearing black trunks... Joe Louis." The noise level spiked with cheers as well as choruses of boos. Louis barely acknowledged the crowd, lifting his arms slightly while two men – trainer Blackburn and another – helped him take off the white robe he wore from the locker room.

The announcer turned to the opposite corner where a group of men huddled around the challenger, feverishly rubbing his back, arms and legs to keep him warm. "From Pittsburgh, Pennsylvania, weighing 174, wearing purple trunks, the... the very capable challenger Billy Conn." And the crowd roared louder still.[81]

From the start, Conn moved like a dancer, darting close and then away as Louis traced him in a circular motion trying to size up a heavy blow. Both men stood about the same height at 6-foot-1-inch, but Louis's arms had a reach nearly three inches longer. While Conn moved quickly, Louis turned like the turret on a military tank following its target but never pausing long enough to take aim and launch a shell. In the opening round as he tiptoed constantly, Conn lunged forward with his left, hit nothing but air and slipped backwards to land on the mat. Louis, ever the gentleman, stood and waited as the referee stepped in to give Conn time to stand up and regain his composure. Despite the fall, Conn's strategy seemed to be working as he absorbed a few hits from Louis but mostly darted out of the way and moved quickly to time his own lightning strikes, hitting the champ amid the flashes of ringside photographers' bulbs. The moves left Louis blinking and pawing as if the "Pittsburgh smoke was getting in his eyes," as one fight reporter put it.[82] For Louis, fighting Conn was like "trying to catch an animated jumping jack who kept thumbing its nose at you and bobbing away," said Washington, the *Courier* columnist.[83]

White sports writers continued to see Louis through the jaundiced lenses of the time, calling him the Negro with "coffee-colored features." When the fight turned against him, one said that the champ sat in his corner facing his trainer, Blackburn, looking like a "little boy listening to his dad."

From the 8th round on, Conn seemed to be dominating, and even Louis started feeling the fight had turned against him. The challenger, two times faster than the champ, rattled left hooks and jabbed at Louis, circling constantly and shooting for narrow openings. Miraculously to everyone except the blokes back in Pittsburgh who had wagered with their hearts instead of their heads, Conn's strategy seemed to be working. Already known for his big mouth in the days leading into the fight, Conn came out of his corner at the start of the ninth and leaned into the champ, saying, "Joe, I got you."[84]

A bemused Louis could only respond, "I know it."[85] Trying to counter Conn's speed, Louis landed hooks to his body in an attempt to slow him down.

Back in Pittsburgh, Conn's sisters and cousins felt the excitement. Everyone in the house had been warned to lower their voices to a whisper so they wouldn't disturb Billy's dying mother, but it was becoming clear that would not be possible.[86] Billy's Aunt Anna McNeely had been too nervous and darted out of the house when the fight started. At the end of the 10th, after listening about Conn still landing left hooks through narrow openings, his sister Mary Jane blurted out, "Yeah, and the smart guys said he wouldn't even last that long."[87]

After another round in which he increasingly swung his left at Louis with confidence, Conn turned for his corner with his right mitt lifted in the air to acknowledge the cheers raining down from the crowd.

Across the ring, however, Blackburn bent over his fighter and whispered into his ear. He warned Louis that he had fallen so far behind that only a knockout would let him keep the title. Louis knew it was true. For the first time in 18 title defenses, he thought he might lose.[88] But the trainer had noticed too that as Conn kept swinging with his left – now in an attempt to knock out Louis – the challenger kept missing and leaving his jaw wide open. Louis would have to find an opening and deliver a decisive blow. Too battered for talking, Louis nodded in reply.

With seconds left in the 13th round, Conn waved at Louis with a left hook that fell six inches wide and the champ moved inside with a hard right to the jaw, followed by seven punches to Conn's body and face. He had thrown very few punches to the face until Conn was in a bad way. Someone from Louis's corner shouted, "Now, now."[89]

Louis felt the challenger's body give, and knew he was going down.[90]

On the front porch of the orange-brick house on Fifth Avenue, Helen Holzappel, the fiancé of Conn's brother Frank, let out a loud shriek, and his sister Mary Jane held her hands up over her eyes. A family friend, Marie Schremer, gasped as she stood holding her hands in prayer. Inside the parlor, Billy's 6-year-old cousin Davey accidentally toppled a stack of phonographic records and shattered them, including a disc with the song "It Makes No Difference Now."[91]

Inside the Rooney house on the Northside, most of the boys had been cheering wildly for Conn and then they fell suddenly quiet – except for the two black brothers from down the street. Silent for most of the night, they now let out a cheer. The oldest Rooney boy, Dan, turned on them: "What are you guys cheering about? Conn's been knocked out!" The boys just smiled and said, "We've got to go home."[92]

The fight crowd at the Polo Grounds had gone from feigned amusement over the challenger's chances, to deep interest as he hung around, to profound amazement as he scored points against the champ and then to sheer delirium as it seemed they were witnessing an upset.[93] Now the 55,000 fans stopped nearly still. Conn tried lifting himself from the mat, slipping first and then rising to his knee, as the referee counted out to ten. The fight he had been winning through nearly 13 rounds ended with him unable to get back to his feet.

"Maybe I had too much guts and not enough common sense," Conn told reporters moments later as his manager reached out with a towel in one hand to wipe a trickle of blood from the challenger's face.[94] In his other hand, the trainer held a bottle of smelling salts, waving it every few minutes under the boxer's nose – and occasionally under his own.

Knowing that the interview was being broadcast and that his sick mother would be listening at home, Conn sent her a special message: "Hello, Mother. I hope you're all right. I'm okay."[95]

Conn sat inside his dressing room inside the Polo Grounds with a towel wrapped around his body, sweat from the ring running on his head and chest, and brownish spots on his right shoulder where he had landed in the ring moments earlier. Friends walked up to congratulate Conn on a great fight but the boxer kept his head low to his chest, sobbing.[96] He had become, as the papers would declare the next day, the only fighter to win and lose a title fight in the same night.

Jacobs, the boxing promoter, had been described as having a heart of granite and no more emotion than a contented cuttlefish in warm water. Yet in the moments after the fight, he seemed to feel Conn's disappointment personally. He walked into the locker room and headed straight for the boxer, kissing him on the cheek and whispering words of encouragement and a promised rematch into Conn's ear.[97]

Another of Billy's aunts, Rose McFarland Shook, had listened to the fight on the front porch with the girls, keeping her eyes closed and her hands tightly folded in prayer as she listened to the fight broadcast. She gasped when Louis dropped her nephew to the mat in the 13th round. And then she had taken the long walk up the stairs to the second floor to tell his mother what had happened.

Waiting quietly in the dark as the house around her rocked first with her son's quick jabs and then filled with the sudden groans and shrieks when he went down, Maggie Conn already knew the outcome. Too weak for much emotion, she said in a whisper, "I'm awfully proud of him."[98]

She would be dead 10 days later.[99]

The stress of listening to the fight had been so great that newspapers blamed at least four deaths on the outcome.[100] Harry H. Downs, 79, a retired claim agent from the New York Central Railroad listened to the fight broadcast at his apartment in Pittsburgh's Fairfax Hotel. He had been suffering a chronic heart condition for years. An ardent fan of Conn, Downs turned to his son, Kenneth, in the 10th round when the upset seemed to be building: "If I can just live to see the end of this fight, I'll die happy." He gasped, collapsed from a heart attack and was dead by the time a doctor arrived.[101]

Pittsburgh fight fans listening to the game at Forbes Field sat in stunned silence as players for the Pirates and Giants trotted back out. At times, it had seemed like the fight was taking place right there in front of the audience. When word of Conn's early successes came across the public address system, the crowd had roared its approval, and at times the shouts and cheers grew so loud that they drowned out the broadcast. As long as the Pittsburgh Kid remained ahead, few people cared. When Conn first slipped and Louis allowed the boxer to regain his feet, the crowd in the ballpark even politely applauded. Then, as at the Polo Grounds in New York, near the end of the 13th round, a disbelieving hush fell over the audience.

The game delay had lasted 56 minutes. The baseball players returned to the field and Melton, the pitcher, warmed up again. Fans in the audience hardly seemed to notice the action had resumed for at least an inning, and it hardly mattered anyway.

The Giants scored a run to tie the game at 2-2, and umpires were forced to call the game in the 11th inning well after 1 a.m. because of a baseball curfew.[102] [103]

By the following day, Conn would be old news even in Pittsburgh. The evening paper still carried a fight story on the front page with the headline, "Conn 'Blows' Great Chance to Win Title." His picture appeared above the fold, sitting in short pants and a sleeveless T-shirt on the ground next to his sweetheart, Mary Louise. Engaged to be married after the fight, the couple had simply disappeared from reporters with her father still fuming and threatening to beat up Conn.

War news returned to top billing. A bold-print headline warned: "Yield or Face Invasion, Nazi Threat to Russia." And President Roosevelt, in a story nearby, had issued his own statement: "We and all others who believe as deeply as we do, would rather die on our feet than live on our knees."[104]

Americans might have been distracted for a moment, but the reality for most had returned as quickly as Louis had reclaimed his title after 12 doubtful rounds.

Each time Louis defended his title, blacks, it seemed, had more to lose than gain from the outcome. Louis had emerged as a black hero. But if Louis went down to a white challenger, many blacks would see it as a setback for them all. Nunn Sr. spoke for black Americans when he described relief over the outcome of the Conn fight: "For our money, Joe Louis is still the greatest champion ever to grace the ring. He proved tonight that he had it in him. With the chips all down … with the cards stacked against him … with 50,000 white folks pleading for Conn and 5,000 Negroes praying for Joe to win … the winner and still champion, Joe Louis … Thank God!"[105]

Blocks away from the Polo Grounds in Harlem, the party continued longer than anywhere else. When it seemed Conn might pull off the impossible, people standing in the streets and sitting in parlors sent up silent prayers for the champ. Some had been there since the early morning, waiting outside the Theresa Hotel to catch a glimpse of their boxing hero as he arrived. That night, they had cheered when he entered the ring amid a chorus of boos inside the Polo Grounds. And as the fight crowd had swelled with the lusty roars of thousands on the verge of witnessing an upset, the street revelers had fallen silent.

In the penultimate 13th round, as the stadium fell still with the static energy of the moment, Harlem had erupted with certainty that its man had overcome again. The fight had seemed closer at times than any of Louis's previous title defenses, and the customary celebration – mixed this time more than ever with a collective exasperated sigh – stretched into the night. Jitterbugs danced on the street corners and a throng of revelers filled Seventh Avenue.

"Another lucky night," shouted one man.

"Yeah, lucky for Conn, Joe didn't kill him," shouted another, with the crowd around him roaring its approval.[106]

In Homewood on his family's front porch, surrounded by white Irish neighbors sitting on theirs, Bill Jr. turned off his radio and quietly went to bed.

Chapter 2. Double Victory

The news of America's entry into World War II arrived on Monticello Street just like the word of Joe Louis's thundering knockout blow six months earlier, over the radio airwaves. A male reporter hammered out the first detailed report of the Pearl Harbor attack with a staccato delivery over WCAE-AM on a cold, gray December afternoon with snowflakes spitting through the air: "Japan's game became crystal clear today. Her desire was war – war with the United States."[107]

Disinterested Americans suddenly took notice. Young male volunteers flooded military draft offices. Mill workers saw the return of steady hours and around-the-clock activity. People across the United States felt an instant pang to defend their country and take the fight overseas before it could return to their shores.

In New York City, bellhop Floyd White felt the swelling fervor of patriotism too. Taking a break from his job, he walked to the nearest American Red Cross blood donor center to roll up his sleeve and help meet the surging demand for blood. He entered the office and presented himself to a nurse at the reception desk. She told him to have a seat. He sat there, next to her desk, wearing his winter overcoat and holding his hat in his lap, for the rest of the afternoon. No one called his name to take his donation. Despite emerging scientific evidence that skin color did not determine blood type, the Red Cross refused to take donations from blacks.

The U.S. Navy limited blacks to serving as messmen. They could shine shoes, swab decks and perform other menial cores – but they could not sail a ship, fire weapons or become officers. They had shed their blood at Pearl Harbor right next to white sailors, but back home, other blacks could not even give blood to help the war effort.

That sort of discrimination cut into black Americans' patriotism. It felt no different than the Jim Crow rules that persisted across the country to keep blacks from swimming with whites in pools or from sitting next to them in theaters. Black children across the South had grown up without ever having a single one-on-one conversation with a white person. Now the same Uncle Sam that told blacks they could not send their children to school with white neighbors wanted Americans to send their sons to die overseas in a fight against racial discrimination. It was too much for some to accept. Called to join the fight, some blacks answered with skepticism.

The *Pittsburgh Courier* gave voice to their concerns: Segregation in the United States had its roots in the same racial superiority that drove the nation's enemies through the "cult and curse of Hitler and Hitlerism, Japanese and Italian fascism."[108]

In the house of the newspaper's managing editor, the feelings were no different. The Nunns asked the same questions as other black Americans: How could people who were told to sit in the back of the bus risk their lives to save others – while gaining nothing for themselves?

Bill Nunn Sr. and his wife already knew the answer. Like others of their generation, they had asked this question before. In the first World War, blacks joined the fight with unwavering patriotism and a fragile hope that risking their lives abroad might lead to better treatment at home. But when black soldiers returned home to the South in their military uniforms, holding their heads high with the pride of defending freedom in Europe, white supremacists pushed them back down. Whites had forced black soldiers to take off their uniforms, tearing them off if they refused and lynching those who put up a fight. The experience left many baffled – heartlessly discouraged and dismayed.[109]

To a new generation of blacks, the problem seemed so obvious. America's own ways made it weaker. The Japanese fought with every resource, but the United States left behind a significant percent of its forces based on the color of their skin. American battle efficiency would be strengthened by forcing the Navy to "enlist and promote sailors on the principle of the best man for each rating, regardless of race, creed or color," Charles Houston, the dean of the Howard University Law School in Washington, wrote in a letter to the Secretary of the Navy on Christmas eve.[110] Without seeing that kind of fairness, many black Americans still would side with the war effort – but only out of loyalty rather than genuine enthusiasm. "Today if those crackers in the South had to choose between a Japanese invasion and devastation of their lands, and giving up their beloved Jim Crow cars and schools, they'd choose the Japanese," black newspaper columnist J.A. Rogers predicted. "No, we have nothing to fight for. Wars may come and wars may go, but Jim Crow goes on forever."[111]

And yet, blacks could not help feeling American either. An attack against the country, threatened everyone. It was as if a member of a bickering family had been punched by a neighborhood bully, black columnist Jule B. Jones told her readers across the country. "The United States is our family," she wrote. "The Japanese brought trouble to our doorstep last Sunday morning … and this U.S. family doesn't like it!"[112]

Blacks had reasons to care about this fight too: The foreign invaders had raised the banners of racial purity. No one had forgotten how the Nazis' white boxer Max Schmeling had come to New York five years earlier to box Joe Louis. He had come not only to win the fight but to dominate the Brown Bomber on behalf of the white race. Schmeling had won the first bout in a stunning upset to Americans and blacks especially. But Louis had settled the score in a rematch with devastating impact, sending Schmeling to the hospital. "The American colored man has a personal score to settle," yet another black columnist Joseph Bibb wrote. "We are not forgetting our grim battle at home to win civil rights, but the paramount thing for us to do at this time is to join in the common cause."[113]

Nunn Sr. and the editors at the *Courier* had to decide where the paper would come down. Blacks across the country would read their advice and use it to make up their minds about what to do. The *Courier* could not ignore black fears or the struggle to win equality and freedom at home – but blacks needed to fight racial segregation wherever it occurred, and sitting out the war effort would cause more resentment and danger when the fighting ended. The coming years would be hard for all Americans, the editors knew. But it would be especially confusing for their readers.

"From the cotton fields and cane-breaks of Dixie, our sweat and our toil has made of impenetrable wildernesses, fertile fields which made this beloved country of ours the most precious gift we have," the *Courier's* top management wrote in a front-page editorial after Pearl Harbor.

Blacks should not forget their battles at home, the paper said, and it pledged "unrelenting warfare against the enemies within our gates."

But it also called on blacks in every part of the country to support the United States' government and its military through the war. This would be a battle with two fronts, at home and abroad.

"Certainly," Nunn and the editors wrote, "we should be strong enough to whip both of them."[114]

Black Americans already were fighting on two fronts anyway.

There were leaked stories of a black Navy messman, believed to be aboard the battleship USS Arizona during the Pearl Harbor attack, who had watched his commanding officer die and then grabbed a gun to fire back at the enemy until he ran out of ammunition and the ship had started to sink. However, military leaders refused to identify the messman or reveal the details of the story.

The War Department might not want to name the man. But the *Courier* did.

Still in high school, Bill Nunn Jr. had his own battles to fight.

Not only had he been allowed to play basketball at Westinghouse High School but he had been named team captain. That had been no small thing. Nunn still had never seen a black teacher. And as in junior high, he and his friends only had been invited to try out for the official squad after starting their own intramural team and displaying their skills. His junior high coach had recommended Nunn for the high school team, but it was said that the freshman student had an attitude, and no one wanted him. That was until they saw him play. As a junior, after he made the team, Westinghouse won its first section title in some 20 years.

By his senior year in the fall of 1942, nine months after the Pearl Harbor attack, the nation's war effort had crept into high school basketball too. One of the team's white starters had been drafted and the coach needed to replace him. Already, Westinghouse had two black starters – Nunn and a younger classmate named Chuck Cooper. The next best guy seemed to be Paul Devon, a black track star who played hoops in the playground summer leagues. But starting him would put three blacks in the starting lineup with two whites. The coach wouldn't do it.

Angry about the injustice – but maybe even more steamed about the team's diminished chances without its best players – Nunn sensed what was happening and called a team meeting before the season started. All of the boys, white and black, knew Devon gave them the best chance of winning.

Nunn stood at the center of the group of boys as they huddled in the high school locker room.

"Look," he said, turning to meet their eyes, "we're not going to have a team unless Coach puts Paul on it."

If any of the white players disagreed, none spoke up.[115]

With the team behind him, Nunn then went to the coach.

"No disrespect…," he said, but the boys had agreed no one would play if the best players did not start – and that meant starting Devon. It was almost unheard of for a high school player, let alone a black player, to give the coach an ultimatum but Nunn had done it.

"Well, Bill, let me think about it," the coach said.

It turned out that he really didn't have the final say anyway. The coach, in turn, went to the principal and let him know Westinghouse would have a team with three black starters – or no team at all.

School administrators relented. Westinghouse won the city championship and Devon ended up as the second-highest scorer in the City League, ahead of Nunn, Cooper and every other player on the team.

The war hurt America's professional sports too. Three National Football League games were being played when the Japanese started the Pearl Harbor attack. A public address announcer at the Polo Grounds in New York interrupted the game between the Giants and Brooklyn Dodgers to tell servicemen in the stands to report to their units. At Griffith Stadium in Washington, announcers paged high-ranking government leaders and military officers without saying the reason. Reporters were told to contact their home offices. The fight had started.

Within a year-and-a-half, so many men had enlisted or been drafted that some NFL teams no longer could keep playing. The Cleveland Rams sat out the 1943 season without enough players, and the Pittsburgh Steelers had just six players turn up for camp.[116] Threatened with the prospect of forfeiting the season too, Pittsburgh's owner Art Rooney Sr. reached out to the owner of the Philadelphia Eagles, which had 16 players in camp – technically enough to field a team, but only barely.

The owners agreed to merge for that fall, playing officially as the Eagles in their green and white colors, but quickly known to reporters and fans by the nickname *Steagles*. With two games in Pittsburgh and the rest in Philadelphia, the team finished with five wins, four losses and a tie.[117]

A month after the Pearl Harbor attack, James G. Thompson, a black, 26-year-old cafeteria worker from Wichita, Kansas, sat down with a pen and paper to sort out his feelings about the war in a letter to the *Courier*. Thompson wanted to join the war effort but feared what would happen if he did. Certainly there would be discrimination in the military, without a doubt. And if black Americans joined the military effort, he wondered, would they lose focus on the fight against discrimination in the United States.

"Should I sacrifice my life to live half-American?" Thompson wrote. "Let we colored Americans adopt the double VV for a double victory: The first V for victory over our enemies from without; the second V for victory over our enemies from within. For surely those who perpetrate these ugly prejudices here are seeking to destroy our democratic form of government just as surely as the Axis forces."[118]

Nunn Sr. and the *Courier* editors agreed, running Thompson's letter along with his photograph. Then they took up the challenge: The editors designed a "Double VV" graphic, and they challenged readers to hang up the symbol, starting a war on two fronts.

While writing his letter, Thompson had made up his own mind about his conflicted feelings.

"I love America and am willing to die for the America I know will someday become a reality," he wrote in closing.

Within 14 months, he had enlisted and was assigned to work as a supply office typist with the 395th Coast Artillery Battalion in Camp Davis, North Carolina.[119] As it turned out, he would be a far distance from the overseas action – but he would be in the heart of the battle for fairness at home.

Blacks' frustration with segregation carried over to football too. The NFL had remained all-white in the decade since 1933, and black college players had few options after graduation to play the game for money.

At the University of California Los Angeles, the football team went undefeated in 1939 and its famed "Touchdown Twins" were blacks – Kenny "the Kingfish" Washington and Jackie Robinson, famous for college football long before reaching immortality on the baseball field. Though Washington finished with 1,370 yards that season – the most of any college player – he was named to only the All-America second team.[120]

Unable to play in the NFL because of their skin color, the college graduates joined teams in the startup Pacific Coast Pro league, which allowed blacks and had teams in Los Angeles, San Diego, Fresno and other West Coast cities. Washington had become so famous for his exploits at UCLA that he became an instant draw for fans. Even before joining the league, he had been the main feature of two exhibition games in 1940 featuring "The Kenny Washington All-Stars." Washington made $1,000 from each game, while another black former UCLA teammate Woody Strode, an end, made $750.[121] Then as soon as he signed with the new league's Hollywood Bears, Washington instantly became its greatest marketing draw with his name printed on the tickets. Washington, again, made good money: $200 a game plus a percentage of the gate, which sometimes paid him as much as $500 per game. That was more than even many white NFL players.[122]

Now with the war underway, the black players found themselves swept up in it too. Washington, Strode and Robinson met on the football field for one last time on New Year's Day in 1942, less than a month after the Japanese attack. Now the former teammates played on opposite teams with Robinson leading the Los Angeles Bulldogs. The game played out under the sunshine in front of 10,000 fans at Gilmore Stadium, the Bear's home stadium, built on a former oil field with views of the Hollywood Hills from the gridiron. A decade later, it would be torn down and become the location for CBS Television City.

Knowing their chances of playing on the same field were dwindling with the draft coming, Washington gave what was touted as the "grandest gridiron exhibition of his sparkling career." With the score tied at 3 late in the third quarter, Robinson led the Bulldogs 76 yards down the field for a touchdown. Then suddenly with the Bears seemingly out of the game, Washington came to life. He had played little of the first half because of an upset stomach inflicted after a particularly vicious hit to the midsection. Now when his Bears recovered a fumble at the Los Angeles 40 yard line, Washington pulled on his snow-white helmet, spat in his hands and rubbed them together before walking into the huddle. Playing quarterback, he ran on the first play for 12 yards and then passed on the next three plays, ultimately scoring a game-tying touchdown.

When Bears got the ball back again, Washington ran a punt return to the opposition's 46 yard line, nearly breaking past the final defenders to go all the way for a touchdown. Instead, he ran on the next play to the 35. And then "giving a true wild-west Buffalo Bill climax to his performance," as the *Courier*'s famed West Coast sports reporter Herman Hill wrote about it, Washington dropped back to pass as Strode streaked toward the end zone. Strode "hurled himself high into the ozone to nestle the swine-skin into his arms" on the five yard line and dragged two tacklers across the goal line for the final score with only a few minutes left to play.

With their ninth-straight win, the Bears had seized the undisputed league championship. Hill, the reporter, looked about him and searched for the words to capture the moment for his readers across the country. None of them, of course, had been lucky enough to see this one last moment play out in person – and no one then could guess the future for Washington, Strode or Robinson.

"Pandemonium reigned," Hill wrote in his column. "The spectators all but went berserk with excitement."[123]

Hailed by many as the "greatest negro player," Washington saw the 1942 New Year's Day game as evidence that he could rank, simply, among all of the greatest players if given the chance to compete against whites in the NFL.

"Maybe I am lucky but just when I thought, 'Well this tops everything,' along would come something else to erase it in my memory," Washington said a year later, looking back on his exploits.

Before the war broke out, he had been invited to play in an all-star game against the Washington Redskins and he had matched up well against Hall of Fame quarterback Sammy Baugh too.

"I was highly elated over my performance," he said, "as it had proved once again that Negro athletes could compare on even terms in the National Pro-Loop if given a chance."[124]

But the league's unofficial race ban did not give black players those moments often. Three months after the New Year's Day game, Robinson was inducted into the army and headed for Fort Riley, Kansas, where he would be stationed.

Washington, who had a military draft exemption because he was married with a child, passed the examinations to become a Los Angeles police officer and entered cadet training with the goal of specializing in juvenile delinquency. Because of a police ruling against outside employment, that meant the end of his football career – at least for the moment.[125]

Bill Nunn Jr. soon faced the end of his athletic days back in Pittsburgh too. After Westinghouse High School's basketball team won the City Championship in 1943, Nunn Jr. and his classmates drew attention from college recruiters and he was invited to play for Long Island University, a private, mixed-race college in Brooklyn.

But his father had other ideas. Nunn Sr., the editor of the nation's largest black weekly newspaper, believed his son should go to a black college. Ever since 1837 when a Quaker philanthropist from the British West Indies came to Philadelphia and started the African Institute, schools that came to be known as historically black colleges and universities grew up around the United States educating mostly black students.[126] [127] As a reporter for the *Courier*, Nunn Sr. had traveled the country meeting black college football coaches, athletic directors and presidents. Now he wanted his son to benefit from those connections – but also to stay true to his roots by going to one of those schools.

Nunn Jr. refused to consider a black college. And his father held firm, refusing to help him attend Long Island University, even on academic scholarship. So the son went to work.

The federal government was spending heavily on steel contracts throughout Pittsburgh's river valleys, even paying to move 8,000 residents of the city of Homestead so it could expand U.S. Steel's mill there.[128] In the nearby town of Duquesne, another 2,900 people living in the city's Castle Garden community were moved to make way for three electric steel furnaces, a conditioning plant and a heat-treating mill. In each case, most of the people who lost their homes were black. Half of the employers in Allegheny County, which includes Pittsburgh, refused to employ blacks or allowed them only to take the worst jobs, as janitors and errand boys. Westinghouse Air Brake Company in Wilmerding, a river town 14 miles outside of the city, was among those companies that still refused to allow blacks to take most jobs.[129]

But with the war effort underway, factories needed all hands, and jobs – even for blacks – were plentiful for once. Nunn Jr. ended up landing a job at Westinghouse Air Brake, working in the company's loud, dirty factory making the brakes used on millions of train cars. He lasted less than a day, never even going back to collect his pay.

Then he landed a job with Union Switch & Signal, another Westinghouse subsidiary making bomb shells, pistols and ordinance for the military in Swissvale, just outside the city limits nearer to his home. There, Nunn Jr. worked in the all-black stock room, sorting and delivering packages throughout the factory. The job meant working 10 hours a day for five days a week and eight hours on Saturday. After a couple of weeks, Nunn thought to himself, "There's got to be something better." But he stayed on the job for a year, until the following summer. That's when he quit that job too and took another, as a lifeguard at the county's South Park swimming pool for blacks.

By then, he had made up his mind – to agree with his father. He would go to a black college.

Three months after the Pearl Harbor attack, the *Courier* had a scoop. Ever since the story of the heroic black messman had broken, Americans had wanted to know the man. But the military, burdened still with its Jim Crow expectations, had continued to refuse to identify him. Radio announcers across the country had come to refer to him as the "unnamed Negro messman hero."

On the cover of its March 14, 1942, edition, the *Courier* surprised its readers: "Add the name of Dorie Miller, 22-year-old mess attendant in the United States Navy, to the illustrious 'honor roll' of Negro fighting heroes," it wrote.[130]

Miller, a former boxing champ aboard the USS West Virginia in Pearl Harbor, had awakened at 6 a.m. on the morning of December 7, 1941, and he was collecting laundry when the alarm sounded to announce the Japanese attack. Because of his physical strength, he was assigned to carry wounded sailors to safety and then he was sent to the bridge where the captain of the ship had been mortally wounded. Miller had never been trained to fire a weapon but he manned a 50-caliber Browning anti-aircraft machine gun until he ran out of ammunition and was ordered to abandon ship. As flames from exploding bombs consumed the West Virginia, Miller and the other survivors climbed down hand-over-hand from ropes hanging from an overhead crane. Later, he described what it had been like to fire the gun: "It wasn't hard. I just pulled the trigger and she worked fine. I had watched the others with these guns. I guess I fired her for about fifteen minutes. I think I got one of those Jap planes. They were diving pretty close to us."[131]

For the *Courier*, this always had been more than just another war story. The paper realized the impact of a black messman – who by Navy rules could not advance past shining shoes, mopping decks and polishing brass – instead taking an active role in defending his ship. The paper had spent weeks running down every rumor about the man's identity. "There flamed in his breast the same fires of patriotism and love of country as burned in the breasts of the gallant crew on the Arizona," the *Courier* wrote. "He saw his duty. He did it!"[132]

Within days of the report, the NAACP sent a letter to the Secretary of the Navy urging him to lift the restrictions on black sailors: "This action by the Navy not only would reward a hero, but would serve dramatic notice that this country is in fact a democracy engaged in an all-out war against anti-democratic forces."[133]

Wendell Willkie, the former Republican presidential candidate, called out the hypocrisy of patriots fighting for freedom in Europe and Asia but not at home: "Won't you, while you are proclaiming the necessity for freedom throughout the world, devote some time to bringing about a correction of this injustice at home, an injustice which makes a mockery of all our fine words?"[134]

Navy Secretary Frank Knox did commend Miller for his actions. Admiral Chester Nimitz, commander in chief of the Pacific Fleet, personally presented a Navy Cross to Miller aboard the aircraft carrier USS Enterprise in May, noting that he was the first black to receive the honor in World War II but probably not the last.

Still, the Navy promoted Miller only to mess attendant first-class, and then later cook, third class. As white heroes from the Pearl Harbor attack came home for officer training or to travel the country raising support for war bonds, Miller was returned back to his mop, duster and shoeshine brush. "The Navy finds Dorie Miller too important waiting table in the Pacific to return him so that his people might see him," the *Courier* reporter in July.[135]

A little more than a year later, Miller was dead, listed as missing in action among 646 men who had been killed aboard the escort carrier USS Liscome Bay when it was hit by a Japanese torpedo and sunk in November 1943.

Congressman John E. Rankin, a Mississippi Democrat who defended segregation and frequently railed against those who were "harassing the white people of the Southern states," took to the Capitol floor a month after the Liscome Bay sank to recall a young white sailor he had recommended for the U.S. Naval Academy. The man had died on the ship. Rankin had no idea that Miller had died in the same attack.

The irony was too great for James A. Wechsler, a white Washington news correspondent, who wrote about it in a Christmas Eve column for his magazine: Rankin's "Mississippi friend and a Texas Negro vanished into the same ocean, victims of the same torpedo, servants of the same cause. The same grim notifications went to a home in Mississippi and to one in Texas. There isn't much that even a Congressman can do about that kind of equality."[136]

Four months after the Allied invasion of Europe, Bill Nunn Sr. traveled to Michigan's Great Lakes Naval Academy to expose its hypocrisy for readers of the *Courier*.

The War Department had created service academies across the country to prepare young men to be pilots and sailors. Then concerned about low morale at home from the diminished quality of football games from teams such as the Steelers-Eagles conglomerate, military leaders insisted that each of the new service academies also field a team. Squads such as the Iowa Pre-Flight Seahawks and the North Carolina Pre-Flight Cloudbusters would go up against traditional college teams such as Boston College and Temple University.[137] Most service academy teams, like the college teams they resembled, remained all white.

At the Great Lakes base 50 miles north of Chicago, Nunn found that it had an integrated infirmary – with black and white sailors lying next to each other. It also had a basketball team with three black players and four whites.

But the Sailors' football team, like the base swimming pool, remained all-white.

The base commander told Nunn some segregation was necessary – to protect the expectations of Southern sailors. He said their self-respect would suffer if they had to live on an equal footing with blacks.[138]

Writing afterwards in the *Courier*, sports columnist Wendell Smith summed up the inequality: It was as if the Navy had said, "We're teaching you to fight for democracy … not play in it!"[139]

It would, instead, take action to integrate football.

That same fall, more than 25,000 football fans watched the all-white Great Lakes Sailors take on the University of Illinois and the team's star player, Claude "Buddy" Young, a black man known as the "fastest human" for being that year's national collegiate sprint champion. Young could not have played for the Great Lakes team even if he had been drafted. But on his team's first play from scrimmage, Young took the ball, stepped around the line – and ran 93 yards for a touchdown. In one moment, he had exposed the weakness of segregation: Given a chance, blacks could play.[140]

Across the field, the Sailors' coach Paul Brown watched Young sprinting for the end zone and knew the boundaries about what he could do with his football team had just been redrawn. Starting out as a high school coach in Massillon, Ohio, Brown had cared little about a boy's skin color if he could help the team win.[141] His mixed-race high school teams had won plenty, giving him the chance to coach at Ohio State University for three seasons before getting drafted. Again in college, he played black athletes such as Bill Willis, a 212-pound tackle known as the "Cat" for his quickness despite his large size.[142] Brown's philosophy had been simple: "I just wanted to win football games with the best possible people."[143]

The Great Lakes academy's rules about segregation made it impossible for Brown to carry his tradition into the military, but Young's sprint had changed the rules.

By the next fall when Young was drafted into the military, he briefly joined Brown as a player for the Sailors. He was not alone either. Feeling emboldened, Brown had found slots for three other blacks, including a running back named Marion Motley. Brown had first seen Motley when he played for Ohio's

McKinley High School. Brown's Massillon team had won the game against McKinley, but fans had gone away remembering the running back on the opposing team. After two years of working in a steel mill, Motley had gone to play for the University of Nevada, where he had scored the longest touchdown run of the 1941 season. He was regarded as the best black player at a white college.[144] [145] When Motley was drafted, he ended up at Great Lakes.

After a short stint with Brown, Young was transferred to Fleet City in the San Francisco Bay. The Navy quickly had set up three training stations,[146] and Young played for the base's Blue Jackets football team.

In early October, 62,000 fans watched Young go against the Second Air Force Flyers. Then two weeks later another large crowd saw the Blue Jackets win 88 to 0 over the Camp Beale Bears.[147] Each home game drew tens of thousands of fans to marvel at the black running back: They talked about the way he played the game, and not the color of his skin.

"Buddy Young does things with a football no back is supposed to do," Lt. Col. Rick Hanley said after watching his team, the El Toro Marines, lose to the Bluejackets.[148]

While Young changed minds on the football field, the *Courier's* Double V campaign continued to build momentum for racial integration off it. After James Thompson wrote his letter to the newspaper's editors and the paper created a logo to demand a victory at home as surely as victories abroad, ordinary people had taken up the cause themselves. Thompson, a cafeteria worker with a pen, could hardly believe what he had started and he had high hopes for more: "Let us hope that this catches on enough so that every home and every car will feature one of these banners."[149]

Cora Lee Barnill, in Muskegon, Michigan, invited local women into her home and they formed a Double Victory club to meet regularly and sing songs in support of the victory at home.[150] Another group in Springfield, Ohio, met to make first aid kits with bandages for the Red Cross. Supporters in Key West, Florida, held a cutest baby contest to raise money for the campaign, collecting a $1 fee per entry. The Double V club in

Connersville, Indiana, pressured city officials to reopen the only playground there for black children.[151] And outside the L.A. Coliseum, where public officials hung a giant V in support of the war effort, Sidney Dones wore a dark suit and a white shirt with a broad collar, holding up the fingers of his right hand in a second V for the battle against segregation at home.[152]

The NAACP backed the campaign, and so did Elks Lodges across the country.[153] New York's Italian Mayor Fiorello LaGuardia sponsored a series of radio programs called "Unity at Home, Victory Abroad," and Milwaukee's white Mayor Carl Ziedler, the son of German and Austrian immigrants, heartily endorsed the Double V effort.[154]

Many Americans actually saw the two battlefronts as one: The United States could not fully defeat foreign aggression without also facing its own demons.

"I am for racial tolerance simply because I love my country," famous radio personality Clifton Fadiman told listeners. "If the German theory of race hatred and race superiority makes any real headway here ... we will have lost the war, no matter how decisively we beat the Germans and the Japanese."[155]

The war created moments no one expected too. Within 18 months of setting the Major League Baseball record for hitting in 56 consecutive games, Yankees centerfielder Joe DiMaggio enlisted in the military and ended up playing exhibition games where he was stationed. In June 1943, his Santa Ana Air Base team in Southern California played an exhibition against the Los Angeles police department team. Kenny Washington, the black UCLA star who had become a police officer, hit a long home run in the first inning, and DiMaggio later singled to extend his military hitting streak to 13 games. The large crowd in the stands that day saw Santa Ana win 10-3[156] – and they witnessed a historic matchup they never could have seen in Major League Baseball.

All the way through high school, Bill Nunn Jr. never had seen a single black teacher. Now after a year of working at the Union Switch and Signal factory, he agreed maybe his father had a point about black colleges. Wendell Smith, the *Courier*'s sports editor, had gone to a small black school, West Virginia State College, 10 miles down the river from Charleston, West Virginia. He wasn't working in a factory. Instead, he was traveling the country to witness the best college football in the fall and chronicling Negro leagues baseball through the spring and summer. That seemed a lot better than working 58 hours a week as a grunt in a munitions factory, and still barely getting by.

West Virginia State graduate Will Robinson wasn't working in a factory either – although no one would say Nunn's basketball coach at the Centre Avenue YMCA in the Hill District had had an easy time. A multisport high school athlete in Steubenville, Ohio, he had endured intense discrimination. His coach had caught hell when he named Robinson quarterback of the integrated high school football team – until they started winning, going undefeated and unscored upon with him as captain. Then when Robinson captained the Steubenville High School golf team to the state championships the next spring, he had to sleep overnight at the local YMCA because the hotel where white players stayed would not allow black guests. During the tournament, he ate in the kitchen of the golf club's restaurant because he could not sit with white diners. Still, he shot a one over-par 73 and finished second. Since then, he had attended West Virginia State on a work scholarship and then the University of Michigan to earn a master's degree in physical education. Unable to find other work, he had ended up coaching basketball at the Pittsburgh YMCA while doing some writing for the *Courier* on the side.[157]

During Nunn's year off from school, Chuck Cooper, a high school basketball teammate who had been a year behind him, caught up. The two had once planned to attend Long Island University together. Now, with Nunn Sr. enforcing a black college mandate for his son, the boys started looking seriously at West Virginia State. There, they could play together again.

As a second lieutenant in an all-black unit at the U.S. Army's Camp Hood in Texas, Jackie Robinson, the black former UCLA sports star, refused to play football for the base when he could not also play on its all-white baseball team. When a commanding officer threatened to order him to play football,

Robinson responded that they could force him to play – but not to play well. [158]

Millions of Americans had been drafted into the military, and at least 800,000 had been black. Robinson was among the few blacks given officer rank. Just before the war, the Army had only five black officers, and three of them were chaplains. Now with the government instituting a universal draft, more black soldiers arrived from Northern cities and the War Department noted that they lacked the "appearance of servility traditionally associated with the Southern Negro." Under pressure from Joe Louis, the boxing star who had enlisted in the Army, the War Department increased the number of black officers.

Coming home one night from the Camp Hood officers' club a month after the D-Day landings, Robinson boarded a local public bus and sat down next to the light-skinned wife of a fellow black officer. The bus driver seemed to resent it, and he told Robinson to move to another seat in the rear. Robinson refused. He told the driver to mind his own business, and they started to argue. When they reached Robinson's stop, a bus dispatcher was there waiting, followed by military police and a small, but growing, crowd of indignant white onlookers. Robinson agreed to go to police headquarters to sort out the problem, and he remained calm until a white policeman ran up and asked if they had the "nigger lieutenant." Robinson snapped, threatening to "break in two" anyone who used that word. Later, the military charged him with showing disrespect to a superior officer and failing to obey a direct command.

Writing in pencil to a black aide at the War Department in Washington, Robinson explained that he did not want unfavorable publicity for himself or the Army – but also that he would go to the media for help if he needed to ensure a fair trial. "I don't mind trouble but I do believe in fair play and justice," Robinson printed in neat block letters. "I feel that I'm being taken in this case and I will tell people about it unless the trial is fair."

The aide, Truman Gibson, also black, noted in his own handwriting on the letter: "This man is the well-known athlete … Follow the case carefully."

By the time the case came to trial, the *Courier* was following the outcome too. Robinson, like other black soldiers, had been asked to fight for victory abroad – but here, again, victory over discrimination at home remained elusive. Already the paper had pointed out that Robinson had been banned from playing sports, or at least baseball, in the military because of his skin color: "Jackie and his racial compatriots could just as easily be Japanese or Krauts, on a basis of the recognition accorded their gridiron talents," the paper's sports columnist Randy Dixon wrote. "Twas forgotten that Jackie is preparing to face those bullets and dive bombers as much as any other of Uncle Sam's nephews."[159]

The court found Robinson not guilty two months later after his military defense lawyer poked holes in the charges, pointing out that it was not even clear whether Robinson had received orders that he had disobeyed. Soon after, as his unit prepared to leave for overseas, Robinson was placed on "limited duty" because of a pre-existing bone spur in his ankle. He was released from the service by November.

His all-black unit, the 761st Tank Battalion, met severe battle conditions in Europe and suffered heavy casualties. Had Robinson continued to serve, it is possible that he could have been killed or maimed – unable to continue playing sports.

After one season of splitting home football games between Pittsburgh and Philadelphia, the "Steagles" football team broke up when enough Eagles players became available for them to form their own team again.

Rooney, the Steelers' owner, still did not have enough players. Plus the league had an odd number of teams, at eleven, with the Cleveland Rams resuming play for the 1944 season. Rooney looked west and worked out a second merger, with the Chicago Cardinals.

Officially the team was known as Card-Pitt. But after losing 10 games without a single win, the team became better known among fans as the "Carpets," for getting walked all over.[160]

The all-white NFL still had another alternative option to replace its missing players. Ray Kemp had been one of the two last blacks to play in the league in 1933 when he was with

Pittsburgh. Now, 11 years later, he pointed out the obvious in a letter to the *Courier*'s Wendell Smith: The league could fill out its ranks by playing blacks again.

"Isn't this America?" he wrote. "Isn't this supposed to be the land of the free and the home of the brave? The land of equal opportunity – regardless of race, creed or color?"[161]

Kemp had a brother serving in the Merchant Marine, four nephews in the Army, one in the Navy and one with a labor battalion in Pearl Harbor, and two brothers-in-law in the Army. Kemp's family had been called to defend freedom and liberty abroad, and they had answered.

Kemp suggested that NFL Commissioner Elmer Layden, a member of Notre Dame's Four Horsemen in 1924, might be sympathetic to playing blacks. After all, Layden had coached Kemp at Pittsburgh's Duquesne University in the 1930s and Kemp had worked as his line coach after playing.

Still, none of the league's owners brought in a single black player.

As the war started winding down, black Americans feared that celebrations for victories in Europe and Japan might not coincide with their other goal of a victory at home. Victory over Japan Day on August 14, 1945, brought jubilation to the streets captured in Alfred Eisenstaedt's iconic photo of a sailor kissing a nurse on the street of New York's Times Square. Blacks shared in the national celebration too – but with a tinge of uncertain anxiety about the future.

"Colored people are joining lustily in the celebrations because the surrender means that loved ones abroad are no longer exposed to enemy guns and treachery and may soon be returned to this country," M.S. Stuart wrote in his *Courier* column, "Southern Say-So."[162] "But it cannot be forgotten that the defeat of fascism not only does not provide for Negroes that full measure of democracy that it does for other types of citizens, but the end of the way may actually intensify and complicate the conditions under which they must live in many places."

After all of the sacrifices they had made, like all Americans, and the gains they had won through a military system that exposed the inequalities of segregation, blacks feared a return to the old ways. With the increased pressure on American factories to supply the war effort, blacks had moved into jobs that had been unavailable to them before. Places that had refused to hire black workers found that they needed them when demand was high and the workforce depleted because of so many young men serving in the military. But the victory over Japan, coming after victory in Europe, allowed the United States government to immediately cut military work orders. Factories responded by laying off workers. In Detroit alone, 250,000 people suddenly lost their jobs. In New York: 130,000. The federal government expected 5 million Americans to be out of work within 60 days. Many feared a return to the desperation of the Great Depression, still fresh in memories. The abrupt halt to the nation's massive industrial machine was "almost equal to the shock of the historic atomic bomb," the *Courier* wrote in an editorial, calling for blacks to give the government time for a period of reconversion. "While the picture may look dark," the paper wrote, "there is no occasion for undue pessimism."[163]

Two other thoughts hung in the balance for black America. On the positive side, word leaked out immediately after the atomic bombs dropped on the Japanese cities of Hiroshima and Nagasaki that young, black scientists had been involved in the discoveries behind the weapons.[164] J. Ernest Wilkins Jr. had entered the University of Chicago at age 13 and earned a Ph.D. in mathematics by 19 before going to work on the secret project to extract nuclear material.[165] Moddie Taylor, a chemist from Lincoln University near Philadelphia had analyzed rare earth metals used in the weapons.[166] Other young blacks such as Jasper Jefferies, an electronics professor who graduated from West Virginia State College, and Benjamin Scott, a chemist from Morehouse College, worked on other secret aspects of the weapon. After working in silence on the project, none of the men would immediately talk about what they had contributed to the nuclear weapon. Robert Patterson, the nation's undersecretary of war, wrote an open letter to all of the scientists who had worked on the Manhattan Project to develop the atomic weapon, thanking them for their service and telling them to remain quiet. No one worker had known the entire purpose of the research or seen the totality of the project until it was used. "The war lords of Japan now know its effects better than ourselves," Patterson wrote.[167] Still, black Americans celebrated that when the nation needed to develop the atomic weapon, it had relied upon the best minds regardless of the color of their skin. "Some of these men are barely out of college, yet the government in its desperate race to beat the Nazi scientists, recognized and made full use of their knowledge and skill," the *Courier* wrote.

Fear weighed down the other side of the scale, opposite of this new-found pride. After World War I, Southern segregation not only had endured but it had flourished. Now as another generation of young blacks prepared to return from war, white racists in the Ku Klux Klan prepared to revive their efforts to enforce segregation again. The secretive organization had peaked with as many as 5 million members in the 1920s but its support for Nazi sympathizers and tax problems with the IRS had forced the group to officially disband by the spring of 1944.[168] [169] In a letter distributed throughout a dozen states, Imperial Wizard James Colescott promised that the group had not really gone anywhere: "We have authority to meet and reincarnate at any time."[170] The *Courier*, again, told its readers not to worry: This post-war period would be unlike the previous one. The country had experienced a spirit of unity through common sacrifice. Blacks could face discrimination with less fear and more courage – and, the paper reasoned, with more whites on their side. "Americans are neither as emotional nor prejudiced as they were in the early 1920s, and therefore not as susceptible to racist propaganda as they were then," the *Courier* wrote.[171]

Playing basketball at West Virginia State College, Nunn Jr. created his own opportunities. Chuck Cooper, his high school teammate, joined him in the little town of Institute, West Virginia, for one semester before getting drafted into the military. Nunn, who did not enlist and avoided the draft, briefly played football. As bigger men came home from the military, enrolled in college on the GI bill and joined the football team, Nunn realized that it was not his best sport. Instead, he continued to excel at basketball.

Nunn had gone to West Virginia State only grudgingly, after a year of factory labor, but when he arrived in Institute, he found that the small, all-black college just seemed to fit. Few white colleges on the East Coast accepted black players, so many of the best athletes ended up in the Colored Intercollegiate Athletic Association, a league of 15 all-black schools in the eastern half of the United States. Nunn started to meet these top athletes as teammates and competitors.

He had been on the campus two years when a tall, gangly freshman arrived from Parker-Gray High School in Alexandria, Virginia. His high school coach had gone to West Virginia State and recommended him to the coach there. The fans called Earl Lloyd the "Big Cat" because of this 6-foot-6-inch frame, his quick natural ability and his habit of turning from a cool, laidback guy off the court into a pouncing attacker on it.

Lloyd felt at home at West Virginia State, too, from the moment he stepped onto campus. Classmates might pass each other four times in a day, but they still took the time to say, "Hey, how you doing?"[172] The college president was friendly and available. Professors were willing to help students with a question, even late at night.

"It was like being at home but in a bigger house," Lloyd said years later. "It was home."

Fresh out of high school at age 19, he had raw, untamed talent. He was so green, Lloyd recalled, that if the coach had thrown him on the ground and poured water on him – he would have grown into something.

Instead, Coach Mark Caldwell planted Lloyd with Nunn by making the star freshman player room with the junior team captain. Lloyd recognized his older roommate's name immediately. Because the local papers in Alexandria wrote only about the all-white high schools, just the *Pittsburgh Courier* and the *Baltimore Afro-American* had paid any attention to the black high school athletes. Lloyd's family had taken the Pittsburgh newspaper, and he made the connection easily between Nunn and his famous father.

The few other people on campus who knew about Nunn's pedigree paid little attention to it, and Nunn rarely talked about it himself. To classmates, he was just a friendly, well-liked guy.

A leader by his actions, Nunn asked first, that his teammates play hard on the court, and second, that they act decently off of it.

The Yellow Jackets basketball team also had men who had returned from military service, including seven veterans by Nunn's final year of college. Bob Wilson had been stationed in Japan, near Yokohama and Tokyo, after its surrender. He had seen a proud, imperialist nation devastated by years of fighting and finally the ferocity of atomic weapons. He also had seen the segregation against blacks persisting in the military. He returned home to marvel at the efficient wealth and comfort of the United States – and to resume his education.

"The environment teaches you a lot of things," Wilson recalled years later. "You learn to live with it and to take advantage of the opportunities when you have them."

A native of nearby Charleston, West Virginia, Wilson stood 6-foot-4-inches and he had played in high school for Coach Caldwell. Together, they had won four state black high school championships. Caldwell asked the Army veteran to just come out and meet the young men he had assembled for West Virginia State's team. Lloyd, a still awkward sophomore, was impressed with Wilson's maturity from the moment they shook hands for the first time.

Wilson felt impressed, too, by the talent that Caldwell had found. It seemed as if he had had a checklist and had gone down it looking for the nation's best black athletes.

Nunn, the calm, confident point guard, fed the ball. "He was just a good guard," Wilson said.[173] "He wasn't a superstar. I was the superstar and he fed me. But he was a good leader."

Joe Gilliam, the Yellow Jackets' star quarterback who grew up across the state line in Steubenville, Ohio, played shooting guard. Lloyd, a tall forward underneath, could put up points. Wilson, a high-scoring center, immediately saw where he would find his place. It was as if while he had been away serving in the military, Caldwell had been building a team around his high school star athlete, waiting for his return.

"We were a true team," Wilson recalled. "We respected each other's ability and used each other's ability. We became a very solid team because we had a coach who knew talent and he put it together."

Traveling around the Colored Intercollegiate league mostly meant long road trips through the Mid-Atlantic and South with road stops carefully planned out to navigate the Jim Crow rules about where a group of young black men could eat or use the restroom.

Even in Charleston, blacks from the campus in nearby Institute knew they could not go everywhere. The state capital, just 11 miles away by bus, could have been 1,000 miles away to the students. Lloyd, who grew up in segregated Virginia, had never had a white classmate or even had a one-on-one conversation with a white person.[174]

"You couldn't eat in some of the restaurants," Wilson said. "They had segregated sections. Hotels were closed to you. In theaters, you had to sit in a certain section, mostly in the top balcony of most movie theaters."

Because the Yellow Jackets could not play the white teams nearby, they traveled for games as far as Johnson C. Smith University in Charlotte, North Carolina, and Delaware State University in Dover.

With five seconds left in the team's first game of the 1947-48 season, it looked as if the Yellow Jackets were not going anywhere. West Virginia State trailed Alabama's Tuskegee College at home until hitting a last-second shot to go up by one as Tuskegee missed a final bucket with time expiring.[175]

When the players pulled out that first win, they never looked back. Nunn ended up never losing in his senior season. The team won 30 games and finished as the only undefeated college basketball team in the country. [176]

"It was just a fantastic year," Lloyd recalled. "That's a year you put on a shelf. You have a nice little niche for it. That year was a happening. It had to be a happening because it had never been done before."

Uninvited to any other tournament, the Yellow Jackets traveled to Washington's Uline Arena to play for the unofficial black college championship in the Colored Intercollegiate Athletic Association tournament. That meant piling into the college's two eight-passenger DeSoto sedans and traveling along two-lane roads without guardrails. For trips to Washington, the players would wake early on game day for breakfast on campus, and then three or four hours later, they would stop somewhere that was expecting them.[177] The black athletes could not afford to be spontaneous on the road and unexpected pit stops were avoided if possible.

West Virginia State easily defeated Johnson C. Smith College by 34 points in the first round, narrowly won against North Carolina College in the second round and faced Washington's Howard University in the championship. The Yellow Jackets took the lead with nine minutes left and won by 11 points.[178]

Ten days later the University of Kentucky won its first National Collegiate Athletic Association championship. The all-white Kentucky squad never played against all-black West Virginia State.[179]

Bill Nunn Jr., center with the ball, captained West Virginia State College to the nation's only undefeated season in 1947-48. Courtesy of West Virginia State University.

Chapter 3. Undefeated

Because of the way West Virginia State's undefeated season ended, Bill Nunn Jr. had options no black athlete ever had before.

His first opportunity came from a Jewish journalism graduate of Boston University. Haskell Cohen had worked during the war as the first white correspondent to write about black servicemen for a black newspaper.

Cohen had found his way to the *Pittsburgh Courier* through sports writer Chester Washington, and after the D-Day invasion in June 1944, he hooked up first with the all-black 92nd infantry group in Italy and then the all-black 332nd fighter group that flew missions over Germany.

"There is little that can obviate the blood tears shed at this or any front," Cohen wrote while traveling with the infantry division.[180] When a mortician serving as a medic was called to deliver the baby of an Italian *signora*, Cohen wrote that "death took a holiday."[181] And he found former athletes were serving as military police officers, such as Jerry Gibson, the brother of better-known Negro leagues' player Josh. He noted that they were the only men to whom boxer Joe Louis, by then an Army private, ever bowed.[182]

Cohen uniquely captured the black soldiers' mixed emotions about fighting the Nazis while dealing with racial discrimination in their own ranks. As the troops marched across Italy, German planes dropped leaflets trying to break morale by telling made-up stories of cheating girlfriends back home. For the black troops, they dropped pamphlets showing a black man being attacked during riots in Detroit and that told the story of "Way down upon the Suwannee River," asking the soldiers what they wouldn't give to be back home again.

"It is quite true the Army segregates us and we have a right to do a lot of beefing," black Private John Trent told Cohen. "But when it comes to a decision between the Nazi creed and the American way, we'll take the American way even if at times we do think it is working against us."[183]

Then when the 92nd infantry arrived to occupy an Italian village that had been liberated from the Germans, they found that the residents had been told by the enemy how black soldiers would eat their babies. They quickly dispelled those fears among people who had rarely if ever seen blacks, and they made friends, providing food and then taking up a collection to buy shoes for a four-year-old boy named Fernando who hung around the Americans and had nothing for his feet.

"Now people can see that we can get along with others of a different race on an equal plane," said one black lawyer serving with the unit. "Perhaps when we get back home, the white folks will have learned from what they observed here and just give us a chance to get by on our own merits."[184]

Cohen covered sports from the front lines too. He landed an exclusive interview with Billy Conn, the "Pittsburgh Kid," in Rome after the boxer had met up with Joe Louis. Both were serving in the military and dreaming of coming home to a rematch that might draw an expected $4 million gate.

"Take good care of yourself, Billy," Louis had said. "Be a good soldier. Come home well, because you and I are going to make a lot of money when we meet in that return match after the war."[185]

And on New Year's Day 1945 in Florence, Cohen covered the Spaghetti Bowl football game that featured white and black players. The Fifth Army defeated the 12th Air Force behind the strength of black running back John "Big Train" Moody. The former black All-American from Morris Brown College in Atlanta scored two touchdowns and kicked two extra points in the 20-0 win that was witnessed by 20,000 soldiers.

"The game was given big time coverage and had a true New Year's bowl atmosphere," Cohen wrote. "… An added thrill came when Sally, the Nazi broadcaster, warned of an enemy bombing of the field."[186]

After coming home in early 1945, Cohen stayed in New York where he had been living before becoming a war correspondent, and he went back to covering sports for glossy magazines. He continued to look at the world with an unusual bent. He convinced the editors of Street & Smith's "True Sports" magazine to include a story on a leading black athlete in every issue, splitting the duties with *Courier* sports editor Wendell Smith. Cohen wrote the first feature about the Harlem Globetrotters all-black team of basketball clowns.[187]

When the Basketball Association of American started in 1946, Cohen fell in with the league's owners and became close especially with Ned Irish, the founding owner of the New York Knicks.

Knowing that Irish already had taken a chance on Wataru Misaka, a Japanese-American point guard who had led the University of Utah to a national championship, Cohen had another idea for growing the league.

As a close member of the *Courier* family, he had followed West Virginia State's undefeated season. Now he suggested to Irish that the Knicks take a black player. Bill Nunn Jr. had been captain and point guard for the black national champion, and he was getting ready to graduate down in Institute, West Virginia.

Eager to grow the league and win games in any way, Irish agreed. He extended an invitation for Nunn to travel to New York City and try out for his professional team.[188]

During the war, tens of thousands of Americans had crammed into stadiums to watch football games featuring black players, and many of them – such as Kenny Washington and Jackie Robinson in California semi-pro leagues, and Buddy "the Bronze Bullet" Young on military teams – had dazzled.

Yet, by January 1946, no National Football League owner had signed a black player for his team since the last two were released 13 years earlier. The owners denied excluding blacks on purpose.

"For myself and for most of the owners, I can say there never was a racial bias," Art Rooney Sr., founding owner of the Pittsburgh Steelers, later said.[189] George Halas, owner of the Chicago Bears, agreed years later that the NFL did not have any sort of agreement to play only whites: "At no time did the color of skin matter. All I cared about was the color of blood. If you had red blood I was for you." [190]

But the players felt otherwise. Many blamed Washington Redskins owner George Preston Marshall for enforcing Southern attitudes about segregation. Ray Kemp, one of the last two blacks who played in 1933, blamed his release on racism: "It was my understanding that there was a gentleman's agreement in the league that there would be no more blacks."[191] Fritz Pollard, star running back of the league's first championship team and its first black coach, blamed Halas for playing him when he needed to draw fans but then kicking him out when his team became more popular.[192]

Attitudes about playing blacks varied widely around the country too. If the Redskins pandered to Southern fans by supporting an unofficial boycott, people in places such as Southern California had grown accustomed to seeing integrated college and semi-professional teams.

When Dan Reeves sought to relocate his Cleveland Rams NFL team in January 1946, he found out just how vast that difference could be.

If the team moved to the West Coast, it would need a place to play. The Rams had just won the NFL championship in Cleveland with Bob Waterfield, a former quarterback from the University of California Los Angeles, throwing two touchdown passes and becoming the first rookie to be named the league's most valuable player.[193] Waterfield was suited to Los Angeles, married to Jane Russell, Hollywood's voluptuous leading sex symbol of the time.

Reeves wanted his team to play in the L.A. Coliseum. Because taxpayers had built and supported the stadium, the Rams' general manager Charles "Chile" Walsh had to go before a public stadium commission to seek permission to play there. When he finished speaking, Walsh turned to the audience to answer questions from the public.

Three reporters from black newspapers sat in the audience: Halley Harding of the *Los Angeles Tribune*, with Herman Hill and J. Cullen Fentress of the *Pittsburgh Courier*'s West Coast bureau. Harding had been a Negro leagues baseball player with the Kansas City Monarchs[194] before becoming the Los Angeles paper's city editor and sports columnist;[195] Hill had been the first black basketball player at the University of Southern

California.[196] The men had been working together for years to press the Pacific Coast baseball league to include black players, once staging an interracial picket line of 50 baseball fans around Los Angeles' Wrigley Field ballpark when team owners said they would give blacks a tryout and the team manager refused.[197] [198]

Harding rose out of his seat, but not to ask a question. He charged that the NFL had long been biased against black players. He reminded commission members that blacks already had played in the NFL and on integrated teams at the Coliseum. UCLA's undefeated 1939 team had featured black players Kenny Washington, Woody Strode and Jackie Robinson.

Harding talked about the aims and ambitions of World War II and the fights against intolerance in Europe and Asia. How, he wanted to know, could the public lease out a taxpayer-funded stadium to a professional team that would not allow black players even to tryout?[199] [200] [201] [202]

Hill and Fentress joined him in an official protest of letting the Rams play in the Coliseum if the team excluded blacks.

Walsh responded by saying the NFL did not have a rule – written or unwritten – against black players. And he immediately invited Washington, Young and other blacks to try out for the Rams.

Later in the day, Walsh met privately with 11 black newspaper writers at The Last Word, a joint on Los Angeles' South Central Avenue that billed itself as the East Side's "smartest sepia night club."[203] [204] On busy nights, it drew hip young blacks with music, soft drinks and the chance to see and be seen: suit and tie for men; stylish dresses and jewelry for women.

The Rams would not sign any black players under contract to another team, Walsh said.[205] The Hollywood Bears held one-year contracts on Washington and Strode, but the team's general manager already had said he would not stop either player from moving to the NFL, as long as the Bears received something in return. Washington, after all, was the highest paid football player in that part of the world.

Talking with Walsh inside the club, the reporters wanted to know what the Rams would do if the team signed a black player and then traveled to Washington, the NFL city where segregation rules were strongest. Walsh told them he was "not worried" about it and that blacks on the roster would play wherever the team went.

Nunn's second offer came from the Harlem Globetrotters.

Sports promoter Abe Saperstein, a short, bald Jewish man from Chicago, had formed the team in the 1920s, giving blacks a chance to play basketball for money.[206] The team had started out as the Savoy Big Five in an attempt to draw patrons to Chicago's Savoy Ballroom before dances.[207] When that did not work, Saperstein renamed the team and took the players barnstorming on the road for paying gigs wherever they could find them. When it formed, the team had no connection to New York's center of black culture and it had not traveled anywhere, let alone out of the country, but Saperstein figured having Harlem in the name signaled that this was an all-black team and that globetrotters sounded cosmopolitan. The team started out playing straight basketball too. But with only five regular players – not counting Saperstein, who wore a uniform under his overcoat so he could step on the court as the team's only substitute – the Globetrotters came up with clowning antics to give themselves a break during the game while still entertaining crowds.[208]

The *Courier*'s Wendell Smith had developed a friendship with Saperstein after covering his attempts to promote black sports, and Smith arranged a chance for the Globetrotters to check out the captain of West Virginia State's black national championship team.

Nunn might have preferred to play for the New York Renaissance, an all-black barnstorming team that played straight basketball, but no one from that team had called.

Instead, the Globetrotters sent scouts to Institute, West Virginia, in the spring of 1947 to watch Nunn tryout. Before leaving, they offered Nunn a two-year contract to join the team traveling the country by bus.

Football needed black players initially because it did not have enough talented whites to fill out team rosters – and that sort of opportunity seemed to be coming around again.

Shut out of joining the closed ranks of the NFL, potential team owners from New York, San Francisco, Los Angeles and Chicago quietly met in St. Louis on June 4, 1944, with Arch Ward, a sports editor from the Chicago Tribune. Ward had a talent for promotion that went beyond his day job: He had come up with the idea for a baseball All-Star Game in 1933, and now he wanted to start a rival football league that would stretch from coast to coast.

The men agreed with his vision, creating the All-American Football Conference with teams in the four represented cities along with two others in Buffalo and Cleveland.[209] What the investors lacked in football experience, they hoped to make up in money: The original investors included an oilman, a lumber magnate, a movie producer, a trucking industrialist and the owner of baseball's New York Yankees. Mickey McBride, the owner of the Cleveland team, had made his money from taxicab companies in Northeast Ohio, real estate in Cleveland, Chicago and Florida, a radio station, a printing company and others. He wanted to own a football franchise for two primary reasons: One, he had not been allowed to purchase the NFL's Cleveland Rams five years earlier, and two, critics said the league never would make it. "I wanted to get into it," he said, "because people said it was impossible."

For his team, McBride wanted the man many considered Ohio's most innovative coach, Paul Brown. He had started years earlier at Massillon's Washington High School an hour south of Cleveland, and he had gone on to coach Ohio State University before getting drafted into the military during the war. In an odd twist that fall, Brown had returned to the college campus as the coach of his Great Lakes Naval Training Station team. More than 73,000 fans had come out to watch the homecoming – and to see the Navy boys hang onto a 6-6 tie into the fourth quarter before losing 26-6.[210]

Many felt Brown would return to coaching college games after completing his military service. He, like many of the time, believed the college game to be far superior to the pros. But McBride made him an offer that Ohio State could not match:

$15,000 a year, plus a monthly stipend of $1,000 for the duration of the war, and part ownership of the team. Brown would be the richest football coach anywhere – and yet he remained torn about what to do.

Wearing his Navy blues as he walked into Ward's Tribune Tower office in Chicago several days later, Brown still seemed uncertain even as he signed his name onto a contract as reporters pressed around the desk.

"I leave Ohio State reluctantly," Brown said. "The time has arrived for me to decide whether I was to continue as a professor or a businessman. I simply couldn't turn down the deal in fairness to my family."[211]

In a contest that year, in early 1945, fans chose to name the team after Brown. The coach initially vetoed the idea in favor of the second-highest choice Panthers. But when a local businessman informed the team that he already owned that name, McBride sided with the fans to create the Cleveland Browns.[212]

One question remained for the new league before playing its first games the following season: Would the All-American Football Conference allow black players?

Commissioner James Crowley answered emphatically that the league had no rules barring blacks. "The AAFC is just what the name implies," he told reporters. "It is All-American in every aspect."[213]

Brown, who had coached blacks at Ohio State and in the Navy, agreed with the sentiment: "I'm only interested in selecting the best football player. I don't care about their color, nationality or religion."[214]

Yet, as the league's teams headed into training camp for an inaugural season, not one of them had a black player.

At West Virginia State, Nunn had distinguished himself not because of his size – at just over 6 feet tall – or his athletic ability, which was strong but did not place him among the very best players in the game.

Nunn's greatest asset was as a team leader. He had developed that ability naturally at Pittsburgh's Westinghouse

High School, forcing the coach and administrators to choose whether to play the best players – even if that meant a majority of them were black. And he had emerged again as the Yellow Jackets' team captain in basketball.[215] When men returning from military service joined the team next to boys just out of high school, Nunn had pulled them all together into national champions. It had not been his style to lead with words and locker room speeches, but rather by his attitude – playing hard, even at practice, studying for classes and smiling through every challenge.

After winning the black national championship, Nunn was ready to graduate as a senior. But Coach Mark Caldwell was not yet done with him.

He offered his team captain yet another option: He could stay in Institute as an assistant coach.

Sitting at the desk of his temporary offices in the Alexandria Hotel, Chile Walsh, the general manager of the newly renamed Los Angeles Rams, went over the contract one last time. In the two months since he had declared to the LA Coliseum commission that the NFL did not have a written ban against black players, Walsh had gone about testing that theory. He had worked out an agreement with the Hollywood Bears for the rights to running back Kenny Washington. Now Walsh prepared to tell the world what he had done.

Team owners and managers in the past had talked about giving black players a chance, but then others had fought the change. To show that everyone on the Rams agreed with this decision, Walsh invited several other people to the announcement – his older brother Adam, who was the Rams' head coach, and other team officials such as the backfield coach, who would be working with Washington, and the team's business manager. As newspaper reporters and photographers gathered around the desk, Walsh held up the agreement with the Bears and announced that Washington would be the NFL's first black player in more than a decade – since 1933 when Joe Lillard and Ray Kemp left the league.

"I have heard many fine things about Washington, both as a player and a man, and I feel certain that he will be a credit to our ball club and to his race," Walsh told the reporters.[216]

But the Rams were not the only team that had to accept Washington. The league's racial tolerance would be tested repeatedly over the coming season, every time the Rams traveled to another city to play an away game. The first chance for Washington to appear in a Rams' uniform would come five months later in the last week of August when the team planned to play against college all-stars at Chicago's Soldier Field. After that, the Rams would play a charity match against the Washington Redskins. Mercifully, the game would be played in Los Angeles.

"I look for other teams in the league to accept (Washington) in good grace, just as he has always been given fair treatment and won the respect of all who have played with and against him, in intercollegiate football and in his professional play on the coast during the past five seasons," Walsh told the reporters.

The Rams could not have just one black player because Washington needed a roommate for traveling on the road. Given the option weeks later of choosing another black player, the running back picked his old friend and teammate, Woodrow Wilson "Woody" Strode.[217]

Strode had married a Hawaiian woman and that created another set of racial concerns for the Rams' owners, but Washington was adamant. "Kenny had power at that point and he said, 'I want my buddy,'" Strode recalled years later.[218] The team relented, and Washington had someone to help him break through the NFL's racial barrier.

Even before the Rams played their first game, Tim Mara, owner of the New York Football Giants, praised the signing of Washington – but he talked in the language of money rather than civil rights. Under increased competition from the rival All-American Football Conference, the NFL needed to expand its popularity, Mara said.

"I am sure we will get thousands of more Negro fans to attend the games at the Polo Grounds this year because they will have an added interest in the league," Mara told the *Pittsburgh Courier* in an exclusive interview.[219]

Unlike Major League Baseball, he added, the NFL already proved that it could have integrated teams.

Mara turned out to be right. With the war over and football returning to full strength for the first time in years, the NFL champion Rams, with Washington in the backfield, drew 97,380 sports-starved fans to the exhibition game in Chicago.[220] Although the Rams had won the NFL championship the year before, the team had changed greatly as men came home from military service: All but six of the team's 59 players, plus team owner Dan Reeves, had seen duty and several of them had been wounded.[221] The college stars won the game 16-0 on the strength of running plays from the University of Michigan's Elroy "Crazy Legs" Hirsch.

A week later, 68,188 fans watched the Rams win their first pre-season home game against the Redskins, raising more than $102,000 for Los Angeles charities.[222]

Despite declaring that it would allow black players, the All-American Football Conference had its own racial problems. Its team in Los Angeles, the Dons, played in the Coliseum as well and it received the same directive to allow black players. But it had not.

Commission members called a special meeting in August to consider rescinding the Dons' lease after protests by Harding, Hill and the other black sports writers. They felt the team should have given a tryout to Archie H. Harris Jr., a former all-Big Ten end at Indiana University who had gone on to fly B-25 bombers as an Army pilot with the Tuskegee Airmen.[223] [224] [225] No one from the Dons came to the meeting but the team's general manager sent a note saying he had interviewed more than 400 players and picked the best ones for his squad. The commission did not revoke the lease agreement.

Other hopes that the new league would allow black players sagged when it admitted the Seahawks in Miami. *Courier* sports columnist Wendell Smith ranked Miami among the "most 'Nazi-fied' of all the cities in the world on matters of racial equality,"[226] [227] and he said the move left little chance for integration.

"It's the same old story," he wrote. "Negroes won't be permitted to play."

Despite all his talk about playing the best players, even Paul Brown showed up to his team's first training camp at Bowling Green State University with only white players. He had formed the team by drawing on his years of experience as a head coach, keeping detailed records of not only his players but also every talented athlete he had seen from Massillon High School, through college and into the military. He gave a long list of names to his assistant and asked him to contact them.[228]

As Brown was building his team, he received a letter from one of his Great Lakes players, Marion Motley. Brown first had added Motley's name to his notebooks when the player was still in high school, and then he had been a key player on the Navy base team. Now Motley wanted to know whether his coach had a place for him again in the pros. Brown wrote back that he did not. The team already had enough running backs.

Then as he was heading to camp, Brown heard from another former player who was black. Bill "the Cat" Willis had been a standout tackle at Ohio State, and he had taken a job coaching football at Kentucky State University, an all-black college. He called to see whether Brown would give him a chance. Again, the coach said he had no need. "I'll give you a call," he answered.

Disappointed but determined to play somewhere, Willis reached out to the Montreal Alouettes of the Canadian Football League. He received a tryout offer and purchased a plane ticket. But by the time he had packed his bags to leave, Willis had a phone call from a sports writer, Paul Hornung, of the *Columbus Dispatch*. The two men had grown close while Willis was at Ohio State, and Hornung called to advise Willis that he should forget about going to Montreal and instead show up at Bowling Green.

"I can't do that," Willis said. "I wouldn't feel right walking into camp without being invited."

"Now wait a minute," Hornung replied. "You just get here. You take my word for it that you can make this ball club. And, as a matter of fact, I'll stake my reputation on it."

Despite losing money on the plane ticket, Willis took the advice and instead drove to the Browns' training camp site. He arrived late in the day on August 1 as practices were ending for the day. Coach Brown looked up from across the field and walked over without a hint of surprise. He shook the player's hand as he asked, "Do you think you can still play football?"

"I don't know," Willis said. "I think so."

"Well, go get a uniform and be out here tomorrow," Brown told him.

The next day, Willis had an immediate impact. Lining up on defense on one snap, Willis reached over an offensive lineman and grabbed quarterback Otto Graham by the belt before he could release the ball. Willis was so quick that Brown ended up having to change Graham's stance from the traditional position with the feet parallel to one with his right foot slightly behind so he could push off from scrimmage quicker. That stance eventually became the norm for football everywhere.

Brown planned to keep Willis on the team quietly until he was ready to make a public announcement. But he needed a roommate for the black player, and despite the large number of running backs in training camp, he wanted someone better. Brown went to his assistant and asked him to call Motley, who was working at a steel mill in nearby Canton, Ohio, while playing semi-pro football on the side.

Motley accepted the offer, saying he would be in Bowling Green by the next day. He packed a bag and hopped a ride to camp with his cousin.

"He could play a game tomorrow," Brown said after watching him practice. "We have the same plays, the same formation, the same signals we used at Great Lakes."[229]

Brown offered Willis and Motley each a $4,000 contract, with a $100 signing bonus. Willis had been making $2,600 a year coaching football, while Motley received $65 a week from the mill, or $3,300 a year if he could get the hours. Both men easily agreed to change professions.[230]

Before the season started, Brown called the men into his office.

"You know that you're going to be in scrapes," he told them. "People are going to be calling you names. They're going to be nasty, but you're going to have to stick it out."[231]

That same summer, Herb Trawick, yet another black football player, was seeking a way to play professionally. He had grown up in Pittsburgh, and he had gone on to play college football at Kentucky State, becoming a *Pittsburgh Courier* black college All-American at tackle and guard.

Like Willis, Trawick sought his opportunity in Canada with the Montreal Alouettes. He was signed as the first black player in the Canadian Football League.[232] [233] [234]

In one summer, all three of North America's major professional football leagues – the National Football League, the All-American Football Conference and the Canadian Football League – had signed black players.

In Los Angeles, Kenny Washington and Woody Strode had each other – but often it felt like they had only each other.

Traveling created the most problems, especially for two men who had grown up in Southern California where segregation was not as strictly enforced as in other parts of the country. Often the Rams would book the team into a segregated hotel and then give the two black players money to stay somewhere else.

When the Rams arrived in Chicago for their first game in that 1946 season, the players stepped off the plane and Washington walked over to his roommate with a pout.

"What's wrong?" Strode wanted to know.[235]

"You know, we can't stay at that stinking hotel," Washington answered.

The Rams had booked the team into Chicago's Stevens Hotel, the biggest and finest place in the city. But it would not allow the black players to stay.

"They're going to give us $100 a piece to go find someplace else to stay."

The men took the money and headed across the city to the Persian Hotel, the plushest black hotel in the city. They checked in and headed for the club downstairs. American jazz pianist Count Basie was playing, and whites had come to hear him. The players sat down at the bar and ordered a couple of Tom Collins drinks.

Around midnight, Bob Waterfield, the Ram's white quarterback, wandered into the bar looking for his teammates.

"You crazy sons of bitches, what are you doing here this late at night?" he wanted to know.

"Just sitting here and enjoying this club," Strode answered.

"Look, we've made arrangements for you two to come up town with us and stay in the hotel," Waterfield told them.

"Forget that, boy," Strode said. "I'm going to be segregated, spend this hundred dollars, stay right here, and listen to the Count play his music."

Waterfield knew he was beat. "What the hell," he said, and ordered himself a drink.

Strode grew frustrated with his role on the Rams, often riding the bench rather than playing in games – a designated roommate more than a valued part of the team. He felt the additional pressure of having a Hawaiian wife and believed the Rams would never give him the chances he deserved.

Asked years later about the experience, Strode was blunt: "If I have to integrate heaven, I don't want to go."

No one – black or white – wants to go where they aren't wanted, he reasoned.

"We're not that far apart, but they try to tell us we're different," Strode said. "I don't know how to beat the drums or chant or do voodoo. I'm no different because we're all exposed to the same culture, the same dreams."[236]

Like the Rams in Los Angeles, the Cleveland Browns led their league in attendance for 1946.

A crowd of 60,135 watched the AAFC's first game when the Browns defeated the all-white Miami Seahawks, 44-0, at Cleveland's Municipal Stadium. During the colorful pregame ceremonies, the stadium announcer identified Willis as part of the starting lineup and he received a standing ovation.

Despite growing up in Pittsburgh, Bill Nunn became an instant fan of the Browns too. Soon, he and his friends started making road trips to Cleveland to watch the game.

"Paul Brown opened up the door," Nunn recalled. "With the number of blacks that they had, you were rooting for Cleveland. It might sound strange, but…"[237]

As he prepared to graduate from college, Bill Nunn Jr. had one other career option. Already he had offers from the New York Knicks, the Harlem Globetrotters and West Virginia State. But he still had one other idea in mind.

Nearly 30 years earlier, his father had been working as a clerk at the local post office when he walked into the offices of the *Pittsburgh Courier*. The newspaper then had just two rooms, next to two others for the law practice of publisher Robert L. Vann. Nunn Sr. had written a sports story and he brought it to show Ira F. Lewis, the paper's manager and president. Lewis read the article and immediately offered the author a position as the sixth person on staff.

Nunn Sr. dreamed about working for the paper, but he worried about giving up a good government job. Taking the offer meant leaving the sure comfort of working steady hours with a regular salary and, if things worked out as they should, a retirement pension some distant day. And yet, he could not let the idea escape. He went first to his co-workers at the post office for their opinions, and they encouraged him to take the chance. Then he turned to his father. He too supported his son's daring ambitions.

When Nunn Sr. joined the newspaper, it had been like taking up a crusade. Yes, the *Courier* reported the news. But its editors aimed to do more than that. The newspaper, with a circulation of less than 5,000 readers, might someday become a national power, they hoped. It would be a pulpit for those who would help the nation's black citizens rise up to equality and fairness. And the newspaper would achieve its goals by telling the truth, unsparingly.

"They told me a real newspaper stressed cleanliness and accuracy in the news," Nunn Sr. recalled decades later after the founders had died and he had ascended to managing editor. "They shied away from the lurid, sensational, imaginative reporting of the times. They planned an unstinting, but highly intelligent crusade for Negroes in the fields of labor, economics, education, government, politics, sports."

His son, then, had grown up in this environment, surrounded by stories of greatness and with a first-hand view of the action. He had experienced the newspaper's triumphs – some small, and others indelible: Vann's 1932 speech in which he called upon millions of black Americans to turn the picture of Abraham Lincoln to the wall and vote for a Democrat. And then the publisher's subsequent trip to the White House to collect on a promise from President Franklin D. Roosevelt to create a Negro division of the government, an early step toward Civil Rights. Nunn had also campaigned to launch black baseball players into the major league and to place black soldiers among the ranks of fighting men. His newspaper had pushed for victory at home and tirelessly worked to identify Dorie Miller, the unnamed messman hero. The *Courier* had moved into its own building too, as its circulation reached across the continent and topped 200,000.

Now the *Courier* offered Nunn Jr. a chance to work with his father. The newspaper had an opening for a sports reporter and wanted him to fill it.

Faced with the choice of where to start his future, Nunn Jr. thought little about the high-minded pursuits of his father and his father's friends. He worried instead about money and stability, and he looked for the place where he could find both.

The Knicks tryout would be no sure thing. Nunn Jr. looked at the roster and figured that the team really wanted big men who could dominate under the basket. That was not his game.

Professional basketball hardly seemed certain either. The Basketball Association of America had teams in New York and Boston, but also Rochester, New York. Several teams such as the Pittsburgh Ironmen and Cleveland Rebels never made it past their first year. Often played in hockey arenas where owners placed wooden boards over the ice, games were occasionally "rained" out when melted water formed puddles on the court or created clouds of fog. Other times owners tried to prevent melting by keeping the temperature so low that fans huddled in blankets and players wore gloves on the bench. Even after the league's first few years, teams drew an average of just 3,000 fans per game – and paid players about $3,000 a year in salary.[238]

Like his father, Nunn Jr. sought out his friends and mentors for advice before deciding. He went to Wendell Smith, the *Courier*'s sports writer, for advice. Smith had spent the previous year following Jackie Robinson through his season as the first black player in Major League Baseball. He had been there when the St. Louis Cardinals threatened to walk out rather than play against a black player until the league intervened and forced them to play the game.[239] Smith had been there too when Philadelphia Phillies Manager Ben Chapman told his players to "give it to" Robinson with every racist and derogatory remark they had.[240] Robinson had become a center of attention even before his first game with the Brooklyn Dodgers, where he emerged from Ebbets Field to flashbulbs that exploded with machinegun-like rapidity and fans pulling him so hard in every direction that they nearly ripped his clothes away.[241] He was in the same position as the "two-headed man in the circus" with some wanting to see him because they were skeptical about his playing ability and others simply because they considered him something new and different, Smith recalled. "Even his own teammates looked upon him with a strange curiosity," Smith said. "Many of them accepted him as the 'real thing,' not as a sideshow 'freak.' But there were others who, deep down inside, objected to his presence. They didn't want him on the club, didn't want to associate with him and didn't want to admit they played on the same team with this 'freak' of the diamond."[242]

If Nunn wanted to try out for the Knicks, he could expect to face the same treatment, Smith warned. Other players would resent him, and fans would come either to swear at him or to marvel at the color of his skin, a black man in a league of whites. Unlike Robinson, however, Nunn would toil in an unheralded league barely struggling to survive. Even if he succeeded, he could not expect to win the adulation of tens of thousands of fans. The

Basketball Association of America just didn't have that many followers.

Given the choice, Nunn figured he would have preferred to play for the Globetrotters. At least he would not seem a freak on the all-black traveling team. Besides, Nunn believed they had a better team anyway – and he was not alone in that belief. Arch Ward, the Chicago sportswriter who had started the All-American Football Conference, had written earlier that year that the "Trotters are still the best team in the world." Heading into a game that February with the Minnesota Lakers, the Globetrotters carried a 103-game winning streak – and they extended it that night against a team that went on to win a season-ending tournament of the top professional teams. During another game with the team ahead by one point and missing two of its five players because they had fouled out, Globetrotters' point guard Marques Haynes simply dribbled out the entire fourth quarter.[243]

But playing for the Globetrotters meant traveling the country on a bus. Because many of the towns they visited had only hotels for whites, it also meant often sleeping on the bus too. Even the team's clowning act drew critics. Although it was designed around the team's dominance over often inferior teams, some critics decried the tactics as part-minstrel show and demeaning to blacks.[244]

When Nunn Jr. looked to his father, he saw the spoils of the reporter's life.

Nunn Sr. lived better than most middle-class whites in Pittsburgh. He had a steady income. The family had a car. And around the time Nunn Jr. graduated from high school, his father had saved up enough money to buy a stretch of property on a bluff at the highest point in the Hill District. He had built a red-brick, two-story home there for his family, with a large park across the street and vistas out the back looking eastward through the city neighborhoods and nearby suburban towns of the Allegheny River valley. Rather than keeping the land for himself, Nunn Sr. divided it into lots and sold the property to other successful blacks to have as neighbors. Jazz singer Lena Horne now lived down the block.

In his working life, as the paper's managing editor, Nunn Sr. routinely found his way to the major events of black life in

America. He had been sitting ringside at boxing title events for years, sometimes catching a plane back to Pittsburgh to file the photos for the next week's newspaper. Events like the Negro league's annual East-West All-Star Game, started by Pittsburgher Gus Greenlee, had become his personal traditions. Over his career, Nunn Sr. had helped grow the *Courier* into not only one of the nation's largest newspapers but also one of its largest black-owned companies.

The *Courier* had given Nunn Sr. and his colleagues a platform to point out inequities experienced by black Americans and to make the case for equality. Their voices were respected by blacks throughout the country – from rich, influential community leaders to poor Southern sharecroppers desperate for the latest news. Their words also were read and understood by whites troubled by the nation's discrimination against others based on the color of their skin.

Robert L. Vann, the *Courier*'s founding publisher, died in 1940, and then when Ira Lewis, the paper's manager, died eight years later, Nunn Sr. took a moment to write about how their legacy would continue into the future through the people they had inspired. He did not have to look any further than the newsroom.

The *Courier*'s "employees, all with good jobs, with good pay, with an American outlook on life, are living symbols of the Vann-Lewis faith in America…and in humanity," Nunn Sr. wrote. "They made Democracy work in America. They lit the torch for 'first-class citizenship' for all Americans!"[245]

When Nunn Jr. went over his choices, he realized that becoming a newspaper reporter offered him the best chance at money, fame and stability.

Nunn Jr. took two weeks off after graduating from West Virginia State, moved back home with his parents at their new home in the Hill District, and then he went to work with his father at the *Courier*.

The decision to become a sports reporter for the nation's leading black newspaper would bring him more riches than he could imagine. But it also would put him in more difficult situations than he could know.

Chapter 4. The Beginning

Bill Nunn Jr. walked out the front door of his parents' red-brick house at the top of the Hill District, down one hill and then up another, about a mile or so to Forbes Field, the ballpark where the Pirates baseball team played. He was working that day, for the *Pittsburgh Courier*, covering Jackie Robinson's return to the city in his second season. But Nunn still had to pay $2.20 for a ticket to sit with the fans.[246] Sure, the Brooklyn Dodgers had a black second baseman, but the Pirates, like every other National League team[247], remained all-white. The white members of the Pittsburgh chapter of the Baseball Writers Association of America controlled the press box at Forbes Field, and they were not ready to sit with a black writer. None of the Pittsburgh daily newspapers had a black sports writer, so the association masked its racism behind a provision that barred anyone from a weekly newspaper – even one with 14 editions and readers in all of the major cities. Nunn would work among the fans, taking notes on what he could see from the stands.

It had been a busy summer since graduation. Nunn already had written a little for the *Courier* in high school and college, but now he leaned heavily on the paper's sports editor and the dean of its reporters, Wendell Smith, for guidance. Nunn's first big break had come when the paper sent him to Chicago to cover the Negro league's annual East-West all-star game. There, in Comiskey Park, with 42,099 fans on hand, Nunn could work like every other reporter. When the West team, with its younger, more athletic players, dominated the game, the young sports writer started finding his voice too: "As the sun set in the golden west here at Comiskey Park Sunday it seemed to take with it into the annals of baseball history the end of an era. The once proud gladiators from the East are no more; and in their wake has stepped a haughty, hustling bunch of ball players from out of the West, intent on showing the baseball world that the Negro American League produces the best that there is to offer as far as the diamond sport is concerned."[248] He meant that the western teams had finally started to build an edge against the once-dominant ones from the east, but he just as easily could have been talking about the demise of the Negro leagues. As soon as Major League Baseball started taking the best black players, it hurt the quality of the all-black leagues.

Nunn had started doing so well that the guys in the office recently had asked him to take over one of the newspaper's plum assignments – at least it felt like a prize for a single, young man with a heart for adventure. Smith had asked Nunn to help cover football games at black colleges throughout the country. With the dry daytime heat of September giving away now to crisply cool evenings, Nunn already had started feeling the tug of fall. Within weeks, he would be driving to cover games in places that he had visited as a player only months before.

For tonight, Nunn joined a sellout crowd of 38,265 fans to see whether the Pirates could handle Brooklyn.[249] The year before, after adding Robinson, the Dodgers had won the National League pennant. The Pirates had finished last. Nunn already had covered the Dodgers and Robinson earlier in the year. The previous "rookie of the year" had seemed to regain his speed on the base paths, Nunn noted: "Watch Jackie Robinson, he's running again."[250] In July, Robinson had scored the winning run over the Pirates by bolting from third base as the pitcher went into his windup, stealing home.

Writing for a weekly newspaper, Nunn looked for stories on players rather than games that could be long forgotten by the time the paper published. A leading story line that summer had been the Dodgers playing of Roy Campanella, the black son of Sicilian immigrants. He had started in the minors with Robinson but he had not joined the major league team until the following April. "Camp," as the players and newspapers called him, made the narrative easy. After starting with the major league team, he had been reassigned back to the minors. Then the Dodgers had fallen into last place and desperately needed some spark. Playing with the Saints minor league team in St. Paul, Minnesota, Campanella had homered eight times in seven days and he had driven his batting average up over .300. Fans of the Negro leagues recognized the swing that once made him a most-feared batter. By the time he came back to the Dodgers in July, the team had lost five in a row and had fallen to the bottom of the league. That day, Campanella had three hits in four trips to the plate. The team still lost, but it marked the beginning of a turnaround. In the seventh inning the next day, the rookie helped his team turn a 5-2 deficit into a win. Nunn had covered it all, finding in Campanella another compelling character for readers of the black newspaper.[251]

Sitting in the stands in early September, Nunn looked for another story line like that to fill his notebook and delight readers with the exploits of white baseball's first black players. Often, the story would reveal itself. On this night the narrative started unfolding in the bottom half of the third inning. Umpire Bill Stewart called a Pirates runner safe at second when Robinson thought he had tagged the man sliding past the base. Robinson had endured racial taunts and injustices quietly through the previous season and a half. Now, for the first time, he erupted. He started a tantrum, vigorously protesting the call – but without any satisfaction.

The next inning as the Dodgers came to bat, the home plate umpire suddenly swung around between pitches, turned toward the visiting dugout as he threw off his mask and shouted out at white catcher Bruce Edwards: "You can leave the game." A fan had been yelling toward the field but the umpire had mistakenly put the blame on the player and tossed him.

Robinson sat nearby, still fuming. Play resumed with the Dodgers batter grounding out to first. Suddenly, the umpire turned again, scarlet-faced as his mask came off again and he motioned for Robinson to leave the game too.

Robinson rushed out of the dugout in a second uproar as the capacity crowd joined in full throat. Watching in stunned shock, Nunn thought to himself that it seemed the Dodgers' second baseman had been "possessed by the devil himself." After all these times of keeping himself together when faced with slurs and segregation, Robinson was losing it over a baseball play. Finally, after winning the pennant and being named rookie of the year, after winning first tolerance and then acceptance by his teammates, Robinson was having a row that had nothing to do with his skin color and everything with what he believed was a blown call, followed by the umpire's accusation against the wrong man. Robinson was getting tossed ultimately for defending a white teammate, the man who had been replaced by Campanella behind the plate. This was a story, Nunn knew, the readers of the *Courier* would love.

When the game ended, Nunn stood outside the ballpark waiting for Robinson. What happened? Nunn wanted to know. Robinson said he had called out the umpire for tossing Edwards, but he wasn't sure anyone had heard him. "Knowing that Bruce had been put out over something that one of the fans said behind the dugout, I replied that 'somebody should get on you,'" Robinson said. "Evidently he heard the remark."[252]

Baseball fined Robinson $25 for the spat with the umpire. Nunn filed an exclusive for his readers.

Kenny Washington carried the ball just 23 times in his rookie season with the Los Angeles Rams, running for 114 total yards – or eighth-best on the team.[253] As a backup quarterback, he attempted eight passes and completed one, for 19 yards. It had been eight years since he, Woody Strode and Jackie Robinson had led UCLA to an undefeated season in 1939. Since then, Washington had undergone multiple knee surgeries. That had been among the reasons he had not qualified for military service, opting instead to travel with a group of celebrity athletes entertaining the troops. Just before joining his National Football League team, Washington had turned 28 years old and undergone yet another surgery. Its lingering effects hampered his playing time.

Fans who had watched him in college, then with the Pacific Coast teams and then again as the leading draw on West Coast barn-storming teams had to wonder just how good Washington might have been if he had been allowed to go straight into the NFL.

"He would undoubtedly have been, with one year's experience, one of the greatest of professional backs and a drawing card from one end of the league to the other," *Los Angeles Times* columnist Dick Hyland wrote. "…Washington has become a beaten-up ball player who is neither so strong nor so quick in his reactions as he was before the war."[254]

Washington's teammate Strode fared even worse with the Rams. He ranked tenth in pass receptions with four catches for 37 yards.[255] His knees felt fine but Strode believed the team had taken him only so Washington would have a roommate. He was in his 30s, and he had been through military service. He was part of a package deal, he understood, and the Rams had little intention of really playing him. The money was good – better than it had been with the semi-pro teams – but Strode still felt embarrassed to sit on the bench.

"I proved I could play, but for whatever reason the Rams weren't interested in using me," he recalled. "When somebody broke down, or they couldn't find anybody with guts enough to go out there and do the job, they'd stick me in and I would shine."[256]

Heading into his second pro season, Strode played just one time in an exhibition game before getting cut. Rams' line coach George Trafton broke the news: "Woody, it's not because of your ability that you're getting fired. They're trying to say you're too old and that they're trying to rebuild. I tried to tell them Negroes don't age like white people."[257]

Strode believed another bit of racial bias played into his release. He felt the Rams never had been able to overcome his marriage to a Hawaiian woman.

After he was cut, Strode went to see Washington who reinforced the idea. "It's your lifestyle," Washington said.

That evening, a group of players came by Strode's house and asked whether he wanted them to argue with the owner and management.

"I've never had a racial incident," he told the mob. "And I don't want to start one now."[258]

Going into this second season then, Washington was alone in the entire NFL as the only black player.

In the rival All-America Football Conference, the Cleveland Browns had won the league's first championship with Bill Willis and Marion Motley. Coach Paul Brown headed into the next season with another black player, Horace Gillom, a punter and defensive end who had played on Brown's high school team in Massillon, Ohio, over two seasons when the players never lost a game.

After seeing the Browns' success, other AAFC team owners were more willing to sign a black player too.[259] And they all had the same one in mind.

Claude "Buddy" Young had been a star at the University of Illinois before the war, and then after he was drafted, he had starred with the Navy's undefeated Fleet City Bluejackets. Tens of thousands of fans often watched a military team that hadn't existed a couple of years before. With Young's service term coming to an end, teams started vying for the "Bronze Bullet."

War victories in Europe and Asia made the country feel giddy. While blacks in the South feared Jim Crow laws rising again, others around the country joined in the national celebration. Even before Young left the military, the *Courier* threw a gala in Los Angeles at the glamorous Park Plaza Hotel[260] to celebrate his athletic achievements, along with those of boxer Joe Louis, baseball's Robinson and the Rams' Washington.[261] The event drew top black movie stars and entertainers including Lena Horne and Nat King Cole. People in southern California already had started murmuring that Young shouldn't bother going back to Illinois to finish his two years of college. Los Angeles had been so warm to black athletes before the war, they said, and UCLA would make a great home for him now. Plus, if the team did well with him, as everyone expected, Young could hope to play in the Rose Bowl on New Year's Day. Teams in the Big Nine league, which included Illinois, did not go to bowl games.

Members of Congress, meanwhile, lobbied the Naval Academy in Annapolis, Maryland, to appoint Young to the team there. He could be its first black athlete.

Young felt an allegiance to Illinois, even though black athletes did not have as many options there. Smith, the *Courier*'s sports writer, noted that Illinois allowed blacks to compete only on its football and track teams – but not in baseball, basketball, boxing, wrestling or swimming.[262] A resident of Champaign, Illinois, wrote to the newspaper advising Young to go anywhere other than back to the college town. "There is an abundance of prejudice here," the anonymous letter-writer said. "It is, without exaggeration, a school that has had far more done for it by its Negro athletes than it would, or could do for them."[263]

Pro teams wanted Young too. The Rams had said they wanted him when they first arrived in Los Angeles a year earlier, even though he was still serving in the military. The LA Dons, the AAFC team that shared the Coliseum and that had made the same commitment to signing a black player, secretly drafted Young.[264] He was technically eligible to play in the startup league because it had been four years since he started college. When he did not show up, however, the Dons did not field any black players in the team's inaugural season.

Young didn't care about the offers and advice. He headed back to his alma mater.

He ended up playing in the Rose Bowl too: against UCLA on New Year's Day. It was the first time champions of the Pacific Coast and Big Nine conferences met in the game. The Illini wore unusually colorful outfits for the game: white jerseys with four black stripes around their sleeves and black numerals, over yellow pants. [265] When they stepped onto the grassy field, which alternated light and dark every five yards, at Pasadena's Rose Bowl Stadium, the crowd of 93,083 fans let out a loud roar to welcome Young back to California.

Kenny Washington, who had just finished his first season with the Rams, looked on in a light-colored, double-breasted suit. He stood next to the president of the University of California and Governor Earl Warren. Half-a-year earlier, no black man had been allowed to play professional football at the highest level. Now as 1947 started, the NFL's first black player in more than a decade was surrounded by white political leaders. It seemed like they could not get close enough to the athlete, and they smiled broadly when they did.[266]

Down on the field, Young took a quick first sprint across the field and thought to himself that it felt like the fastest turf he ever had seen. It would be a harbinger for his day. When he catapulted across the goal from the two yard line in the second quarter, Young became the first black man to score in Rose Bowl history. Later, when he sliced off the end and headed for a second touchdown, it seemed that he scored before some Bruins players even realized he had the ball. In the press box, one wag called it the "Bruin ruin." Illinois won the game 45 to 14, and Young solidified his place as the nation's most exciting young football player.

His successes also underlined the weaknesses of segregation. The St. Louis Post-Dispatch noted a week later that neither Young nor any of the other three blacks in the game could have played at the University of Missouri or studied there — even if they had been born in the state, to tax-paying parents. "They happen to have been born with darker skins than those who set the rules for admission," the paper wrote.[267]

When the game ended, Young did not immediately head back to Illinois. He missed the victory celebration in Champaign and the first week of classes in the spring semester. With a wife and child, Young had other things on his mind.

He had another decision to make. After the Rose Bowl, the LA Dons immediately offered him $20,000 to play.[268] Another AAFC football team, the New York Yankees, reached out to Young as well. The team offered him a $25,000 signing bonus and $125,000 over three years.[269] That would make him the highest-paid player in the game, making more than even the top white player, Charley Trippi, who had flirted with the Yankees before going to the Chicago Cardinals for a $25,000 signing bonus and $100,000 over four years.

Technically, the Dons and Yankees were prohibited from negotiating with a college player, but Young had put his amateur status in question. He had agreed to play in California for a charity game against other professionals. Louis, the boxer, was hosting the event and had agreed to pay Young $5,000 for an appearance. White players from the Pacific Coast League backed out when they found out how much the black star would be making, and the game never took place.[270] [271]

Again, the Courier's Smith had advice for the young player. This time, it was about the Yankees' offer: "Grab that money like a drowning man grabs a safety belt."[272]

Five months later, Young turned up in New York at the offices of the Yankees. The Amateur Athletic Union had declared him ineligible for college football after he accepted a plane ride with his wife for the exhibition game that never came off. Illinois also had declared him ineligible because he had skipped mid-term exams for the spring semester.

By May, Young had received offers from seven professional teams. He chose the Yankees not only because of the money, he said, but also because the team had signed seven of his teammates from the Fleet City naval team.[273]

Young was among nine black players that AAFC teams signed before the start of the league's second season.[274] The impact of Brown's decision to play the best players in Cleveland, regardless of color, was being felt throughout the start-up league.

The Yankees had been desperate to change their fortunes. In the AAFC's inaugural season, the team had easily won the league's eastern conference. But then it had lost 14 to 9 to the Browns at Cleveland Stadium. By adding Young, the Yankees hoped to gain an edge.

Growing up, Bill Nunn Jr. had wondered where his father spent all of his time. He slept-in most mornings, waking late and then coming down to the kitchen to stand at the sink, looking east over the river valleys carved into the earth over the centuries. Some days, that would be the only time with everyone at home, a quiet moment to start the day. But then Nunn Sr. always found his way to the *Courier*'s offices. Every day. Even when the paper wasn't going to press. He would stay there late, rarely making it home for dinner and often lingering until 10 or 10:30 at night, the last one to leave. Even if he went golfing in the afternoon, he would find his way back to the newspaper before coming home.[275]

Now as he too joined the working world, the son started to understand. No wonder his father had stayed out so often. The streets were alive with stories – where everyone seemed to have a bit of gossip to share, and wanted to be the first to tell a newsman. To feel that satisfaction of watching the reporter's eyes grow big with wonder over a good tale. To see him reach into a back pocket to pull out a long, narrow notebook and then jot down a few details or maybe a juicy quote. No one likes telling a yarn only to have the reporter shake his head and say he has heard it before.

Nunn felt freedom too when he started working at the *Courier*. The newsroom sat on the second floor of the paper's own building on Centre Avenue, amid a warren of narrow streets and close houses. Reporters and editors sat in a separate section, away from the clacking and whirring of the linotype machines[276] that literally spit out lines of type, rather than individual letters, that were used to design the paper. Then the presses roared as they pulled great rolls of paper and printed the latest edition amid a drenching smell of ink that made the head feel light.

Inside the newspaper's offices, no one but the girls working as stenographers and receptionists really watched the clock. Everyone else came and went as they needed to get the work done. The rest of the time, they filled their hours with the reporting life. Work almost always was done out on the street anyway. Nunn's family had two cars but he preferred to walk. Along the way, he passed barber shops and bakeries, little groceries, bars and churches. The paper sat across the street from the YMCA, where black entertainers and athletes stayed when they were turned away from white hotels. Nunn had spent enough time on these streets to know many of the people. The reporter's life, it turned out, had a lot to do with trading stories, hearing some secrets over here and trading them over there. Nunn counted his sources among the police and the pimps, the numbers writers collecting money for the unofficial daily lottery and the ministers trying to fill their pews. He knew which cops were on the take and the ones that stayed honest. Everyone had a story to tell – and everyone wanted to find out which news the *Courier* had not yet heard.

The weekend for newspaper reporters started on Wednesday night when the last copies of the final city edition rolled off the presses for Pittsburgh readers. On Thursdays, no one had to come into the office but many did anyway, partially out of habit but also to read over the latest edition with clear eyes. They felt the satisfaction of seeing the finished paper – with its scoops and strong editorials, breaking news and latest investigations – mingled with the dread of finding a typo or, even worse, a glaring error in a headline. On Fridays, most employees allowed themselves a day off as the anticipation of filling the entire paper over again started creeping back. By Saturdays, everyone had returned to the offices putting that fear to ease with new information once again as details started trickling in from the newspaper's distant offices. When the presses started to run Sunday morning for the national edition, they kept going through the night into Monday morning, turning out stacks of bound papers for the waiting trucks that would carry them to the railroad for delivery across the country. Employees basically worked a double-shift that day, with the week already half over, before it began.

Covering sports, Nunn spent time in baseball's Negro leagues that first summer, and they already had started showing signs of fraying. Robinson was the first, but others followed. After starting Robinson the previous April, the Dodgers lured black pitcher Dan Bankhead away from the Memphis Red Sox by August of that year. He had beaten the New York Yankees in an exhibition game in the spring while pitching for a team in Caguas, Puerto Rico. In his first appearance at Ebbets Field, he gave up ten hits over three innings to the lowly Pirates – but hit a home run in his first major-league at-bat.[277] In between, three other blacks made it into Major League Baseball that first season: Larry Doby was leading the Negro leagues with a .458 batting average when the Cleveland Indians signed him in July, 11 weeks after Robinson's first appearance. That month, the St. Louis Browns, the worst team in baseball, purchased from the Negro leagues' Kansas City Monarchs the contracts of Henry Thompson and Willard Brown, making them the major league's first black teammates.[278] The Dodgers added Campanella at catcher the following season, in 1948, and the Cleveland Indians trotted out Satchel Paige at age 42 after a successful Negro leagues career.[279]

No other team would add a black player for another year, and many held out far longer than that. But the impact was being felt – both in the Negro leagues that were losing their best players and in the Major League where owners were seeing fans pass through the turnstiles to see blacks play. The Dodgers' Branch Rickey had proved with Robinson that the Negro leagues held gold: Brooklyn set a National League attendance record his first season. Then Cleveland, with Doby and Paige, broke every attendance record ever set by a Major League team.[280] The pocketbook was the weakness of the white supremacy program, black Chicago lawyer Joseph D. Bibb wrote that fall. He had seen a throng of 51,013 fans crowd into the White Sox's Comiskey Park to watch Paige pitch a complete game shutout of the home team.[281] "Frothy sentiment and archaic phobias are rapidly being hurled into discard," Bibb wrote.[282] "It is cold-blooded business. And adroit business men in sports, at least, have found out that color pays off."

But as summer turned to fall, as the Indians streaked toward the pennant, Nunn turned his attention to college football. The summer had been one of liberty and discovery. But it had nothing on the adventure that waited.

Buddy Young immediately impacted professional football. The Yankees again won the AAFC's eastern division in his rookie season. With the Cleveland Browns dominating in the west, the two teams met for a championship rematch that December.

Standing on the sidelines, Coach Paul Brown pulled his big fullback Marion Motley to the side. Look up at the stands, he said. More than 61,000 people had come out to Yankee Stadium despite a bitter cold. More than 3,000 had come from Cleveland, including the mayor.

"Marion, you see all those people out there?" the coach asked. "Guess what they're here for."

Motley gave the obvious answer, to watch a football game.

"No, Marion," Brown replied. "The thing they want to know is whether you or Buddy Young is a better man."[283]

Over four quarters, Motley and the Browns provided a definitive answer. They controlled the game with Motley's running, by holding onto the ball and by keeping it away from the Yankees' star. Motley ran 51 yards to set up Cleveland's first touchdown late in the first quarter. Cleveland won the game 14-3, its second league championship in only the league's second year.

"Marion Motley, bulldozing fullback of the Cleveland Browns, proved the old axiom that 'a good big man can always beat a good little man,'" reporter Haskell Cole wrote in the *Courier*.[284]

Hundreds of Cleveland fans swarmed the field after the game, and a group of blacks lifted Motley on their shoulders, carrying him halfway to the locker room. He shouted as he bounded inside: "Great, great, great! Well, we beat them because we played together. Did you ever see any team pull together like ours out there? No fussing, no arguments. We played football like we knew we'd win."[285]

Scouting football for the first time, Nunn turned his eye toward his former opponents and teammates. He knew that college football meant more than just a game to the black schools and their fans, yearning for a financial, academic and athletic equal footing. Rutgers and Princeton played the first football game in 1869[286], but black colleges had adopted the game for their own by 1892. That's when Charlotte's Biddle University[287] traveled 45 miles up the road to Livingston College in Salisbury, North Carolina, amid bitter cold and four inches of snow to play a game that only one or two of the participants had even seen before.[288] In place of sweaters, the players bought bolts of brown cloth and made blouses to match their pants. No one wore pads or helmets to protect their heads. But they brought a great spirit. The Biddle Bulls shouted a rhyming, Latin-laced fighting yell before kickoff.[289] And after the 90-minute game, split into two 45-minute halves, when the visiting team won a 4-to-0 victory with the points coming from a touchdown but not a failed extra-point conversion, the men from both squads met for a turkey dinner and social.

By the fall of 1948, the black college game had grown. The spirit had remained strong with a focus on the outcome of each game, of course, but also on the social aspects that grew up around it. At Louisiana's Grambling College, Coach Eddie Robinson was building perhaps the country's best-known black football program. The school had the nation's leading running back in Paul "Tank" Younger, who had topped all black players with 110 points and 1,207 yards the year before. But Grambling's growing fame had as much to do with its public relations program as the play on the field. Collie J. Nicholson, a prolific and talented public relations director, wrote sensational press releases and the occasional newspaper story for outlets such as the *Courier*. "Coach Eddie Robinson rolls his Grambling College gridders out of the hay every morning at an hour when most burglars are returning home from a hard night with the crowbar and wedge," he wrote on one occasion.[290] At another, he said, "Robinson, a mild-mannered perfectionist is known as the 'Cinderella coach' of Negro football."[291] Writing for the *Courier* at the start of the 1948 season, Nicholson described fullback Younger as the "heart and soul of many a winning drive during the campaign," evoking military language in the post-war years.[292]

But Grambling was just one of many black colleges with rich football traditions. Even if white America wasn't watching, the talent seemed obvious to anyone who actually looked. Nunn saw it as soon as he opened his eyes as a scout: "There was no doubt about it," he said years later. "Hey, I had been around athletes all my life. I could see. I could see speed. Naturally one of the things that was part of it was segregation."[293]

Each year, the *Courier* chose the black college national champion. Sometimes that was the winner of the Orange Blossom Classic, a game in Jacksonville or Miami hosted by Florida A&M. More often, the paper picked the team or teams with the best record, sometimes choosing more than one top school. Tennessee State had won the previous two black college national championships, losing just one game over two seasons. Baltimore's Morgan State College already had won five championships behind Coach Edward P. Hunt. Heading into that fall, coaches at Alabama's Tuskegee Institute, North Carolina's Shaw University, Lincoln University near Philadelphia and Ohio's Wilberforce State College, among at least a dozen others, had national championship ambitions.

Football helped those schools build a sense of belonging in an America still uncertain about accepting blacks as equal partners. When Atlanta's Morris Brown College opened a $250,000 football stadium that year with seats for 15,000 fans, blacks across the country heralded it as not only a fine place to watch a game – but as an ambition achieved. The stadium served as proof that an all-black college, using its own money with support from successful alumni, could achieve status taken for granted by white schools. Nunn's father traveled from Pittsburgh to the opening and captured the meaning of the moment, calling it a "milestone of progress and achievement" and an "epoch in community and civic development." As he sat in the press box watching the kaleidoscopic picture of high schools bands, track stars and the Elks drill corps of Atlanta commemorating the new building, Nunn Sr. saw more than concrete and steel. "It is impossible," he wrote to *Courier* readers across the country, "not to think of the driving spirit and the enervating genius of those intrepid characters who had made of this stadium … a dream come true!"[294]

His son brought a similar emotion to chronicling the college game. And in the process, he started to define his own belief system. One in which football evoked its own lyricism. There was the game. And then there was its broader meaning, as a competition and as a way of celebrating black culture, independent of the white game and the larger America that followed white players. Before covering his first game – Richmond's Virginia Union University versus his alma mater, West Virginia State – Nunn predicted winners for that week's games. He chose his school to "barely nose out" Union[295]. He also articulated a philosophy that would define the rest of his life:

"As the golden brown leaves of autumn begin their earthward flight back to the soil from which they came, the sounds of clashing helmets, bone crushing tackles and nerve defying blocks begin to penetrate the air."[296]

Football, then, as part of the life cycle. Ashes to ashes, and football season to football season.

Nunn made one other telling observation that would be equally important to his outlook: Not everyone wins.

"By the time December creeps in," he wrote, "many a coach will have seen his dreams of a great football machine fade away into the nothingness that goes hand-in-hand with mediocre teams of the past."

With Nunn sitting in the press box at Institute, West Virginia, his alma mater dominated for three quarters – but then Union started passing the ball and won on a field goal with 2:15 left in the game.[297] The young reporter had been accurate about the nature of the game, but he had backed the wrong winner. Enough of Nunn's other picks, however, were accurate enough for him to keep his job.

That fall, he traveled mainly through the Mid-Atlantic and Appalachia. He covered the biggest mid-season game in black college football when defending black national champion Tennessee State met Wilberforce State College in Washington, D.C. Wilberforce made up for its only loss to Tennessee the year before.[298] Nunn watched his alma mater in November ruin Virginia State's perfect season, relying on the arm of quarterback Joe Gilliam despite a driving rain storm that left the field soaked with a half-inch of water.[299] And he traveled to Frankfurt, Kentucky, to see Tennessee State's final indignation, a 19-0 shutout loss to Kentucky State over the Thanksgiving holiday.[300]

The *Courier* named the first black college All-America team in 1925, and the paper's editors and reporters took the responsibility seriously. They tried to see as many games as possible – from Texas to the Deep South of Mississippi and Louisiana to small college towns throughout the Northeast and Mid-Atlantic. Correspondents from across the country covered games too, and coaches and athletic directors filled the *Courier*'s mail boxes with colorful information about their best players. Ultimately, someone in the newspaper's main office had to decide. Wendell Smith and Chester Washington had been making the picks for years. They traveled in the late summer to watch practices and then headed out over the fall to see one marquis game each week. Over the years, the paper claimed its top sports editor might travel 15,000 miles over the football season to see a dozen or more games.[301]

But a black man traveling around the country on his own, particularly through the Jim Crow strongholds of the South, faced unique challenges in an age before rental cars and cell phones. At the time, blacks could not just stay at any hotel. Ray Sprigle, a white reporter who already had won the Pulitzer Prize, chronicled the challenges for black travelers when he spent the summer of 1948 posing as a black man crossing through the South. He left out of Union Station in Washington, D.C., and traveled through Georgia, Mississippi, Alabama and other states, riding in Jim Crow rail cars, eating in blacks-only restaurants and staying with Negro families.

"Discrimination against the Negro in the North is an annoyance and an injustice," he concluded. "In the South, it is bloodstained tragedy."[302]

For Nunn, like the other *Courier* reporters who traveled to the South by plane out of Pittsburgh, the culture shock could be severe. It could feel like traveling back in time, from a place with one set of rules for blacks to another with entirely different, more-severe practices.

"You had to be aware of it," Nunn said, "when you could fly out of Pittsburgh and go to a black college, and then get off the plane and you had to get on a bus that's segregated."

That fall when two white schools, the University of Alabama and Vanderbilt University, played the first game at Ladd Stadium in Mobile, Alabama, blacks were allowed to purchase tickets – but only after it became clear that not enough whites would attend for a sellout. Even then, after paying the same $3.80 per ticket, blacks sat farthest from the field and were not allowed to use the toilets.[303]

Two weeks later, 41 members of West Virginia State College's football team were traveling by Pullman rail car on their way to Nashville when they tried to get something to eat in the dining car. Conductors told the players they would have to eat behind a curtain, shielded from the white diners. The railway men even offered to move the curtains halfway up the railcar to make more room. But the players refused, choosing instead not to eat anything over the eight-hour ride. For the trip back, the team brought along 82 sandwiches.[304]

Nunn, like his predecessors at the paper, knew a few tricks to make the traveling easier. It helped that wherever he went, he always arrived as the living manifestation of the *Courier*. For blacks, even in remote college towns, the paper carried news of the outside world. And the arrival of a reporter for that newspaper on campus was cause for a little special attention. Nunn might have to ride in the back of the bus until he arrived on campus. But from that moment, he received special treatment. Unable to stay in white hotels, Nunn often instead would end up sleeping at the home of the college president or athletic director. School officials would be eager to see that he had a good time, providing meals, covering expenses and keeping him entertained.

"I had no desire to even go to restaurants because everything was happening right there on campus," Nunn said. "...It was basically like I was a celebrity."[305]

Typically, he would leave Pittsburgh on a Friday, be at the college Saturday for the game of the week, stay overnight and return home Sunday, headed straight for the paper's offices. Already, the *Courier* would be going to press. Nunn initially was responsible just for his own stories but eventually he ended up laying out the sports pages, rewriting copy from across the country and editing the *Courier*'s Detroit edition. With so many papers to produce each week, there was always plenty to do. Not all of it had to do with sports.

Rosa Lee Ingram, already a widowed black mother of 12 children at age 40, looked up from working on the Georgia farm her family worked as sharecroppers – raising animals and crops on someone else's land and giving up a share of their harvest in return. She saw a white farmer from next door heading her way with a .32 caliber rifle in his hand. John Ed Stratford had found the Ingrams' mules and hogs in his corn field again, and he grabbed the rifle to shoot them. Then he saw Rosa Lee and headed in her direction instead.[306]

In one version of events, the white farmer confronted the black mother along a road between their homes and started beating her around the head with the rifle. She snatched the gun and hit him back. Then he started hitting her with an unopened knife. With blood running down her face, she screamed and pleaded for him to stop. At least two of her sons, maybe more, came to her defense and attacked the white farmer.

That turned out to be the only version of the event. Stratford ended up dead. One of the sons had grabbed the gun and hit Stratford two times in the head. He fell to the ground. His wallet, with $133 in it, ended up buried behind the Ingrams' barn.

Scared, Rosa Lee and her children all ran to their house. She sent a son, Wallace, 17, to tell the folks in town what happened. The sheriff and lots of white men came to the road. They arrested Rosa Lee and four of her sons. One was charged with stealing the wallet and one was let go. Rosa Lee and two older boys – Wallace and Sammie Lee, 14 – were charged with killing the neighbor. A special grand jury was convened to indict them. Two days later, a special court tried, convicted and sentenced the mother and sons to die in the electric chair. At home, another son James, 11, was left to take care of the 17-month-old baby and the other children. Their oldest sister was picking beans in Florida.

That's when the *Courier*'s J. Richardson Jones showed up. He interviewed Rosa Lee from prison. She stammered through trembling lips with tears falling from her eyes: "My children need me! I need my baby!"[307]

The newspaper found evidence that had been overlooked. The mother's sweater had been torn in the struggle. She told another reporter that the white farmer had "persistently tried to 'go with me.'" In response, the NAACP sent defense lawyers to Georgia and *Courier* readers took up a defense fund.

A judge stayed the executions – and the *Courier* took credit for saving their lives.

"The Pittsburgh Courier takes pride in feeling that it has helped to negotiate another milestone along the highway toward civil rights for ALL Americans," Chester Washington wrote.

Editors and reporters for the *Courier* believed they had a responsibility not only to tell the news – but to crusade on behalf of black Americans.

That same year, 1948, the paper exposed racial bias in Washington, D.C., by focusing on slum conditions within sight of the Capitol and directly behind the Senate Office Building. Nearly a quarter of black residents in the capital lacked flush toilets.[308] One in ten did not have running water. Three percent still went without electricity. These were health benefits and conveniences that nearly every white resident of the city took for granted. A government report in response to the *Courier's* stories found that the capital actually had been getting more segregated while blacks were making gains in other parts of the country. "More and more Negroes have been confined to a ghetto or to ghettoes which expand but do not disintegrate," the paper wrote in a Christmas Day editorial.[309]

Separately, the paper continued its push to end segregation in the military[310], and it sent its own reporter George S. Schuyler to canvass the South. Unlike Sprigle, he did not have to pose as a black man. He was one. Three-quarters of the nation's blacks lived in the South, so Schuyler traveled 10,000 miles through 14 states to examine their quality of life.[311] He too found a dire situation, focusing in part on the inadequate schooling for blacks in their separate, if not equal, education system.

Robinson had proven in baseball that whites would overcome racial stereotypes when there was a buck to be made, Schuyler concluded. If blacks could make a similar case throughout the South – that they contributed to the economic success of their communities – they might make a stronger argument for equal rights everywhere. He finished his series with an editorial that laid out a strategy to make that case: "First, intelligent campaign should be waged against segregation in transportation because that is the least defensible, and inroads have already been made via interstate travel."[312]

Few people outside of Montgomery, Alabama, would know anything about a seamstress and housekeeper named Rosa Parks for another seven years.

That same month in Los Angeles, Kenny Washington ran onto the field at halftime of a game against the Pittsburgh Steelers for the biggest reception of his two-year career. The time between playing at UCLA and the pros – with the barnstorming games and work as a police officer – had been too long. Woody Strode, his black teammate, already had been cut at the start of the season. Now Washington heard the crowd of 27,367 fans cheer for "Kenny Washington Day" in Los Angeles, to mark his retirement.

Members of the Kenny Washington Day Committee were waiting at mid-field. They gave him a new Ford automobile, money for his children's college fund, a trophy and a television set. Washington's teammates had taken up a donation to buy him an inscribed watch. A group of boys from El Centro, an agricultural center along the Mexican border, had won that city's touch-football championship, and they presented Washington with a sports shirt and a crate of lettuce.[313]

Washington turned to thank the crowd. The applause he received over his 16-year football career had gone to his heart, he said, but never to his head.

After the game, Washington would go on to an acting career in Hollywood and to business. The NFL, meanwhile, would go back to being all-white. At least for the moment.

Black college football was winding down too, and Nunn for the first time would get to help with the *Courier*'s All-American picks. His predictions for the season mostly had panned out. Southern University in Baton Rouge, Louisiana, had not been among his favorites in August – but he had been right that many other coaches' ambitions for a great season had fallen apart.

Southern had shocked a lot of people. Coach Ace Mumford's team not only won its third-straight Southern Conference championship but it had been so dominating with 12 wins and no losses that the *Courier* staff had chosen the Jaguars as the black college national champion.

Instead of playing in a bowl game to end the season, Southern traveled to play all-white San Francisco State College in an inter-racial contest – with more than bragging rights on the line.

"A convincing victory will mean much for Negro colleges," Wendell Smith, the sports columnist, wrote. "On the other hand, a humiliating defeat will mean that Negro colleges do not play the brand of football some of us like to believe they do."[314]

Southern ended up winning 33 to 0.[315]

Two Southern players made the *Courier's* All-American team, among 22 men who had "written their names in gold across the football heavens," in the paper's typically hyperbolic language.[316]

But no words had been too bold for one member of the all-star team, Grambling's Paul Younger. Nicknamed the "Tank" at 220 pounds, big for that day, he had scored over his career 60 college touchdowns and a record 362 points. Among all the honored players, he most deserved a shot at the pros, the *Courier* wrote.

That December, boxers Joe Louis and Billy Conn faced each other one more time.

Their first bout had followed them through the war, with Americans eager for a rematch that had to be put off until the fighting ended. Then the two men agreed to box a second time in June 1946. Conn hoped once more to use his speed against the champ and win on points. Louis famously responded: "He can run, but he can't hide." Louis again won by knockout. This time, Conn immediately retired while still sitting in his dressing room. "I'm convinced I haven't got it anymore, so I'm quitting," he told reporters.

But both men made out. The spectacle brought in a gate of nearly $2 million and a national television audience, a first for a heavyweight championship.[317] Promoter Mike Jacobs had priced ringside seats at $100, at a time when a gallon of gasoline cost 21 cents and bread was 10 cents a loaf.

The money brought the boxers back a third time.

Louis had signed onto a series of exhibition matches that would pay him $100,000. Conn agreed to fight him one more time, for six rounds with no title on the line. Ringside seats would cost just $7.

"You can't expect them to charge top prices for an exhibition...," Conn said. "But whatever I get will be extra gravy, and if I look good I'm sure to get another big money fight by the time summer rolls around."

Louis seemed to agree: "If you could make $100,000 this year on your job, would you quit or keep on working?"

Conn lost on points. And he finally retired for good.[318] [319]

Despite the advances won by Robinson in baseball or Washington and Strode with the NFL, and Motley and Willis in the AAFC, racial discrimination continued to play out.

Lafayette College in Easton, Pennsylvania, had won an invitation to play on New Year's Day in the Sun Bowl, but its faculty declined to accept when organizers told them the team's star halfback, who was black, could not play. Jack Rhodes, a tackle for the University of Texas at El Paso, which also had been invited to the bowl game, said he could not understand the controversy: A couple of years earlier, he had fought with black soldiers against the Nazis.[320]

Then in Toledo, Ohio, that month, organizers of the "Banquet of Champions" invited some of the year's top athletes to the Hotel Commodore Perry. They had gathered baseball's Joe DiMaggio and Stan Musial, top football players from the Chicago Cardinals and Brooklyn Dodgers, golf's Ben Hogan and Olympic champions, among others. But not one black athlete.

R.A. Stranahan, co-founder of Champion Spark Plug and the evening's host, stood before the audience and declared without irony that the assembly exemplified America – "the one country where there are no castes. Where ability, achievements and character are the common denominators and all admire and prize each other."[321]

Preventing blacks from playing in sports now that they had found athletic success – and after owners had started making money from the increased interest – felt like holding back time. In Grambling, Louisiana, that next spring the momentum toward sports equality grew stronger, if imperceptibly to all but those caught in its pull.

Paul Younger, the "Tank," waited along the train tracks for the colored-only railcar that would carry him to Los Angeles. Eddie Robinson, his coach, stood nearby. They had been together for years, since Younger was an unusually big 16-year-old boy – at more than six feet tall and 200-plus pounds. Robinson had recruited him to play for Grambling. Together, they won 33 games against 13 losses. That success rate, along with Nicholson's public relations efforts, had made black people across the country pay attention.

Some whites had noticed too. With Washington retiring, the owners of the Los Angeles Rams wanted a new black star. Scout Eddie Kotel had come to Grambling in the spring of 1949, just after graduation, and he had offered Younger a $6,000 free agent professional contract. He had settled on the contract offer after Robinson and Grambling's president had hounded him to offer an amount they thought was appropriate.

Blacks had appeared in both professional leagues but they remained uncommon. The NFL and AAFC agreed to merge later that year, adding the Cleveland Browns, San Francisco 49ers and Baltimore Colts to the NFL. By then, five of the seven AAFC teams had a black man on the roster. The NFL had been slower to integrate, with just three teams fielding a black player – the Rams, Detroit Lions and New York Giants.[322]

But none of the black professionals had come out of an all-black college. Younger would have the first chance.

"You've been voted the best football player in the country from a black school," Robinson said as they stood waiting for the train.[323] "You are now going to play for the Los Angeles Rams. And if you don't make it, they can always say, 'We took the best you had to offer, and he wasn't good enough.' And in all likelihood, it may be years before another black guy gets an opportunity."

Younger looked his coach in the eye. "If they're playing football," he said, "I'll make it."

As a Ram, Younger went on to play in four Pro Bowls as a league all-star, play in four championship games and gain almost 5,000 yards as a runner and receiver over ten years. "He made the most of an opportunity," Robinson recalled years later.

Two years after Younger went to the Rams, members of the New York Giants staff were sitting in their draft room discussing potential picks. Owner Wellington Mara walked into the room holding a copy of the *Pittsburgh Courier*. It was the edition with the black college All-America list.

Nunn had started picking the players in 1949[324] when Wendell Smith received an offer to work for the Chicago Herald-American, a white paper with no black sports reporters at the time. The *Courier* had celebrated Smith's departure as breaking down another racial barrier. And Smith had let it be known in Chicago that he would not be just the paper's black writer. "I'm not going to just write about blacks in sports," he told his new editors.[325] "If you want me to be a sportswriter here, I'm going to write about all sports, and I'm going to do it fairly."

Mara, talking with his scouts, laid out his copy of the *Courier* and pointed to the name Roosevelt "Rosey" Brown, a black All-American lineman from Baltimore's Morgan State College.

"Take this guy," the owner said.

Brown, too, given a chance, made the most of it. He played in nine Pro Bowls over 13 seasons, was named lineman of the year in 1956 and entered the Pro Football Hall of Fame as only its second offensive lineman.

Bill Nunn Jr. had found Brown before anyone in the NFL ever had heard the player's name.

By then, Nunn had been fighting his own battles against discrimination.

More than two years after Smith helped convince the Dodgers' Branch Rickey to play Robinson in 1947, the *Courier's* reporters still could not sit in the press box at Pittsburgh's Forbes Field. The local chapter of the Baseball Writer Association of America continued to hide behind the rule that it would not allow anyone in the press box unless they worked for a daily newspaper. Because the *Courier* published just once a week, its reporters had to sit in the stands.

"That, of course, is simply evading the issue," Smith wrote in 1949, while he was still working for the paper. "It's a technicality used conveniently under the circumstances."[326]

Vince Johnson, a white sports reporter for the *Pittsburgh Post-Gazette*, agreed. He attempted to force the issue from within the ranks of the baseball writers association – but its

Charles "Teenie" Harris, American, 1908–1998. Bill Nunn Jr., Chicago Cubs baseball player Ernie Banks, Milwaukee Braves player Hank Aaron, and Mal Goode, examining baseball bat on Forbes Field for 1959 All Star game, July 1959. Black and white: Kodak Safety Film, H: 4 in. x W: 5 in. (10.20 x 12.70 cm), Carnegie Museum of Art, Pittsburgh: Heinz Family Fund, 2001.35.5931.

members responded by asking him to resign from the group and to leave the press box too.

Black reporters for the *Courier* already had become members of the American Newspaper Guild, a local chapter of the Congress of Industrial Organizations union. Its executive committee voted in the fall of 1949 to investigate the baseball writers' discrimination against guild members who had been excluded from the Forbes Field press box.[327] The union leaders also agreed to test the ranks of the all-white local Women's Press Club, which had refused membership to two black writers for the *Courier*.

Still, by baseball's opening day in 1950, when Nunn wanted to cover a visiting black player, he had to buy a ticket and sit with the fans.

Then on a spring night in May, with the Boston Braves visiting Pittsburgh, the baseball writers granted Nunn "special privileges" for the first time. Boston had just signed its first black player, centerfielder Sam Jethroe, the month before. The baseball writers agreed that any time one of the three National League teams with a black player – the Dodgers, Giants or Braves – visited Pittsburgh, Nunn could sit in the press box. Despite the association's argument that it had banned *Courier* reporters only because the paper came out just once a week, its members ironically had made an exception to the rule based only on the issue of race.

"Strangely enough, upon entering the press box Tuesday night, no brass band struck up 'Hail, Hail, the Gang's All Here,'" Nunn wrote to readers of the *Courier* that week.[328] "The many sepia fans on hand to see Jethroe perform didn't stand up and holler, 'There he is,' and, believe it or not, the seats didn't catch on fire when I sat down. Actually no fanfare was involved. That's the way it should have been."

Nunn still could not join the Baseball Writers Association. He would not be allowed access to the press box when the all-white Pirates played opposing teams that had only white players. But progress had been made. Another barrier broken.

"That doesn't mean we've quit the battle…," Nunn wrote. "Actually the battle has just begun."

Charles "Teenie" Harris, American, 1908–1998, Portrait of Bill Nunn Jr.
seated at desk with documents and typewriter, in office with North
Carolina Mutual Life Insurance Company calendar on wall, possibly in
Pittsburgh Courier Newspaper office, c. 1950-1960. black and white: Kodak
Safety Film, H: 4 in. x W: 5 in. (10.20 x 12.70 cm), Carnegie Museum of Art,
Pittsburgh: Heinz Family Fund, 2001.35.44714.

Chapter 5. Broken

Johnny Bright led the country in total offense as a sophomore at Drake University, a small Bible college in Cedar Rapids, Iowa, in 1949. The following year, as a junior, the quarterback topped all college players in rushing and passing yards again. Then by his senior year, he had covered more ground than anyone in the history of the college game. And Bright was black.

When he started against Oklahoma A&M College as a sophomore, Bright became the first black athlete ever to take the football field in Stillwater. At the time, few people knew him and the moment passed without much attention.

Returning two years later, he had emerged as a top national star. The game likely would determine the eventual champion of the Missouri Valley Conference, a rapidly evolving league that stretched from Detroit to Houston, cutting through the middle of the nation and crossing over a wide range of attitudes about race. And this time, as Drake's senior quarterback, Bright would not be missed.

Walking into the stadium, Bright looked around at the 22,500 people in the stands. That was more than five times as many people as Drake had enrolled as students. Oklahoma A&M's players and fans were celebrating parents' day, which stirred emotions even before Drake arrived with its black star. The night before, while his white teammates stayed at a hotel, Bright had not been allowed to join them and he spent the night at the home of a local black preacher instead.

As the game started, an Oklahoma businessman and his wife sat in the stands behind two members of the Aggies' practice squad. One of the players turned and shared the team's strategy: "We're gonna get that nigger." [329]

But the team's plan had been an open secret on campus all week, at least to anyone who had watched practice. Oklahoma's coach had rehearsed his players with a simple mantra: "Get that nigger."

On the first play from scrimmage, Bright stood under center near his team's 30-yard-line, took the ball, turned around and handed it to the fullback behind him.[330] [331] As the runner scampered to his left for a first down, Bright relaxed and drifted backwards as he watched the ball carrier.

Oklahoma A&M defensive tackle Wilbanks Smith never turned his eyes away from Bright. He charged unseen toward the quarterback, balling his fist and cocking back his right arm as he closed in from a yard away. Players did not wear facemasks at the time. As Bright looked to his left with his arms hanging at his sides, Smith's fist swung around and crashed into Bright's jaw.

The quarterback crumpled to the ground.

Drake's trainer ran onto the field, followed by the team's coach a moment later. Bright staggered to his feet and rubbed his left jaw, feeling the bones move.

As he stood there on the field, Bright waved off any question about coming out of the game.

On the team's second play, from its 39 yard line, Bright took a direct pass from center, stepped a little to his right, stopped and braced, throwing a long pitch down an alley where his teammate had cut straight down the field and emerged behind the Oklahoma A&M safety. The receiver turned to his left, running in full stride, caught the ball with two hands and turned toward the end zone untouched.

Drake had needed 35 seconds to score. Bright stayed in the game.

The Aggies came back to score a touchdown moments later but missed the extra point.

Bright returned to the field for another drive. In a play almost identical to the one that opened the game, Bright took the ball from center, turned and handed off to his right halfback who scampered to the left for two yards.

Again, Bright watched the play. And again, Smith charged in unseen and clobbered the defenseless Bright.

He fell to the turf again. This time, he stayed down until the trainer helped him to his feet. The quarterback rubbed his jaw again. Undeniably, it had broken.

Again, Bright remained in the game.

The next play, Bright took the ball and kept it, running four yards to his right. He was tackled cleanly on the play.

Finally, he could not stand back up. The pain felt too great. He stayed on the turf until the trainer ran back out once more. A Drake offensive lineman helped Bright get on his feet. He and the trainer guided the quarterback toward the sideline.

After 5,690 yards in a record-setting college career, Bright had been stopped by two illegal blows to his jaw.

The entire game so far, the referees had not called a single penalty.

But photographers for the *Des Moines Register* had captured the two muggings on film in a rapid sequence of shots. They had enough time to take photos during the first 10 minutes of the game before rushing to the airport, catching one of the newspaper's "Good News" propeller planes and returning to Des Moines in time to print the photos for the next day's edition.[332]

A series of six photographs showing the first play of the game ran across the front page of the Sunday sports section with a detailed cutline: "Bright's head goes back like a fighter being knocked out. And this was the end of John Bright – probably for the season. He was half carried, half led off the field."[333]

Oklahoma A&M went on to win the game, 27 to 14, but as the *Register*'s sports writer said, the victory "must have been a flat, tasteless one."[334]

Drake's school administrators had felt helpless watching from the stands. Their frustration grew in the weeks after. The president of Drake's athletic council went to the Missouri Valley Conference with papers, pictures and films of the incident. Yet its members were unwilling to act, refusing even to look further into what had happened.

Drake withdrew from the conference and immediately canceled all future games with Oklahoma A&M.[335]

Philip Becker Jr., president of the athletic conference, resigned over the members' inaction: "I, too, held to the slender threads of hope that someone, somewhere would see the light and prevent what has taken place," he wrote to Gardner. "But alas, the villain has stolen the scene and now all is serene."[336]

When Bright looked back on the game, he saw the same thing the practice players had predicted: "There's no way it couldn't have been racially motivated."[337]

That same fall, in 1951, Bill Nunn Jr. was still plotting his own future, writing about black athletes but also falling in love. He did not marry the girl next door. Frances Bell lived across the street.

She was four years younger, and they did not date while he was in high school. But after he went to West Virginia State and she headed to Howard University in Washington, they found each other back in Pittsburgh.

More accurately, the *Pittsburgh Courier* found Frances. With a pretty smile, she had drawn the attention of the newspaper's photographers when she posed one year in an Easter dress.[338] She eventually worked for a time at the newspaper too.[339] She was one of the dozen girls in dresses and skirts who wrote up memos on big black typewriters, answered phones and ran errands.[340]

Before long, she put the deadline on Nunn too. It wasn't a hard decision.

On their wedding day in August 1950, the bride wore white.[341] And so did the groom, dressed in a white tuxedo jacket over black pants, with a narrow black bow tie and a white carnation boutonniere.

The bridal party included five bridesmaids, four groomsmen, Bill Nunn Sr. and a young flower girl. The ceremony took place at a large church, with organ pipes that reached to the 30-foot ceiling and an enormous, intricately carved wooden altar. The bride and groom stood before a center pulpit decorated with sprays of ferns next to potted gladiolas.

When the minister declared them husband and wife, Frances turned to Bill. The maid of honor, wearing long white gloves, held back the bride's long veil. The groom's father stood beside him, smiling with crinkles at the corners of his eyes. A little girl behind the high altar rail turned her eyes to watch

Charles "Teenie" Harris, American, 1908–1998. Bill Nunn Jr. and his bride seated in back seat of car, c. 1940-1955. Black and white: Kodak Safety Film, H: 4 in. x W: 5 in. (10.20 x 12.70 cm), Carnegie Museum of Art, Pittsburgh: Heinz Family Fund, 2001.35.23979.

the newlyweds. And the bride and groom kissed deeply, lost for a moment, away from the packed rows of family and friends watching them.

A moment later, the couple walked back out the narrow aisle. Frances smiled broadly with her head high, looking into the faces of women in big hats. She rested her left arm in the crook of her new husband's right arm. Bill guided her, letting her have this moment as he twisted his body forward so they could both fit between the rows of pews. He smiled awkwardly.

The newlyweds climbed into the narrow backseat of a car wide enough just for two, and rode to the reception at his parents' house. With the *Courier*'s photographer Teenie "One Shot" Harris taking pictures, the bridal couple posed on the lawn with the bridesmaids and groomsmen.[342] Heading inside, the bridal party set up a receiving line in the Nunns' living room. That night Bill cut the four-tiered, white wedding cake, with Frances holding his hand, and the guests partied late on the back lawn, overlooking the river valley.

After the wedding, the bride and groom moved into their own apartment. A daughter, Lynell, was born there a year later, on October 28, 1951. A son, Bill Nunn III, came within a year, on October 20, 1952. For eight days each year, the children would be the same age.

At work, Nunn covered black athletes for the *Courier*. It hardly mattered that he only could go to the Forbes Field press box on days when the Pirates were playing the Giants, Dodgers and Braves. They were the only visiting National League teams with black players, and they were the only ones Nunn wanted to cover.

When another Pittsburgh fighter Ezzard Charles, who was black, took on "Jersey" Joe Walcott at the ballpark in July 1951, Nunn chronicled the weeks of training leading up to the fight. The men had met twice before: in 1949, when Charles won the heavyweight crown vacated by Joe Louis who had retired, and in March 1951, when Charles won again.

The two men had become known as great fighters in a time when Americans hungered for great fights. The third match would bring them each a big payday, and the anticipation was great. Walcott trained at Rainbow Gardens, a small amusement park with a swimming pool, drive-in movie theater and wild mouse ride in the Pittsburgh suburb of McKeesport. Some days, 1,600 people came just to watch him spar.[343]

At Forbes Field that summer, Walcott finally wrested the title away from Charles with a seventh-round knockout.

More often, Nunn's job required him to look for character stories on black athletes at a time of firsts for them.

George Taliaferro, a halfback out of Indiana University, became the first black drafted by a National Football League team when the Chicago Bears picked him in the 13th Round in 1949.[344] He ended up playing with the Los Angeles Dons of the All-American Football Conference instead. So Wally Triplett, a Penn State University halfback, became the first black draftee to play in the NFL, with Detroit.[345]

Arthur Dorrington became the first black professional hockey player in the United States when he signed with the Atlantic City Seagulls of the Eastern Amateur League in 1950.

Althea Gibson was the first black woman to play in a U.S. Lawn Tennis Association[346] national singles tournament at New York's Forest Hills in 1950. She also became the first black woman at Wimbledon a year later.

The American Bowling Congress gave into a court order in 1950, requiring it to remove a clause limiting membership to whites. And the Professional Golfers Association removed a restriction against blacks in 1951.[347]

In basketball, Nunn had passed up a chance at breaking the race barrier. Now his friends had opportunities to go where he had not.

Chuck Cooper had been Nunn's teammate at Westinghouse High School, and they had played together at West Virginia State for one year before the Navy drafted Cooper for World War II. Military service had taken him as far as the West Coast where he played basketball for the Fleet City team. Back home in Pittsburgh, he enrolled at Duquesne University, a Catholic school where he became the first black to make the basketball team.

Nunn wrote about his friend with a detachment that revealed nothing about the time they had spent together: Cooper "seems a sure bet to end up with some professional basketball aggregation at the end of his college days," Nunn wrote in the sports pages.[348]

Cooper scored a school-record 1,000 points and led the Dukes to two appearances in the National Invitation Tournament.[349]

When the National Basketball Association held its closed-door draft at Chicago's Hotel Morrison in April 1950, Boston Celtics' owner Walter Brown announced, "Boston takes Charles Cooper of Duquesne."

The room fell silent until another team owner shouted, "Walter, don't you know he's a colored boy?"

"I don't give a damn if he's striped or plaid or polka-dot," Brown answered. "Boston takes Charles Cooper of Duquesne!"[350]

In that moment, Cooper became the first black drafted into the NBA – taken with the first pick of the second round, 12th overall. But he would not be the first black athlete to sign with an NBA team or to play in the league.[351]

After the Celtics drafted Cooper, Washington Capitols coach Horace "Bones" McKinney drafted another of Nunn's former college teammates, Earl Lloyd, in the ninth round, with the 100th pick overall. McKinney also took Harold Hunter, a black player from North Carolina State College in the tenth.

"We want to win," McKinney said. "…They will be given the same chance to make the grade as the others, and will rise, or fall, on their merits."[352]

Throughout his life, Lloyd had lived apart – a black man, in a black world, segregated from whites. He had gone to an all-black high school and he had played college basketball at an all-black school, mostly against all-black opponents.

Suddenly, he became the only black man on an all-white team, in a league of white players. Oddly, for the first time, it seemed his skin color did not matter.

"There were very few times in my life when the playing field was level," Lloyd recalled years later.[353] "The first chance

I got at the field being level, I ran across a coach who drafted me for the NBA in 1950, Bones McKinney. He never said a word about it. And he never said, 'Don't do this. Don't do that.' He just threw us in there as players. His concern was, 'What kind of player am I getting?'"

Due to a quirk of scheduling, Lloyd became the first black to play in an NBA game, one day before Cooper appeared with the Celtics. Hunter had been the first black player to sign an NBA contract, but he never made it out of training camp.

In that first game, Lloyd scored six points and had a game-high 10 rebounds as the Capitols beat the Royals of Rochester, New York. Unlike with Robinson in baseball four years earlier, the breaking of basketball's color barrier drew little attention. George Beahon, beat reporter for the *Rochester Democrat & Chronicle*, did not even mention the significance of the moment in his game story.[354]

Lloyd appeared in nine games with the Capitols before he got drafted again. This time, by the Army. The Korean War had started and, unlike Cooper, Lloyd had not already served.

"Uncle Sam came for me," he said. "Look, I can't be worried about something that I know is gonna happen. If they were voting on whether or not you were going, you'd be a little nervous. But, look, it's just a matter of when that paper comes, you know, 'Greetings from the president,' now you know something's up."[355]

In the fall of 1951, the University of San Francisco Dons college football team won all nine of its games and became eligible for the Orange and Gator bowls in Florida and New Orleans' Sugar Bowl. The Dons had a stacked team that season, with eight future NFL players, including three hall-of-famers – Gino Marchetti, Ollie Matson and Bob St. Clair.[356] Coach Joe Kuharich had been a star player at Notre Dame and was embarking on the start of a long career of coaching college and professional teams. Even the Dons' public relations man, Pete Rozelle, was poised for greatness: He would go on to serve 30 years as NFL commissioner, turning the league into a national pastime.

But going to any of the bowl games that season meant leaving behind the team's two black players, Matson, a halfback with Olympic medal-winning speed, and Burl Toler, a middle linebacker being scouted by the pros.

"We were all angry over the fact that they would even suggest that we would even consider doing that by leaving our two black players behind," St. Clair recalled.[357] "These were teammates. These were brothers."

It was no big deal at home in Northern California for the Dons to have black athletes, but the team's players knew that not everyone felt the same way across the country. When they had played in Tulsa, Oklahoma, two years earlier, Matson and Toler couldn't stay in the team hotel or eat with the white players in restaurants. From that experience, the players learned what it felt like to be separated by skin color, and they did not want to feel that way again.

This time, the players – white and black – refused to be divided.

"That's the relationship we had with one another," Toler said,[358] "if one can't go, don't ask for anyone else because we are a team and we are going to stay like that, as a team."

Orange Bowl officials especially wanted the Dons. But none of the bowls would cave on the issue of the black players. So the Dons stayed home. The players' motto became: "Undefeated, untied and uninvited."[359]

The impact on the University of San Francisco was permanent. The athletics department barely had been able to afford football that season, and it needed the cash from a major bowl game. Without it, the school ended its football program.

At Christmas that year, Harry Moore, a black school principal, and his wife, Harriette, enjoyed a quiet holiday evening as a dense fog gathered around the one-story, wood-frame home he had built deep within the orange groves of Mims, Florida, along the Atlantic coast east of Orlando.

The couple's grown daughter, "Peaches," had come home to be with them, as had Harry's mother. Harriette's brothers and their wives had been in the house earlier in the day for a holiday celebration. The Moores enjoyed playing cards and might have played a game of Bid Whist before heading to bed just after 10 p.m.[360] [361]

At age 46, Harry had gained a reputation for challenging the inequalities of segregation in Florida. A decade before the U.S. Supreme Court struck down whites-only primary elections, he was preparing his school students to read a ballot. He had called on the state to raise black teachers' salaries to equal whites'. He had formed a local chapter of the National Association for the Advancement of Colored People 17 years earlier, and then he had used it as a bully pulpit to challenge injustice. Moore led his own investigations when a 15-year-old boy was lynched in a nearby county, and then again when a man was hanged by another mob years later. When the local sheriff that fall shot two handcuffed black men in the back of his squad car after their rape convictions were overturned, Moore wrote to the governor and federal officials calling for the sheriff to be indicted.

Living alone with his family, unarmed among the orange groves, Moore knew he had taken risks. The Ku Klux Klan in that part of Florida had enforced segregation by terrorizing blacks. Anyone considered "too big for their britches" might be kidnapped off the street, taken somewhere remote and given a "treatment" – a beating with a leather strap, often so severe that it killed the person. Other victims had been beaten and then shot. The Klan counted among its members political leaders, local businessmen, attorneys, doctors. County sheriffs and their deputies openly joined the Klan, some showing up to meetings in uniform, still carrying their weapons. Even Florida Gov. Fuller Warren had admitted to once being a Klansman.

But on Christmas night, Moore felt no fear. He kissed Peaches as she headed to her bedroom next to his own, and he said good night to his mother as she went to her room down the hall. Moore went to his room, undressed, set his watch on the dresser and climbed into bed next to his wife, Harriette. As his head rested on the pillow, he whispered with his wife about their day and then he listened to his mother and daughter settling into sleep. A quiet deepened by the fog outside fell across the home.

Without warning, a loud crack exploded from underneath the bedroom as the floor suddenly rose up with a bright flash of light and wood splintered through the air. The bed where the Moores had been sleeping flew up against the ceiling and crashed back down. The back of a wooden rocking chair had been blown into the attic while its other parts blew into the room next door. A light bulb twisted into the ceiling socket remained intact but the socket was thrown from its bolts. Light bulbs in the other rooms and the front porch shattered, and the bottom of a fish bowl cracked open with its water running out. The chimney on the house lifted into the air and settled back into place. The explosion left a two-foot crater in the sandy soil eighteen inches below the Moores' bed, and an egg-sized hole in the roof above.

Peaches crawled out of bed, stepping around the glass shards on the wet floor in her room. She reached the doorway of her parents' room and met her grandmother as they looked in at the damage. Harriette was out of bed too, able to stand on her own.

But Harry could not. The bomb had detonated right below him, and he was badly hurt.

George Simms, Harriette's brother, had been staying with his wife at a house down the road. When he heard the blast, he got out of bed, dressed and drove in his Buick sedan toward the Moore's home. When he arrived, George helped Harriette walk outside and he went back in to carry her husband to the car. It felt like every bone in Harry's body had broken.[362] He laid the man in the back seat of the Buick, with his head resting on his mother's lap. Harriette sat in the front seat, and George drove them to the hospital 30 miles away.

As his mother patted his head, Harry talked to her in whispers.

"If I die, I was only trying to help my people," he said. "If I go that way, I will go as a hero. Somebody has got to do the work."

By the time they reached the hospital, Harry was gone. His wife made it there alive.

Sheriff's deputies arrived at the Moore's home first. They alerted the FBI's Florida field office, and agents arrived in the orange grove around 3:40 a.m. The fog was dense by then. People who had come to help and those who had come just to look had walked around in the sandy soil, destroying much of the evidence. Investigators found a few small, shallow footprints leading toward a road nearby. Apparently the bomber had run toward a waiting getaway car.

John Diaz, a reporter for the *Pittsburgh Courier*, showed up that night to investigate too. He headed to the hospital to find Harriette.

"I have a couple of ideas who might have done it," she said. "But when people do that kind of thing, they have someone else do it."

Her words ran in bold type across the front page of that week's newspaper, above photographs of the Moores' bomb-blasted home and bedroom: "I know who did it."

Harriette lived another nine days. When they laid out Harry's body for burial, doctors told her not to go. She was too weak to leave the hospital, they said. But she went any way. Later, the doctors said the trip to the church might have contributed to her death, from a blood clot.

Six hundred people attended Harry Moore's funeral at St. James Missionary Baptist Church on New Year's Day.[363] FBI agents combed through the building before the service, fearing someone might have left another bomb inside. Fifteen members of the Civil Rights Congress attended from New York and Philadelphia. The president of Bethune-Cookman College[364], a black school in Daytona Beach where Harry had graduated, called him a "man of great personal conviction and courage." The president of the NAACP did not make it to the funeral but he sent a telegram: "It has never been more true than in his case that the blood of the martyr is the seed of the church."

Harry and Harriette were buried together in a community cemetery, amid orange groves.

Diaz, the *Courier* reporter, had stayed in Mims after the explosion. He was at the church when Harriette saw her husband for the last time. He wondered whether she ever told anyone who she suspected in the bombing. She had been too afraid, it seemed, to say their names.[365] The attackers might come after her daughters or her sisters and brothers next.

A photograph of Harry's body being lowered into the grave ran on the front page of the newspaper, along with a portrait of his mother, holding her head in grief.

"The state of Florida is in 'one hell of a fix,'" Robert Ratcliffe, *Courier* news editor, wrote[366]. "Her gun-toting and bomb-tossing hoodlums have gone too far in the Klan-like and gangster-type attacks on Negroes, Jews and Catholics. The entire state is a bunch of nerves, and pressure from the outside is beginning to take its toll."

By coincidence, the stories about the Moores' burials ran next to an article about Rosa Lee Ingram, the Georgia sharecropper, who had been sentenced to die with her sons in the death of their neighbor.[367] They had been in prison three years already. A state judge had changed their sentences to life in prison under pressure from the NAACP. By state law, they could apply for parole after seven years but a lawyer for the NAACP had won another exception, allowing them to have a parole hearing sooner than that.

The *Courier* sent reporter Bill Fowlkes to the parole hearing in Atlanta.

As the paper promised its readers on the front page that week: "If and where it happens, the *Courier* is there."

Three weeks after the Moores' bombing, NFL owners met at New York's Hotel Statler for the 1952 draft.

Blacks had been back in the league six years, but heading into the draft that year, half of the NFL's 12 teams remained all-white. After the L.A. Rams and Cleveland Browns reintegrated professional football in 1946, the Detroit Lions, New York Giants and San Francisco 49ers added black players two years later. The Packers, in 1950.[368]

Major League Baseball remained even more segregated, with 10 of its 16 teams refusing to sign a black player.[369] For Nunn, getting access to the Forbes Field press box still mattered only when three National League teams came to town.

The rest of the time, the *Courier* did not care much about white baseball – except when it affected blacks.

Nunn wrote one story about the Pirates after he discovered that manager Billy Meyer had gotten drunk and then yelled at a black railroad worker while the team was boarding a train for New York. Meyer had been the National League's previous manager of the year. And yet, he saw blacks as a threat to his career.

"Those niggers are being moved up too fast and will soon have our jobs as managers and coaches," he said, after yelling at the railroad porter.[370]

Meyer apologized days later, after Nunn confronted him. The manager said he held no prejudices against black ballplayers.

"We are interested in any ballplayer that we figure will help our ball club," Meyer said, "but we figure they should come up through the proper channels and not make that big jump from Negro ball up to the majors."

Meyer offered the porter $100 in cash for embarrassing him. The railroad worker turned it down.

And the Pirates remained all-white.

In football, at least, more barriers to black athletes were about to come down.

With the third overall pick in the 1952 draft, the Chicago Cardinals chose Ollie Matson, the star halfback from the University of San Francisco.[371] Two picks later, the Philadelphia Eagles chose Johnny Bright, Drake University's quarterback with the broken jaw.

Both men, again, would be called to break barriers. They would have to put up with the racial taunts and the segregated hotels and restaurants while traveling.

Matson signed with the Cardinals. He ran that summer in the Helsinki Olympics, winning a bronze medal in the 400 meters and a silver medal in the 400-meter relay.[372] Matson went on to play 14 seasons in the NFL, with the Cardinals, Rams, Lions and Eagles, and he entered the Pro Football Hall of Fame in 1972.[373]

Bright, with his jaw still healing, wasn't interested in integrating the Eagles. He turned down the team's offer and headed for the Canadian Football League. He played 14 seasons for the Calgary Stampeders, a team that had signed its first black player in 1949, and later with the Edmonton Eskimos. He entered the Canadian Football Hall of Fame in 1970.[374]

The Eagles ended up with two other black players that season. The Bears, Texans and Steelers added black players in 1952 as well.[375]

Only the Redskins, catering to fans in the segregated South, remained all white. And the team had no immediate plans to change.

With a wife and two young children, Nunn needed more space for his family.

His father had purchased a long tract of land at the top of Pittsburgh's Hill District neighborhood, where he built his own house. He divided the land into lots and gave the one two doors down to his son.

Nunn's parents had built a two-story, red-brick house. When the family had lived in Homewood, in the house previously owned by the *Courier*'s publisher, it had stained glass windows on the second floor that set it apart from the neighboring houses. Here, on the bluff overlooking the Allegheny River valley, Nunn Sr. gave his home its own distinction. It was the first house on the land, and he made sure it would stand out from others. A round turret at the entry, strong gables and shingled dormers gave the house charm. It looked like a house from one of the city's wealthier middle-class suburbs.

Nunn Jr., of course, had his own vision. He might build his house down the street, but it would have a totally different aesthetic. Germany's Bauhaus movement before the war had created a new modern style, characterized by flat roofs and clean straight lines. After the war, some American architects carried the idea forward, and Nunn found one for his home. It would stand out too. But the house would look distinctive for its lack of ornamentation. The modern front elevation featured stone, a grid of glass panes stretching from ceiling to floor and a flat roof. From the front, it would appear to be one-story but, nestled into the hillside, a second floor opened beneath in the back, looking out to the dramatic view.[376]

Around the same time, the *Courier* promoted Nunn Jr. to sports editor. He still would be traveling to games and reporting from around the country, but he also would oversee the sports pages. For the first time, he would be in charge of choosing the black college All-Americans and the black college football champion.

The *Courier* referred to its top team each year as the "mythical" black college champion. And at times, Nunn would find choosing just one winner to be nearly impossible. Without the teams meeting in playoffs or even a clearly defined bowl series, Nunn had to decide which team was best – often after seeing each play just once or twice in a season. In his first year, the *Courier* named four champions when multiple schools ended with one-loss seasons. Then again two years later, in 1954, five teams had just one loss. "Not often is the football might among the Negro colleges so evenly distributed," Nunn said then, hamstrung over who to choose.[377]

Louisiana's Grambling State College was about to make Nunn's job a whole lot easier, even if he had no idea what was about to happen.

Willie Davis arrived in Grambling, Louisiana, in the summer of 1952. He had been born in a rural part of the state but he had grown up in Texarkana, Arkansas, playing football at Booker T. Washington High School. The rules had been generally unwritten but clear: "Blacks had their own special bathrooms, and all that," he recalled. "...It's almost like everybody had lived with it if they grew up in the South. You just didn't go anywhere expecting anything much different than what you got."[378]

But expectations were changing.

Grambling Coach Eddie Robinson had been at the school for more than a decade, and he had recorded twice as many wins as losses but still few people knew about his program. Davis had been no exception, even when Robinson came to his home on a recruiting visit. Davis's mother worked as a professional cook, and she won over Robinson with her roasted chicken. The coach, in turn, convinced her to give over her son by promising to have him in church every Sunday.[379]

During the first season that Davis spent in Grambling, the Tigers won eight games against two losses. But football soon would have to fight to keep his attention.

That winter across the state in Baton Rouge, the city council passed an ordinance allowing blacks to fill up city buses from back-to-front if no white riders were sitting there. Until then, even if no whites were riding, blacks had to leave open ten seats in the front, and black riders would crowd into just half of an otherwise empty bus. Passing the rule alone, though, didn't change behavior. Bus drivers generally ignored it and few black passengers felt brave enough to sit down in the white section on their own. That was, until June.

By then, Davis and many of his classmates had returned home for the summer, but the events of that summer would draw their attention and keep it. Blacks never had seen a drama like this play out across an entire city seated in the Deep South.

That month, drivers were ordered to comply with the new rule after one driver manhandled a black woman who sat down in an empty seat reserved for whites. Drivers went on strike for four days, until the state attorney general determined the bus rule violated state laws enforcing segregation.

The drivers came back – but the riders did not.

Blacks in Baton Rouge, led by local pastor the Rev. T.J. Jemison formed a United Defense League, and they went to a radio station to announce a boycott of the buses after organizing a rideshare program so black riders still could get around. The next day, June 20, 1953, no blacks rode on city buses.

The Ku Klux Klan burned crosses at Jemison's church, Mt. Zion Baptist, and his home. But the boycott held for four days, until local leaders reached a new compromise: Only the front two seats on every bus would be reserved for whites and the long seat in the back would be set aside for blacks. Anyone else could sit in between.[380]

The first bus boycott of the Civil Rights Era brought quick results.

When Davis returned to Louisiana for football camp at the end of that summer, the drama had ended but its impact lingered. He and his black classmates felt galvanized.

Coach Robinson had grown up in Baton Rouge, and he had watched the boycott with concern. The moment was important, he told his players, but they needed to focus on what they could do.

Right then, that meant football. As players, they could make their statement on the field and in the classroom.

"The most important thing for you is to stay focused on getting an education, and not get caught up in some of those things," Robinson told the players.[381]

The bus boycott mattered. Football did too.

By Davis's senior season, the Civil Rights movement had picked up strength – and Grambling football had grown, even if few had noticed yet. When Nunn wrote up his preseason expectations for 1955, he prayed for one team to emerge as the clear winner but he expected several black colleges to vie again for his attention and the *Courier*'s mythical championship title.

"The turbulent situation that prevailed among Negro college football teams on a national scale ... can hardly be expected to continue," he wrote.[382]

Nunn mentioned Grambling, but only as an afterthought. The school would merely be among the teams playing games, he thought, and not a legitimate contender.

While Nunn worried about football in early September 1955, other news dominated the *Courier*. By then, the U.S. Supreme Court had ruled against segregated classrooms for black children and the federal Interstate Commerce Commission had banned segregated interstate travel and waiting rooms.

Practices remained harder to adjust. In Savannah, Georgia, whites and blacks sat in the same train station waiting room, but on opposite sides of a brass rail running the length of the room. Blacks in Nashville entered the train station through the same door as whites, but then sat in a side room set aside for "colored." And in other places, such as New Orleans, blacks were supposed to know by custom alone where they could, and could not, sit.[383]

Still, few people could imagine how bad things would get.

Living in Chicago and working for the Air Force, Mamie Bradley knew her uncle lived in another world as a Mississippi sharecropper. When her 14-year-old son begged to visit his family there, she tried to explain to him that the rules for what a black kid could get away with would be entirely different. The boy, Emmett Till, had suffered from polio and spoke with stutter, but he also looked big for his age, almost like an adult to some strangers. Emmett told his mother he understood about the South as she kissed his cheek, and then he boarded a train to spend the late summer in Money, Mississippi.

Three days later, on a Wednesday afternoon, Emmett was hanging out with his cousins when they teased him about going into a local store to see an attractive white woman working there behind the counter. He went inside and when she walked by, he gave a little whistle of appreciation. In Mississippi, it was enough to get him killed.

Early Sunday morning, the woman's husband and his half-brother drove out to the house where Emmett's uncle lived. They snuck into the room where the boy slept next to his cousin, shined a flashlight in his face and pulled him out of bed, dragging him to the front door as his aunt pleaded for them to leave him alone. If the boy had done wrong or stolen something, she cried, the family would pay the men to leave him alone. They ignored her as they dragged Emmett out the door.[384]

No one would see him again until his body floated up in the Tallahatchie River, 10 miles away. He had been beaten and shot in the head. His body was tied with barbed-wire to a large fan from a cotton gin so it would sink. [385]

Back in Pittsburgh, Nunn stayed focused on football. His predictions for the black college football season ran in the same edition as a cover story in bold type about 100,000 mourners passing through a Chicago church to see Emmett Till's body in a pine wood coffin.

"Let the people see what they have done to my boy!" his mother told the *Courier*.[386]

Grambling Coach Eddie Robinson stayed committed to football too. He invited his former player Paul "Tank" Younger to help run drills that summer.[387] Younger had been the top player on the *Courier* All-America team when Nunn first started as a reporter. In Los Angeles, Younger had emerged as the NFL's first star athlete from a black college, playing at running back for the Los Angeles Rams.

Now, back in Louisiana, he had become a symbol for rising above the challenges of segregation. He had become a pro just six years earlier. In that time, the expectations had started to change. More black players believed they could go where Younger had gone. Football mattered.

Grambling's players responded to growing expectations by starting to win. That fall, as the trial for Till's killers played out 200 miles away across the Mississippi state line, Grambling dominated teams.

Nunn arrived in Grambling for the third week of the season, planning to see one of his preseason favorites, Tennessee State University, start making its case for the national crown. Instead, he arrived in Louisiana to hear Robinson talking with his players about putting together an unbeaten season and a national championship of their own. Grambling's public relations machine was running in high gear – and the players were backing it up. Grambling won the game, 12-0, with Willie Davis and his defensive line mates refusing to let Tennessee State move the ball. Nunn was stunned by what he saw: "Grambling was magnificent in victory," he told *Courier* readers across the nation.[388]

A week later, Grambling scored 12 touchdowns and defeated Alabama's Bishop College 80-0. Two weeks after that, with three games left in the season, the Tigers won the Midwest Conference championship.

The team had set its goals higher, on winning a national championship. By the end of the regular season, Grambling had allowed opposing teams to score just five times – and no team had scored more than once. The combined tally: 302 points for Grambling; 33 for its opponents.

Uninvited to the major white bowl games, black college football teams invented their own.

Most years, the Orange Blossom Classic in Miami determined the national football champion, pitting whatever team had the best record against Florida A&M. Nunn at the *Courier* would make the actual determination, but a undefeated team winning the Classic could make his job easier.

Grambling already had done the first part. Now it needed to defeat Florida A&M, which had top running back Willie Galimore. The team had tied one game during the season and not lost once either.

As Nunn arrived in Miami for the game in early December, Civil Rights news dominated the front page of the *Courier* again. A black woman named Rosa Parks had refused to give up her bus seat to a white woman in Montgomery, Alabama, and black activists led by the Rev. Dr. Martin Luther King were looking back to the Baton Rouge bus boycotts for lessons learned. A columnist in the *Courier* that week exhorted blacks to keep up the fight until every Jim Crow-statute is overturned. "The Till murder is proving as bad to America as Hitler's treatment of the Jew was to Germany," he wrote.[389]

Then on the day before the Classic was to be played, controversy erupted over another football game in the South, the Sugar Bowl, scheduled for New Orleans on January 2. Georgia Tech had agreed to play in the game against the University of Pittsburgh, which had a black fullback and linebacker named Bobby Grier. Pitt vowed that Grier would not only take the field but that he would "sleep, eat, practice and play with his team."[390] The school also had arranged with Sugar Bowl officials to sell 10,000 tickets to a non-segregated section of the stadium for its fans. Pitt planned to bring its band, which had black members, and they would travel through the South on integrated Pullman rail cars. The Sugar Bowl would be racially integrated for the first time.[391]

Incensed that Georgia Tech would play against a team with a black player, Georgia's Gov. Marvin Griffin issued a statement asking the school's board of regents to withdraw from the game: "The South stands at Armageddon," he wrote in a telegram on Dec. 2, 1955. "The battle is joined. We cannot make the slightest concession to the enemy in this dark and lamentable hour of struggle. There is no more difference in compromising integrity of race on the playing field than in doing so in the classrooms. One break in the dike and the relentless enemy will rush in and destroy us."[392]

Students at Georgia Tech unexpectedly lashed out against the governor. They wanted the team to play against Pitt and its black linebacker. They marched on the capitol and the governor's mansion, burning him in effigy. Their response, in the heart of the Deep South, marked progress, the *Pittsburgh Courier* resolved.

"Things are changing," a columnist wrote. "Years ago, Georgia Tech would have said to Pittsburgh, 'Leave Grier home,' and Pittsburgh would have left him home."[393]

Nunn stayed focused on his job, which at the moment hardly seemed like work.

Similar to the Orange Bowl that would dominate Miami around New Year's Day, the Orange Blossom Classic in early December featured parades and floats, parties, marching bands and girls. The Florida A&M marching band, in orange and green, had prepared a halftime show based on the theme "Highlights of Opera."[394] The hosts had guaranteed Grambling the largest payout in black college sports, at $15,000, and Classic organizers expected a record turnout for the game.[395]

When the city of Miami first opened the Orange Bowl stadium in 1937, blacks were allowed to sit only in one roped-off section of the end zone.[396] But with the Classic, the city had made racial history by allowing blacks to sit on one side of the main bowl, coincidentally keeping the south side all white. Earlier that year, 1955, the Orange Bowl even had hosted its first integrated game when the University of Nebraska played Duke University on New Year's Day.

Coming from Pittsburgh, Nunn saw the hibiscus-scented Classic as an easy draw: "When the ingredients of football, girls, music and Florida's soothing breezes are involved, even selling becomes easier," he wrote into his story.[397]

The Classic that year had its largest gate ever, drawing nearly $82,000[398] from 40,319 fans despite rain-filled skies.[399] Nunn found the action on the field "spine-tingling." On the game's second play, Grambling running back Edward Murray dashed up the middle, picked up two key blocks on his team's own 29-yard line and ran for a touchdown, giving the Tigers an early lead.

Florida came back and kept the game close until the final four minutes when Galimore fumbled in his own end. Grambling scored a final touchdown, to win 28-21.

Nunn had his national champion.

After that, Grambling's program rose to national status and Robinson found a bully pulpit. With the help of his public relations man[400] and the good fortune of peaking at a moment when black college players were starting to be noticed, Robinson talked about racial inequality and the strengths of black athletes. For white audiences throughout the country, Robinson would become the most famous black college football coach.[401] [402]

Two weeks after the Orange Blossom Classic, Nunn sat at his desk in the *Courier*'s offices to come up with the black college All-America football team. As it did every year, the list weighed heavily on his mind. It was possible, as always, that he would miss an unheralded star – a player without the public relations strength of Grambling or the high-profile program of Louisiana's Southern University or Prairie View in Texas. Nunn could not attend every game, or even visit every school. And, of course, the games were not on television.

"We believe that we have come as near as humanly possible to selecting the best eleven players in the country," Nunn clacked into his typewriter.[403] But "possibly there may have been an omission here and there," he conceded.

As his mind went back through the fall season, the Classic continued to play. Murry, the Grambling back who broke open the game within 50 seconds, made the team as just a sophomore. Galimore, the Florida A&M back, made the cut too, despite his costly fumble in the final minutes. Davis, who had anchored the Grambling defense through a season in which it gave up few points, ended up on the list as well.

Other All-Americans that year came from across the South – Texas, Oklahoma, Mississippi, Florida, Tennessee – and Ohio.

Nunn set a high standard for the team: "It takes daring, experience, plus super-human effort," he wrote.

A month later, NFL teams validated Nunn's picks. They chose four of his All-Americans: The Cleveland Browns claimed Davis, and the Chicago Bears took Galimore.[404] They were among 27 blacks drafted that year.

While Grambling celebrated its win, the University of Pittsburgh followed through on its intentions to play with Bobby Grier in the Sugar Bowl. Pitt's team members stayed together by sleeping at Tulane University, allowing them to avoid New Orleans' hotels that refused black guests.[405]

As the game started, Grier ran onto the field for Pitt. And in the end, he played a key, but controversial, role in the game. Officials flagged Grier on defense for pass interference, setting up the only score of the game, giving Georgia Tech a 7-0 victory. Many blacks saw conspiracy in the outcome, pointing out that four of the six officials – including the one who called the penalty on Grier – came from the South.[406] The final score, though, meant less than the fact that the game even had been played.

After the Sugar Bowl that year, lawmakers in the Louisiana State Legislature unanimously passed a law banning interracial sporting events in the state. Members of the state's White Citizens' Councils pushed for the bill to prevent another northern school from repeating what Pitt had done, but sports fans knew the outcome would be devastating to their aspirations. Louisiana State University no longer could hope to play most Big Ten teams, which by then had at least one or even a few black players; the Sugar Bowl would be limited in which teams it could invite; and Major League Baseball, which had been holding spring training games in the state, would stop coming back.[407]

Nunn followed the case with Grier closely, but he had long believed that Pitt did not do enough to support black athletes. One game wasn't going to change that. And just as he covered baseball games only when a team with a black player came to town, Nunn favored black college football over mostly white teams sprinkled with a few blacks.

Nunn made just two references to Grier in his column. He noted the game among the "sports thrills" of 1955.[408] And later he mentioned that Grier had attended a banquet for the players of both teams after the game at New Orleans' St. Charles Hotel. When a dance started after the dinner, Grier excused himself so he could attend a separate event on the campus of Dillard University, a historically black school in the city.[409] It made sense, Nunn mused, that Grier would choose to attend "festivities where those 'cultured ladies of the South' would be present."[410]

Even as Nunn stayed focused on his job, he could not avoid the changes taking place all around him, especially as he traveled through the South. The next fall, in 1956, he visited Itta Bena, Mississippi, a short drive from where Emmett Till had been snatched out of bed in his uncle's house. Nunn had gone there in early October to cover a football game between Jackson College and Mississippi Vocational College, [411] the two teams he estimated to be the "mightiest of the mighty among the grid powers in Mississippi."[412]

It was Nunn's first visit to Mississippi Vocational, and an old friend, Bill "Dead Eye" Cochran, met him at the airport.

"You're here," Cochran said to him. "I gotta tell you this story."

Cochran and his brother, Earl, had attended West Virginia State with Nunn and were black.[413] The boys' mother was black too and worked as a cook. But their father was white, a plantation owner, who acknowledged his sons and gave them his last name. Bill Cochran had grown up to run the NAACP in that part of Mississippi, while his father was known as perhaps the most powerful white man in the area.

Nunn stayed the first night in the home of the college president. He spent the second at a black hotel owned by

Cochran's family. Mississippi remained a dry state where alcohol sales, imports and manufacturing were illegal. But the hotel served as a place for folks to get whiskey, and even the local white cops came to drink.

Later that evening, after dark, Cochran turned to Nunn: "I want to show you something."[414]

The two men climbed into Cochran's car, shiny black and new. They drove out into the countryside, cloaked in dark shadows under a new moon.[415] Nunn thought to himself that he had no idea where they were, surrounded by farm fields along the Tallahatchie River, the waterway where a fisherman had found Till's bloated and bruised body, with his head blown open from a bullet and a 70-pound fan tied around his neck with barbed wire.

Suddenly, Nunn spotted an opening in the trees by the side of the road and Cochran pulled inside. The car stopped in front of a country barn and the two men got out. They walked into the barn, where crates of whiskey and beer sat stacked as high as their heads. Local white folks came here to purchase illegal alcohol. A black man ran the place.

"Cochran, whadda ya want?" he said.

Cochran turned to glance sideways at Nunn. "I got enough," he said, "but just give me two cases of whiskey."

The man grabbed the cases and handed them to Cochran. He turned back to the car with Nunn following silently behind, his eyes wide. Nunn climbed back into the passenger seat as Cochran slid behind the wheel.

"I just wanted to show you that," he said.

The next morning, Nunn and Cochran went out for a ride again and as they head back to the hotel to pick up Nunn's bags for the flight back to Pittsburgh, Cochran's car ran out of gas. The car's tires crunched on gravel as it rolled to the side of the road. Cochran glanced in the rearview mirror.

"Goddamn," he said. "Here comes somebody."

A white man with his wife pulled up beside Cochran's car. The man drove a beat-up jalopy, so old that it still had a rumble seat in back above the trunk. Cochran leaned out his window and told the man he had run out of gas. Then he asked a favor.

"Hey," he said to the man as he pointed his thumb toward Nunn. "Take him up to my hotel?"

Nunn looked over at the white man with his wife. The story of Till's murder, just the summer before, flashed again through his mind. Still, he climbed out of Cochran's car, walked around the rear and reached for the back door of the white man's car. The man looked over his shoulder and waved for Nunn to get up front. His wife slid over and Nunn sat down next to her. Till had been murdered for less, just catcalling to a white woman.

The hotel sat a short bit up the road, and Nunn rode silently next to the man and his wife. When they pulled up to the building, Nunn thanked the man and offered to pay him for the lift.

"No," the man said, waiving him off, "you're a friend of Cochran's."

Nunn walked inside the hotel, packed his bags and waited for Cochran to turn up. He arrived a little while later, with gas in his car.

"I didn't want to tell you," Cochran said about the white man who had driven Nunn to the hotel. "That's the guy. His brother was the one that killed Emmett Till."

Nunn stared back, stunned. He shook his head. His perceived notions of the South, where the rules seemed so stark – black and white – had been churned again. Cochran smiled back at his friend.

"It happens that way down here," he said, shrugging his shoulders and throwing his hands in the air.

Chapter 6. Feted

Moments after Pirates second baseman Bill Mazeroski hit a Game 7, ninth-inning, walk-off home run to win the 1960 World Series, Bill Nunn Jr. rushed into the team's clubhouse to cover the celebration. By then every Major League Baseball team had at least one or two black players, and Nunn felt comfortable reporting from the press box, the locker room or anywhere else members of the press could go.

When the series between the Pirates and New York Yankees started, Nunn noted for his readers that the two teams had five "tan" players among them – but really only one regular starter. The *Pittsburgh Courier* frequently used colorful language to describe blacks in its pages and the World Series preview story was no exception, saying that the Yankees' two black players – Hector Lopez, from Panama, and Elston Howard, who was born in St. Louis – were "very useful hombres," but often replaced by whites at left field and catcher. The Pirates started Roberto Clemente, a dark-skinned Puerto Rican, in right field almost every day when he was healthy but the newspaper noted that his "two pigmented pals," Joe Christopher and Gene Baker, saw action "only in emergencies."[416]

As Nunn looked around the locker room, Pirates players soaked themselves in champagne, quickly opening new bottles and dousing them over each other.[417] When the Yankees won games during the series, they crushed the Pirates, taking Game 2 at Forbes Field by 16-3 and the next game in New York by 10-0. But the Bucs had stayed in the series with strong pitching, winning close games to remain even. Then the final game had seesawed back and forth – with the Pirates taking an early lead, scoring four runs in the first two innings, and the Yankees coming back to score seven unanswered runs. Even when the Pirates scored five runs in the bottom of the eighth inning to retake the lead, the Yankees came back and put up two more runs in the top of the ninth to tie the game. As the home team came to bat in the bottom half of the inning, Mazeroski, who had grown up nearby in West Virginia as the son of a coal miner, came to the plate. The first pitch was a ball. "Maz" swung at the second and hit a line drive to left field. The Yankees leftfielder turned to collect the carom off the ivy-covered wall but the ball kept sailing over the fence into a grove of trees. Mazeroski watched it disappear as he headed toward second base, and he pulled off his helmet, waving it in his right hand as he ran around third. Fans – two boys and a grown man in suit and tie – had run onto the field, and they jumped up and down near the base as Mazeroski turned for home where a mob of players and other daring fans waited for him to touch the plate so they could swallow him into a buzzing hive of celebration.[418] The party carried from the field to the more than 40,000 fans in the stands and out into the streets where countless more people would claim for decades that they too had been there to see the home run in person. The image of the moment had been so clear in their minds.

Inside the clubhouse after the game, Nunn looked around for Clemente. The rightfielder had been with his teammates when they rushed onto the field to celebrate after the dramatic home run. But now Nunn found Clemente standing alone in a corner, clearly contented but unconcerned with all of the festivities around him.

Nunn had been drawn to Clemente from the moment the player arrived in Pittsburgh. He did not neatly fit into anyone's definitions of racial stereotypes. Despite his dark skin, Clemente never thought of himself as black until he came to the mainland and started playing baseball, first in Montreal, for the same Brooklyn Dodgers' farm team where Jackie Robinson had broken the game's racial barrier nearly a decade earlier.[419] Sports writers, fans and even people on the street constantly reminded Clemente that they saw him as black first, not as an athlete or even as a Puerto Rican. But Clemente realized that he confounded blacks in America too whenever he opened his mouth. He might have looked like them, but when he talked, he did not sound like many Americans at the time, speaking his native Spanish and struggling to speak in broken English.[420] Nunn decided early that it did not matter what language Clemente used because he communicated to fans best on the baseball diamond: "Although he speaks only a little broken English, there is nothing about the bat Clemente's been carrying around which doesn't put him near the head of the class when it comes to being heard," Nunn wrote when the ballplayer was just a Major League rookie with the Pirates in 1955.[421]

Since then, the men had become friends off the field. They lived just blocks away from each other in Pittsburgh's Hill District neighborhood, and Nunn saw Clemente socially away from the game. Because of the confusion over Clemente's skin color and language, rumors had spread that summer before the World Series that the rightfielder did not like black people. Frustrated, Clemente had turned up at the *Courier*'s offices looking for Nunn to set the record straight. That week in June, the paper ran a first-person story under Clemente's byline, using his own broken words to express his feelings: "Som' Co-lored people I understand saying 'Clemente, he do not like co-lored people. This is not the truth at all. Look at me. Look at my skin. I am not of the white people. I hav' color the skin. That is the first theeing I straighten out. I like all the people, both co-lored and the white; and since I am co-lored myself, in the skin, I would be seely hate myself."[422] Clemente had been pleased that the paper gave him space to express himself, even in his own way.

As he walked toward Clemente in the dressing room, Nunn noticed that the player had quickly showered and was now stuffing his clothes into a heavy traveling bag to leave.

"What's the hurry?" Nunn called out as he got close.[423]

"I catch plane at 6 o'clock for New York," Clemente answered back, tucking his glove into the bag. "I stay there tonight and then I head for home."

"What about the victory party they're holding for the team?" the reporter asked. "You certainly belong in this group."

Nunn already had made the case in his mind why Clemente should have been named most valuable player. The baseball writers had chosen Dick Groat, the Pirates' shortstop who had grown up in nearby Wilkinsburg, attended Duke University and always had a moment to share an articulate comment or quote with the media. By contrast, Nunn felt few of the English-speaking reporters had taken the time to understand Clemente, calling him at times a "showboat" or "hot head." When Nunn rang up the tally on each player, he kept coming back to the Puerto Rican for MVP: Clemente was the only player to hit safely in every World Series game, coming up with a clutch eighth-inning single in the final game that set up a three-run home run. Over the season, Groat had a .325 batting average to Clemente's .314, but the rightfielder led in almost every other category – 16 home runs to 2; 94 runs batted in to 50; 261 total bases to 226.[424]

Now as the reporter and player stood talking, someone walked over and handed Clemente a cup of champagne. He smiled his thanks, took a sip from the cup and set it aside. In the next moment, he waved to the Pirates' other Caribbean player, Diomedes Antonio Olivo, a pitcher who threw for batting practice after he did not make the World Series team. A month earlier, Olivo had appeared in the majors for the first time – a rookie at age 41,[425] after spending most of his career in Mexico's Double-A league. Before Clemente, few Latino players had a clear path to Major League Baseball. The two players planned to travel to New York, spend the night and then head back to the islands the next day. Clemente zipped up his bag and picked it up, along with a large box. It held a trophy for being the most popular player among Pirates fans. The sports writers might not have understood Clemente, but the fans surely did, shouting, "Arriba! Arriba!" whenever he came to the plate, using a Spanish word to cheer him on.

When Olivo motioned he was ready too, Clemente turned to Nunn: "Come on a ride home with me," he said. By that, Clemente meant that he wanted the sportswriter to give him a lift to the airport. Nunn agreed.

The three men headed for a side exit under the stands that players used to avoid crowds. Clemente stopped for a moment to shake hands with Gene Baker, one of the two other blacks on the team. Then as they walked out of the locker room, Clemente told Nunn he expected to be back the next season. The player had been unsure about returning because of contract negotiations, but the Pirates general manager had worked out an offer days earlier.

As they reached the street, the men suddenly stopped talking. A crowd of fans spotted Clemente and swarmed toward him, patting him on the back and excitedly shouting out praises toward him. The player smiled, nodded and slowly kept walking. It seemed to take hours just to walk the short distance to Nunn's car. Finally as they climbed inside, Clemente sat back and relaxed.

"These are the best fans anywhere," he said to no one in particular. "They make all of this worthwhile. They are the reason I'm glad we won the World Series. They are the ones who deserve this championship."

Pulling away from the curb, Nunn realized Clemente had enjoyed his victory celebration a lot more on the streets of Pittsburgh, surrounded by the fans who had chosen him as their favorite player, than in the clubhouse with his teammates.

Five months later, Nunn found himself again trying to understand Clemente's complicated mindset to share the player's true feelings with readers. Nunn had traveled to Florida for Pirates spring training practice. For years, black players had accepted unequal treatment when major league teams headed to the South before the regular season. Nunn knew the treatment was wrong – and, now that the Pirates were world champions, he committed to doing something about it. As a young reporter, he had watched his mentor Wendell Smith use his words in the *Courier* to push for the integration of Major League Baseball. Nunn realized his own words could have impact too. He planned to write about the real conditions black players faced in Florida.

As he rode a public bus into Ft. Myers, Florida, Nunn looked out the window and saw a sign welcoming visitors to the "Home of the World Champion Pittsburgh Pirates."[426] But he knew the city would not be equally welcoming to everyone. Arriving at the team's practice facilities, Nunn found a divided team: Players who had worked with each other to create a magical World Series win in Pittsburgh once again found themselves in the South, unable even to eat together or to sleep in the same place. The white players stayed at the Bradford Hotel, a white-washed, three-story building along a lively downtown thoroughfare lined with gas lamps and neon signs advertising shops and restaurants. The white players used their free time to swim, play golf and go to the beaches. Many brought their families to Florida with them.

The same privileges were off-limits to the black players. Nunn joined them after practice as the men drove in a rented car to the private home of local resident C.B. Earle,[427] where three women prepared the players' evening meals. They all stayed with local families and met up for dinner. The men ate well and the host families worked hard to make them comfortable. But problems with the segregated housing became obvious as soon as Nunn pulled out his notebook and started asking questions.

"We go to the ballpark, play cards and watch television," Clemente said to Nunn.[428] "In a way, it's like being in prison. … The only thing we can do is put in time until we head North."

Gene Baker, the team's black veteran infielder, spoke up. He liked to talk with his teammates during the day about the races at the nearby dog track. Like a lot of other players, he went to watch the races at night.

"But when it comes time to enter the track," he said, "I have to go my separate way. My entrance is marked 'colored.'"

The same was true for Terry Park, the stadium where the Pirates played their games. Black fans could use only the restrooms marked for them and sit in a separate section along the first baseline. The funny thing Nunn realized when he went to the stadium was that the "colored" seats were among the best in the house.

The Pirates were not unique. Major league teams that had integrated in their northern home cities continued to allow local rules about segregation control how they treated players and fans during spring training. The attitude often came down to a reluctance to challenge local officials, as if the teams were guests in a foreign land. Players often found the situation confusing: How could the same people who cheered for them on the field during a game, also refuse to let them sit in a local restaurant immediately after the game ended? Worse, how could team owners allow the practices continue to happen?

Bill White, a player for the St. Louis Cardinals, spoke for players throughout the league: "How could Major League Baseball treat us – and pay us – like first-class citizens in the ballpark and then turn its head when we were treated like second-class citizens after the game was over?"[429]

Nunn found the transition from Pittsburgh to the Deep South jolting too.[430] Early one morning on his way to the Pirates' practice fields, Nunn climbed into an idling public bus parked at its first stop of the day. No other passengers were there yet, so Nunn struck up a conversation with the driver and sat down in a nearby seat. After a few moments of small talk, the men turned quiet and Nunn closed his eyes, nodding off. "When I wake up," Nunn recalled years later, "no one's sitting next to me. Whites are behind me, and in the back are all blacks." Nunn looked to the driver. The bus was segregated, but Nunn forgot about the local practice because no other passengers had been there when he entered.

"Should I move?" Nunn asked the driver.

"Nah, stay where you are," the man answered back.

What bothered Nunn as much as the segregation at spring training was that the Pirates' team officials seemed willing to accept the differences. At first, in February, a month before Nunn traveled to see the conditions for himself, Pirates spokesman Jack Berger insisted no housing problem existed: "The Negro players," he said, "understand perfectly, too, the segregation problem in the South and accept it as such."[431]

The black players, of course, disagreed when Nunn called them on the phone.

"I am definitely not satisfied," Baker told the reporter as he took notes. "…I believe that any player who makes the grade in the major leagues should be treated as a major leaguer. We are all on the same team and should be treated equally."

Then when Nunn traveled to Ft. Myers, team managers admitted they wanted to do better by the black players, but local officials wouldn't allow it. General Manager Joe L. Brown spoke to Nunn with conviction and apparent sincerity but conceded he had not been able to change the rules. The Pirates were under a contract. He had met with city leaders and told them the segregated living conditions were creating friction for Pirates teammates. But the team had no leverage to pressure local leaders.

"I didn't go to these men to make demands," Brown told Nunn.

Brown understood the problems with segregating players, and he explained how he had asked the city to integrate the Pirates' living space and ballpark. It had seemed like progress, he told the reporter, when city leaders said they understood his concerns. Even so, no one made any effort to fix the situation. They instead continued to fall back on local rules, saying a city ordinance prohibited mixing of the races. The Pirates controlled the playing surface at Terry Field and could integrate the team during games – but the city controlled the rest of the stadium, and it would not allow blacks and whites to mingle in the stands or restrooms.

Before coming to Ft. Myers in 1955, when the city expanded the ballpark to 2,500 seats and later added lights for nighttime games, the Pirates had wandered to different spring training homes every year.[432] The situation always had been the same. Even if Brown and the other team officials truly wanted to resolve the separation of players, they did not want to spurn Ft. Myers, the only city in recent memory that had felt like a regular destination.

As Nunn packed his bags and headed for a flight back to Pittsburgh, he felt even more determined to tell readers across the country about the discrimination. He left Ft. Myers believing segregation had become a way of life in the town and that it would not change any time soon. He also believed the Pirates had simply given in to the pressure, rather than taking a stand over the issue.

"The real tragedy of the situation, however, is the Pirates," Nunn wrote into his typewriter when he returned to the *Courier*'s offices, "who despite all of their noble talk, seem ready to accept things just the way they are next year, the year after that and only God knows how far into the future."[433]

Nunn was right that local leaders were reluctant to change practices – but he hadn't realized how attention generated by him, Wendell Smith and other writers would have an impact. Their words emboldened black players to speak out.

By the 1961 All-Star Game in Boston,[434] the Cardinals' Bill White traveled with another black player to the game to meet with player representatives. The players wanted their white teammates to support them in demanding changes.

"If the players are going to pussyfoot over this thing, I'd just as soon not attend the meeting," White told Nunn by phone from Boston. "If they are serious about doing something and really want to hear our side of the problem, then I will be glad to cooperate."[435]

White players were willing to hear the other side of the problem. And the combined pressure worked. Or at least it started to work. By the following spring, seven of the 14 major league teams with Florida spring training camps found ways to keep their players together.[436] The Dodgers resolved the issue by taking over a former military base in Vero Beach. The Baltimore Orioles negotiated an arrangement with a hotel in Miami. The Yankees and White Sox each invested about $1 million to secure living facilities for their players. The Cubs actually purchased the Sarasota Terrace hotel in Sarasota so the team could set the rules for who stayed there. White's team, the Cardinals, leased a small beachfront motel for the entire team. The place actually became a tourist attraction when local residents started driving past just to see the unprecedented sight of black and white men with their families, living together, eating in the same dining room and even swimming in the same pool.[437]

The Pirates still were not among the teams that made any changes. Team officials continued to believe they could convince local leaders in Ft. Myers to eliminate segregation simply by asking. Besides, the team remained under contract. But the pressure from other teams made it impossible for the Pirates' owners to plead ignorance or even intractability. Within two years, by 1963, the team agreed to lease out the entire Edisonian Court Motel in Ft. Myers.[438] The team's contract had run out by then. When the Pirates threatened to leave the city, local leaders agreed to make an exception. In return, the team agreed to renew its contract for four years.

The tradeoff about staying at the smaller team hotel, however, meant that none of the players would have room to bring their families. They would have to work out separate arrangements.

Brown, the Pirates' general manager, seemed as relieved as anyone to have the issue of spring training segregation finally resolved.

"This is something we've worked on and wanted a long time," he told Nunn. "We've always believed in equal facilities for all of our players. Unfortunately there were elements we had to overcome before we were able to put our thoughts into action in Florida."

Many professional football team owners and managers seemed sincere about wanting to knock down barriers to black players too. But again, Nunn believed few of them were moving fast enough to do something about it. Mostly, he felt frustrated that so many of his black college All-American choices continued to be overlooked.

He also realized that things were improving. Perhaps not as quickly as he and black leaders wanted. But still. Black players had to look for openings whenever they occurred. Oddly enough, it seemed that a four-hour flight by propeller plane from Miami to Dallas had created more chances for black players than anyone could have imagined.

Lamar Hunt, an heir to an oil fortune in Texas, had been on the plane and he desperately wanted an NFL franchise for his hometown of Dallas.[439] His father had been known in 1948 as the richest man in the world, and while Hunt seemingly had little talent or interest in taking up the oil business, he had dabbled in running sports franchises and believed strongly in the future of professional football. Hunt started out wanting to buy the Chicago Cardinals, but when the Wolfner family who owned it held out for more money, Hunt shifted tactics to pushing for an NFL expansion team. The league seemed poised to grow but team owners would not add franchises as long as the Cardinals' owners still pondered a sale, as stubborn as they might be.

Boarding a flight back home after yet another failed meeting with the Wolfners, Hunt reconsidered his options and realized that he was not alone in wanting to expand professional football. Potential owners existed in Houston, Denver, Minnesota and a few other cities. All had been rebuffed by the Wolfner family and the NFL. But what if they started their own league? Writing in clear short strokes on American Airlines letterhead that he received from a stewardess, Hunt sketched out the plans for a new league to challenge the NFL. When potential owners of teams met for the first time at the Imperial South Suite on the 20th floor of Chicago's Conrad Hilton Hotel on August 14, 1959, they agreed to revive the American Football League name for their new venture.[440]

Just as before, the creation of a new league meant more opportunities for black players. Teams in the newly formed AFL needed men to play the game. Before the year ended, Abner Haynes, a football star at North Texas State College who helped break that state's color barrier at the previously all-white school in 1956, announced he would turn down offers from the NFL's Steelers and the Canadian Football League so he could stay in Dallas with Hunt's new team, the Texans.[441] The new league meant more opportunities for players from black colleges too. Before the start of the AFL's second season, black colleges sent 50 men to professional training camps, with the players divided almost evenly between the leagues.[442]

Suddenly, Nunn started to feel even more pressure to make the right picks for his All-America teams – and for those players to perform up to expectations if drafted anywhere. Before, black college players often had no higher honor than making the *Courier*'s list, and Nunn had no way to measure the strength of his selections. Now the list would be tested like never before: If the newspaper named a black college player as the best among his peers and he could not play with whites or blacks from larger schools, the All-Americans and black colleges would lose credibility.

"With more and more emphasis being placed upon the Negro college graduate by the National Football League, the American Football League, as well as the Canadian League," Nunn wrote into his typewriter at the end of 1962, "it becomes increasingly apparent, with each passing season, that these standout gridders, through their outstanding play, are the young men upon whose broad shoulders rest the proof of the caliber of football being played by minority schools."[443]

Nunn knew, too, that the stakes remained high despite recent gains. Some team owners, coaches and fans still refused to accept black players. Few seemed more stubborn than George Preston Marshall, owner of the Washington Redskins NFL team.

During World War II when the league still had no black players, Marshall vowed that it would always remain that way: "Negroes will never play in our league again, because the white players would not stand for it," he told the *Courier*.[444] Then, as Kenny Washington and Woody Strode reintegrated the NFL after the war, Marshall again told the newspaper his team would remain segregated. "I have nothing against Negroes," Marshall said. "…but I want an all-white team. I believe in states' rights, both in government and in football."[445]

Marshall stood by his promises, even to the detriment of his team. By 1961, the Redskins had recorded just three winning seasons in the 15 years since the L.A. Rams started the reintegration of the NFL.

Nunn, like many sports columnists, saw the team's racial bias as its biggest weakness.

"Numerous citizens in Washington, D.C., are laughing out loud over the sad showing of the Washington Redskins' grid team the past season," Nunn wrote at the end of 1960, after the team finished with one win, nine losses and two ties.[446] "The Redskins remain the only professional football team that refuses to use Negro personnel."

That criticism was not limited to the black press either. Shirley Povich, sports editor of the *Washington Post*, leveled a similar criticism at the Redskins' owner after the season: "Marshall has been doing a disservice to all of his coaches and putting them in an unfair posture against the other coaches in the league. This is his adamant position against drafting Negro football players."[447] Regardless of how Marshall felt about black players, the Redskins could not hope to compete by ignoring a whole group of talented athletes, said Gordon Coddledick, sports editor of the *Cleveland Plain Dealer*. "This isn't an argument for social equality," he told readers in northeast Ohio. "It's a matter of practical football policy."[448]

Like the Coliseum issue that forced the L.A. Rams to take black players, stadium economics ultimately forced Marshall to reconsider his support for athletic segregation too. The Redskins had signed a 31-year lease to play at the new, publicly financed, $24 million D.C. Stadium, located in a portion of the National Capital Parks system called Anacostia Flats.[449] When President John F. Kennedy's administration came into office in January 1961, Stewart Udall, the new secretary of the Interior Department, saw an opening. A group using "any public facility in a park area" had to abide by the agency's rules against job discrimination. That now included the Redskins if the team intended to play in the new stadium.

Nunn's sports pages in the *Courier* celebrated the moment with a headline that taunted the football league's owners: "Govt. Does What NFL Wouldn't."[450]

Marshall resisted. "I am surprised that with the world on the brink of another war they are worried about whether or not a Negro is going to play for the Redskins," he said, citing Cold War rhetoric.[451] And then he claimed the team had made only a "business decision" to recruit players from segregated white colleges across the South. He found some, perhaps unwelcome, support too: The American Nazi Party paraded outside the new stadium that fall, carrying signs showing swastikas and slogans such as "Keep the Redskins White!"

The team finished the 1961 season with an even worse record: one win, 12 losses and a tie. During the offseason, other team owners refused to play exhibition games against the Redskins in segregated southern cities. Under growing pressure, Marshall agreed to draft one black player for 1962. His team ended up with four.

In the Redskins' first game, Bobby Mitchell, a black running back that the Redskins received in a trade with the Cleveland Browns, ran back a 92-yard touchdown and scored on two passes.

Even with at least a couple of black players on every team, professional football remained far from fully integrated. Teams might take black players – but coaches still did not have to play them, especially at so-called skilled positions at quarterback or center.

Going through his usual work to evaluate black college players in 1961, Nunn had traveled to Houston, expecting to see Texas Southern University win a conference championship in front of a homecoming crowd of 10,000 fans. Instead, he watched an upset in amazement as the little-known quarterback of Mississippi's Jackson State College literally ran away with the game. Roy Curry rushed for two touchdowns in a 12-7 win, elevating his team to that year's Orange Blossom Classic championship in Miami.

"Curry was a one-man floor show," Nunn told readers of the *Courier*, "as he scored both of Jackson's touchdowns and called his plays with enough diplomacy to win himself a seat in the United Nations."[452]

Jackson State lost the national championship weeks later, but Curry won a spot on Nunn's All-America team.

The next season, Curry came back and led the Tigers to a national championship as the most valuable player of the Orange Blossom Classic, and he earned a second consecutive slot on the *Courier* all-star team. By then, Nunn had learned not to be surprised by what Curry could do on the field.

The reporter also had gotten to know the player better by talking with an old friend. Nunn's college teammate Joe Gilliam had been a two-time All-American at West Virginia State College, and now he was working as assistant coach at Jackson State. Both men believed Curry deserved a chance under center as a professional – and they felt the NFL and AFL were overdue for a starting black quarterback.

A generation earlier, Gilliam had pressed for that chance himself. After Gilliam finished at West Virginia State, Green Bay Packers owner Curly Lambeau offered him a $7,000 contract to play safety on defense. But Gilliam played quarterback. Before deciding whether to accept the offer, Gilliam called Lambeau and asked for a chance to play under center on offense instead.

"There are no colored quarterbacks in the NFL," Lambeau replied.[453]

Gilliam felt certain he could play in the pros. West Virginia State threw the ball a lot, and he had been a standout player. He asked Lambeau again.

"I'd like an opportunity to play quarterback," he said.

"I'll tell you again," Lambeau answered. "There are no colored boys playing quarterback in the league."

If he couldn't have even a chance to lead an NFL offense, Gilliam decided he would not play at all. He talked over the decision with his wife and decided not to accept the Packers' contract. He instead went onto coach black college players, serving as defensive coordinator at Tennessee State University when the school had four undefeated seasons and seven black college championships.

The Packers later took a chance on a black college quarterback, Charlie "Choo Choo" Brackins, in 1955. He played only a few minutes at the end of a 41-10 loss, throwing two incomplete passes and getting released after the game. Nunn believed that Brackins had defeated himself, giving into distractions off the field that hurt his ability to play football.

In Curry, Nunn saw the best black college quarterback in a decade, since Brackins had graduated from Prairie View A&M College in Texas.

"Curry is a natural leader," Nunn told people that fall, "with the ability to pass brilliantly and, if needed, to run with the ball."[454]

Members of the Rooney family, who owned the Pittsburgh Steelers, heard Nunn talking. The team drafted Curry in the 12th round, although the Canadian Football League's Saskatchewan team wanted him too.[455] Curry decided to stay in the United States on the promise that he would get a shot to play as a quarterback in the NFL. The Steelers had suggested that veteran quarterback Bobby Layne, at age 36, should retire, and that created a slot for someone new. The team said Curry would get a chance.

But when training camp opened, Steelers Coach Buddy Parker played Curry at wide receiver. Teammates said they never knew Curry could even play quarterback.

"Roy was a gifted athlete who was very fast and could catch anything," recalled Andy Russell, a Pro Bowl linebacker drafted by the Steelers in the 16th round that year, 56 picks after Curry.[456] "I had no idea he was a quarterback in college. It wasn't easy. There were very few blacks and Coach Parker hated rookies."

Sandy Stephens, a black quarterback at the University of Minnesota, ran into a similar wall when he graduated and looked for professional work in 1962. In college, he had led the Gophers to an 8-1 record and a Rose Bowl victory. He had been the nation's first black All-American from an integrated school and was a finalist for the Heisman trophy.[457] It still was not enough. While he was drafted by both the NFL's Cleveland Browns and the AFL's New York Titans, neither team wanted to play him at quarterback. Browns running back Jim Brown broke the news in a phone call after the draft: "Sandy, if you think you're going to be the quarterback of the Cleveland Browns, you're crazy."[458] So instead of going to Cleveland, Stephens went to Canada and played there.

Nunn and other black sports reporters were growing frustrated. The way they saw it, talented black athletes were being denied a chance to prove themselves simply because of their skin color. The *Courier* called out professional teams for the oversight, albeit in the flowery language of the time: "The three-generations-old belief that Negroes are as gifted in muscular synchronization as they are subnormal in mental coordination has long needed to be removed."[459]

Curry made the Steelers in the fall of 1963 – but as a receiver. Late in the season on a cold day in Philadelphia, he sped up to chase an overthrown ball and pulled up short with a strain in his hamstring. He reinjured it the following week, and never fully recovered. The Steelers kept him on the roster for the rest of the season and invited him back for training camp the next summer. But he did not make the cut a second season. Curry then tried out with the Chicago Bears and a team in the Canadian Football League, but the hamstring injury persisted and he never played again professionally.

For Gilliam, the answer was easy: "The NFL was not ready for a black quarterback, period."[460]

Nunn agreed. He found himself feeling cynical about the way professional teams looked at all athletes. It seemed that the only color owners truly could see was green. If a team owner believed he could make more money by playing a black quarterback, maybe he would. But the player would have to be good enough to overcome public stereotypes. A few men already had overcome those challenges – Kenny Washington with the L.A. Rams and Jackie Robinson with baseball's Brooklyn Dodgers – but more would have to keep pushing against bias.

"Every white man is not a bigot," Nunn said as he thought about the situation.[461] "And then there are plenty of white guys who might be a bigot but still know, 'I want to win, and this is a way for me to win.' ... And then there were some people who said, 'Hey, this is a way for me to make some money. Cheap too.'"

The sports pages of the *Courier* reflected Nunn's dismay. "One of the great fallacies of our time, in which college-bred people are surprisingly guilty of racism, is the continuing bar on the use of Negro quarterbacks," the paper said in an unsigned sports editorial.[462]

Nunn knew from experience and observation that some changes simply would not take place without public pressure. Some pro team owners had noticed the *Courier*'s All-American picks. The New York Giants' Wellington Mara back in the early 1950s used the list to find tackle Roosevelt Brown at Morgan State College. Since then, Brown had been named an All-Pro player 10 times. But moments like that had been too rare. Black players, especially those from small black colleges, still were considered a novelty. A few might be good enough to play as professionals, owners reasoned, but most were not worth a second look. A man had to be so obviously talented at his position that white owners, coaches and teammates would overlook the color of his skin. And even then, as in the case with Curry, that still might not be enough.

Nunn would help them see the talent in the black colleges – and make sure the public saw it too. He began plotting a way to bring more attention to the *Courier*'s black college All-America team.

Charles "Teenie" Harris, American, 1908–1998. Pittsburgh Steelers football team coach "Buddy" Parker, posed with hand on shoulder of trainer Wallace "Boots" Lewis, on athletic field at Slippery Rock State Teachers College, July 1961. Black and white: Kodak Safety Film, H: 4 in. x W: 5 in. (10.20 x 12.70 cm), Carnegie Museum of Art, Pittsburgh: Heinz Family Fund, 2001.35.1711.

❖❖❖

The following summer, in 1964, became known as "Freedom Summer." White college students headed into the South to work with black volunteers at registering blacks to vote in Mississippi. That June, three activists – James Chaney, a black volunteer from the South, and two white, Jewish New Yorkers, Andrew Goodman and Michael Schwerner – were murdered in an event that came to be known as "Mississippi Burning."[463]

A month later in Washington, Congress passed – and President Lyndon Johnson signed – the Civil Rights Act of 1964, prohibiting discrimination based on race, skin color, religion, sex or national origin. It also outlawed segregation in schools, at work and in public places such as hotels, restaurants and sports stadiums.[464]

Also that summer, Bill Nunn Jr. decided his All-Americans deserved more than just having their names appear in the newspaper.

Nunn started organizing an event for the players – a "Night of Stars" that would take place after the season at the Pittsburgh Hilton Hotel.[465] The setting would be as glamorous as any the city could offer, with the hotel sitting at Pittsburgh's front step, across the street from a large grassy park where the rivers come together to form at Point State Park. In his mind, Nunn already could see the scene coming together: On a Friday night in late December, long black cars carrying the *Courier*'s All-Americans and other high-profile guests – hundreds, in all – would pull around in front of the building, under a long portico. Upstairs in the hotel ballroom, each of the 22 players would receive a plaque, a watch and a blazer identifying them as *Courier* black college All-Americans. The event would be so glamorous and high profile everyone would notice.

More importantly, he knew, the event would serve as a coming out party – for the black college players, of course, but also for everyone who had come before them too. The night would honor the history of the *Courier*'s black college All-Americans, tracing back 39 years to when Nunn's father started the tradition. It would honor the memories of men who had played the game for nothing more than the love of the sport and the chance to see their name in the newspaper.

When Nunn pitched the idea, he convinced the Royal Crown Cola Company of Columbus, Georgia, to pick up the tab. And he helped others share his vision. Eddie Robinson, the coach at Grambling College in Louisiana, saw it right away: "For years, I've felt our All-Americas weren't receiving the honors they really deserved," he said. "I think a banquet of this type is long overdue. It will give the All-Americas something to remember for the rest of their lives."[466] Jake Gaither, the coach at Florida A&M, the team that hosted the annual Orange Blossom Classic in Miami felt it too: "Negro football is producing some of the top players in the country. I think it is time they get the type of recognition deserved by outstanding athletes." [467]

By the 1960s, top coaches at the small black colleges had learned the importance of hyperbole when it came to promoting their players and teams. But in this case, Gaither could make a strong argument for his claim about supplying some of the nation's top players. Black athletes had started turning up in notable numbers in both of the professional football leagues. Together, the leagues had 76 black players, with a third coming from the smaller black schools where the *Courier* found its All-Americans.[468] That fall too, for the first time, half of the rookie all-stars in the NFL were black.[469] Mississippi's Jackson State College, alone, had eight players signed to professional teams.

In the weeks leading up to the dinner, Nunn interviewed players and their agents about starting salaries and signing bonuses. "Bullet" Bob Hayes, a rookie All-American from Florida A&M, had spent the summer proving at the Summer Olympics in Tokyo that he was the fastest man in the world, tying the world record in the 100 meter dash and anchoring a 4 x 100 meter relay team that set a new world record. That fall, Hayes signed a rookie contract with the Dallas Cowboys that paid him $100,000 over three years.[470] Other, less-heralded players, received contracts with a mix of financial benefits: One received a $10,000 signing bonus, the keys to a new Ford Thunderbird and a salary of $15,000 a year.[471] As an added incentive, the team paid his mother $1,000 and his girlfriend

$300. Another player received $12,000, an Oldsmobile and enough money to pay off the mortgage on his mother's home.

Nunn realized the moment for black college players finally had arrived, and he wanted nothing more than to remind the world that these players had been there all along, hidden in plain sight. He sat down as his typewriter in the *Courier*'s offices as the planning for the banquet continued around him.

"It is sad that it took the professionals so long to wake up to this source of raw talent," Nunn wrote to his readers.[472] "Yet the fact that these men were eventually allowed to be discovered at all is to the credit of those far-sighted Negro college presidents who believed, all along, that sports was a means for our young men to reach for the stars."

On the night of the banquet, December 18, nearly 300 guests arrived in the early evening at the Pittsburgh Hilton. Most were men, wearing dark suits over starched white shirts with narrow long ties. A few wore bow ties.

From the podium at the front of the ballroom, Nunn called forward his latest All-America picks, reminding listeners again how hard it was to choose just 22 men from across the country.[473] As always, he worried about the player he might have missed.

Over 15 years of choosing the best black college players, Nunn's idea of an All-American had crystallized in his mind. Above all, each man needed the desire to excel. "This, we think the members of this team have in abundance," Nunn said about the class of 1964.[474] [475]

But desire could never be enough. Many black college athletes wanted to play well, especially as more of them saw a chance to make money from the game. With more players getting scouted for the pros, a *Courier* All-American truly needed to stand out. Nunn looked out across the ballroom at the selected young men he had gathered for the dinner in Pittsburgh.

"All had the size, speed, maneuverability and football savvy to standout above the rest of the crowd," Nunn said. "This, they did to their own justification, as well as that of their team and their schools."

J.T. Williams, the president of Maryland State College, a historically black school on the state's Eastern Shore, gave the keynote address. He had been a member of the *Courier's* first All-America squad in 1925 as a player at Oklahoma's Langston University.[476] [477] The men on that team had been born too soon, everyone in the room knew.

Ric Roberts, a *Courier* sports writer, reminded everyone about the history of the All-Americans. He talked about Paul "Tank" Younger, the NFL's first black college player in 1949, with the Los Angeles Rams. Younger had opened a door, Roberts said, "the door to financial independence, the absolute 'must' for any nation, any people, any person – in our secular society. Younger lighted that first torch, in a quest for human dignity…and gold." [478]

Nunn also gave out awards to his former picks now playing as professionals. During training camp that summer, two former black college All-Americans playing for the Chicago Bears – Willie Galimore, from Florida A&M, and John "Bo" Farrington, from Prairie View A&M – died in a car accident.[479] They had been out late near the Bears' training camp at St. Joseph's College in Indiana. Nunn created two awards in their names, recognizing the top black college rookie and veteran in the NFL and AFL. The men's widows, Audrey Galimore and Vivian Farrington, sat at the head table inside the Hilton ballroom.[480]

Art Rooney Sr., owner and team president for the Pittsburgh Steelers, stood to receive the NFL rookie award on behalf of his team's new lineman Ben McGee, who had returned home to Jackson, Mississippi, for his wedding.[481] Other winners – the Giants' Roosevelt Brown, Tommy Day of the Buffalo Bills and Mack Lee Hill of the Kansas City Chiefs – stood to receive their trophies.[482]

For the first time, Nunn also handed out a large trophy to the black college national champion football team. He always had referred to his pick as the "mythical" champion. But now the winning team would have an actual piece of hardware — a wood and metal trophy decorated with figures of little football players — to take back home.

For the second year, Prairie View A&M finished as the undisputed top team with nine wins and no losses. The team's coach Billy Nicks was named the *Courier*'s coach of the year. Its quarterback, Jimmy Kearney, not only made the *Courier*'s All-America list but won a separate award for being a top offensive player. A month before the dinner, the NFL's Detroit Lions had drafted Kearney in the 11th round, with the 151st overall pick.

As Coach Nicks stepped to the podium to receive the championship trophy, he could not stop thinking about his star quarterback in the audience – and the uncertain professional future that awaited him.

"A lot of people tell me we Negro coaches have it made now," Nicks said, speaking to the ballroom audience. "They point out the fact that our youngsters are signing big professional contracts and proving they can play football with the best.

"I'm here to tell you, we still have a long way to go."

Nicks looked out to where Rooney, the Steelers owner, sat with his son, Dan, the team's vice president, and Buddy Parker, the Steelers coach who had refused to let Roy Curry take any snaps at quarterback just a year earlier.

"While we are accepted in most phases of pro football," Nicks said, "there are still positions closed to us. One of those is quarterback."

Nicks turned to his star player, Kearney.

"In front of me is a youngster who could make the grade as a quarterback. He has been signed by the Detroit Lions. But you know what they're going to do? They'll make him a running back. Here is a youngster who has never taken a handoff in his life. The kid can run and he can throw. He's always been a quarterback. Now they talk about making him a running back? It doesn't make any sense."

Nunn sat in the audience quickly taking notes. He had created this "Night of Stars" for a moment such as this. He needed to make sure Nicks' words were heard not only by Rooney and the other people in the room – but also by readers across the country. If they thought the fight was won because some black college players had made the pros, he would quote Nicks to remind them the battle had to continue.

That next week, the *Courier* ran stories praising the success of the banquet. The night had been a long time in coming. Nunn and his staff wanted to savor the moment just a little longer, and make sure they had enough momentum for it to become an annual event.

The paper ran an entire page of photos. One showed Nicks lifting the championship trophy, and a story nearby carried the words from his speech. Everyone had been elated, Nunn wrote, that Nicks had spoken up for his star quarterback – and for black college players everywhere.

"His speech was on the lips of many individuals until the small hours of the morning," Nunn wrote.

Months later when the Lions opened training camp the following summer, Jimmy Kearney did make the team – but not as a quarterback or even running back. The Lions, instead, moved him to defense, where he saw little action. He lasted two seasons before going to the Kansas City Chiefs and becoming a regular starter, again on the defensive side of the ball.

Nunn still was enjoying the success of his All-America banquet less than a month later when the American Football League's best players started arriving in New Orleans for an all-star game. The black players among them would realize again just how far they still had to go.

League officials had chosen the city because its civic leaders desperately wanted a professional team – and also because they had promised that Louisiana had changed. Less than a decade earlier, the University of Pittsburgh upended interracial sports in the state by insisting on playing in the Sugar Bowl with a black player and a fully integrated student section. The state's new rules against interracial sporting contests after the game left it more isolated, but they had been superseded by federal law. Business and political leaders desperately wanted to show that New Orleans could be a big-league city.

Dave Dixon[483], a New Orleans businessman who hoped to own a professional football franchise, assured the AFL all-stars the city would be safe and that people would treat them with respect. Locals could serve as warm hosts for all of the league's best players, regardless of color, he said. As proof, the city had hosted the Sugar Bowl less than two weeks earlier, with Syracuse University fielding eight black players in a loss to all-white Louisiana State University.

"They told us, 'Bring your wife and kids,'" said Clem Daniels, a black Oakland Raiders halfback who had graduated from Prairie View A&M.[484] "'There will also be a golf tournament.' It sounded like a big picnic."

Trouble started as soon as players arrived at the airport the weekend before the game. Some taxi drivers refused to take players to their hotel or, if they did, dropped them far from it. Clubs on Bourbon Street denied admittance to black players. At one, the bouncer pulled a gun on the San Diego Chargers' Ernie Ladd. Later his teammate Earl Faison overheard two locals debating whether he was Ladd. "Ernie Ladd's a bigger nigger than that," one said. "That Ladd is a big nigger."[485]

Back at the team hotel, Ernie Warlick, a tight end with the league champion Buffalo Bills, started comparing stories with other black all-stars. Many had similar experiences, being turned away or insulted. As the group started getting larger, one player suggested they should boycott the football game by simply refusing the play. Others agreed. They chose Warlick to notify the commissioner.

Joe Foss, the AFL commissioner, had been staying in Chicago, back at the same Conrad Hilton Hotel where team owners had formed the league. He was there to attend a banquet by the Chicago baseball writers association, honoring black major leaguers Ernie Banks, Willie Mays and Bob Gibson. Months earlier, Gibson had willed the St. Louis Cardinals to a game-seven victory in the World Series.

Warlick called Foss around 8:30 p.m. on Sunday night. He said the black players were seriously thinking about pulling out of the all-star game because people in New Orleans had been insulting them in every possible way. They didn't want to play in a city where so much prejudice prevailed.

Foss listened to Warlick and said he understood. He would abide by whatever the players decided.

"But don't do anything hasty," he told Warlick.[486] "Think this over for a while longer and then call me back with your final decision."

Warlick said he would call again in an hour.

All 21 black players met up at the Roosevelt Hotel, the headquarters for the East team. Warlick said they should take a vote among themselves to make sure everyone agreed. All but four supported the boycott. Two dissenters spoke up, saying they were afraid to lose their jobs if they embarrassed the league. Warlick and his Buffalo teammate Cookie Gilchrist[487], a fullback, stood in front. They understood why the holdouts were afraid but they believed there would be safety in numbers. "The majority ruled," Warlick said.[488]

The black players needed to let their white teammates know what they had decided. No one knew how the white players would react. Ron Mix, a white tackle on the San Diego Chargers, was among the first to answer: If the game was going to happen without the black players, he told them, he would not play either. "I felt I would be wrong in not playing," he said later, "but that it was important for at least one white player to join them, to say, 'We're with you.'"[489] Soon all of the other white players agreed in a statement of solidarity.

Foss was eating his dinner at the Chicago Hilton when a waiter walked over to the table and said he had a long-distance phone call from New Orleans. The commissioner immediately left the banquet and rushed back to his hotel room. Warlick was on the line again.

"Commissioner," he said, "we're not going to stay here and play. We've voted on it, and the majority is against playing. We're all pulling out of here immediately."[490]

Foss again said he understood. He told Warlick the players had every right to boycott. He also asked them to stay in touch because the league still intended to play the game, just not in New Orleans.

Nunn was at the *Courier*'s offices in Pittsburgh laying out that week's sports pages when Wendell Smith, his mentor and former colleague, called from Chicago with word that the AFL's black all-stars were pulling out of the game.

The league commissioner would be holding a press conference Monday morning to announce his backup plans. That would be too late to get the news into the *Courier*'s national edition that week, but Nunn realized the impact immediately. Smith had moved into television as a sports anchor for WGN but he continued to write on the side. Nunn asked him to cover the press conference and write up something for the *Courier*.

Foss looked exhausted as he stood inside the Hilton's Imperial Suite the next morning. Reporters crowded around him with notebooks out and a battery of television cameras trained lenses on him. He spoke in a soft but emphatic voice as he explained how Warlick had called him twice the night before, finally saying that none of the players, black or white, would play in the all-star game in New Orleans.

"I do not blame our Negro stars for doing what they did," Foss said.[491] "I doubt that New Orleans is ready for the big league. If they can't treat big leaguers with the dignity and respect they deserve, then the city will have to suffer the consequences."

Instead, the commissioner had stayed up all night making arrangements to move the game to Houston, home of the league's Oilers franchise.

Nunn hardly could believe it when he heard about the alternate location. Houston had been among the least accommodating cities for black football. Black fans had been boycotting the Oilers for three years because of the team's insistence on segregated seating. Even after the Civil Rights Act was passed, players in Houston felt the team owners were not overly sincere about signing black players. At the same time, Nunn knew the Texas city actually had emerged as a relatively friendly place for blacks, allowing integration at most restaurants and hotels even before the federal government required it.

Sitting at his typewriter, Nunn felt pride in the black players' tough stand. He could not remember a time when so many black athletes had banded together to fight injustice – nor when their actions had been so warmly received, even by whites. The *Courier*'s Double V campaign during World War II twenty years earlier had solidified blacks, but it had been scorned as anti-American or even seditious by many whites. This time, much of the nation seemed to agree with the sense of outrage. Foss, the AFL commissioner, had not hesitated for a moment to move the game.

"The Negro athletes who refused to bow in the face of segregation in New Orleans last week are to be commended," Nunn wrote to the newspaper's readers across the country.[492]

"To a man, the individuals who put principal above playing in a football game have shown that courage can pay big dividends. When the 21 Negroes decided as a group that they would not perform in a city where they weren't accepted as citizens, they had no idea of the repercussions they might face. Despite this they went ahead and made their move."

A week after the American Football League moved its all-star game, the New Orleans Aviation Board ruled that any taxi line guilty of discriminating against black passengers would be banned from operating at the city's airport.[493]

Wendell Smith predicted the league's decision would keep the city from receiving a major league franchise for a long time. "The town has no chance whatsoever now," he wrote in his own column for the *Courier*.[494] "No sports promoter in his right mind will go there. The town hasn't grown up. It's not ready for major league attractions … and won't get them."

Dixon, the New Orleans businessman who lured the AFL all-star game to the city and hoped to land a professional franchise, had been embarrassed. But he also learned from the mistakes. More could have been done to prepare cab drivers, club owners and the city's residents. Federal laws had changed, and national expectations had shifted too.

Ernest "Butch" Curry, a reporter for the *Courier*'s Louisiana edition, had watched the situation up close and decided the city had benefitted from the boycott.

Charles "Teenie" Harris, American, 1908–1998. Samuel Wolfolk and Jimmy Harris looking at baseball signed by Willie Mays held by Bill Nunn Jr., in Pittsburgh Courier newspaper office, May 1964. Black and white: Kodak Safety Film, H: 2 1/4 in. x W: 3 1/4 in. (5.71 x 8.26 cm), Carnegie Museum of Art, Pittsburgh: Heinz Family Fund, 2001.35.59254.

"As painful as it was," he wrote, "the cancellation gained allies for the city's forces of good."[495]

Two years later, the NFL awarded a franchise to New Orleans as part of a deal to win Congressional approval for the league's merger with the AFL.[496]

By opening doors for others, Nunn inadvertently opened one for himself too.

Team owner Art Rooney Sr. grew up with black friends and always felt well-regarded by Pittsburgh's black community. But sitting at the *Courier*'s All-America banquet in 1964, Rooney had an epiphany. He realized perhaps for the first time just how much professional football teams had imposed an unfair burden on black players – not scouting them hard, overlooking many players at the smaller black colleges and even then never really considering black athletes for every position.

He saw that the teams had hurt themselves too. Teams that ignored black athletes were missing out on a whole pool of talent because of the color of the players' skin – and because of the scouts' discomfort on black college campuses.

When the Detroit Lions turned James Kearney, the Prairie View A&M star quarterback, into a defensive back and then place him on the team's practice squad, Rooney remembered the speeches at the *Courier* banquet. He had his son Dan reach out to the Lions about a trade. The teams could not agree on a deal, but Rooney said his eyes had been opened.

"I am convinced that color has nothing to do with individual capabilities, in any endeavor," the team owner told the *Courier* soon after, "and wish it understood that the Steelers will use any brilliant quarterback we can recruit, regardless of color."[497]

That did not mean the Steelers actually had a black quarterback on the team, or even on the draft board. But the Rooneys, father and sons, had a plan to change that too. If only they could find the right scout – and convince him to help their team.

Chapter 7. Drafted

Dan Rooney felt uncertain every time he attended one of the *Pittsburgh Courier*'s All-America banquets. The son of the Steelers owner didn't know exactly how much racism had contributed to the National Football League's ignorance of black players. League insiders always gave the answer that teams scouted the top colleges in the major conferences: If those schools had a black player, then the scouts would know about him.

At the second *Courier* All-America banquet, former defensive end Lowell Perry spoke to the audience. The Steelers had drafted the black defensive end out of the University of Michigan in 1953 – in the eighth round, 90th overall – and he had seemed like a potential star until fracturing his pelvis in just his sixth regular-season game.[498] Perry had gone on to become an executive at Chrysler as the company's first black plant manager, and he had sold Bill Nunn Jr. his first car right off the factory line. Perry stood inside the ballroom of the Pittsburgh Hilton and praised Art Rooney Sr., thanking the Steelers' owner for fortifying his belief in the "American dream."

As he listened to the speech, Dan could count the ways his father believed in the dream too. As a young man, the Steelers founder had black friends and he supported their causes. As a North Side ward heeler, from what locals still called the old Allegheny City's 1st ward before Pittsburgh annexed the neighborhood, Art Sr. spent time with political boss Gus Greenlee in the city's Hill District. And when Greenlee's Pittsburgh Crawfords Negro National League team needed support, Art gave him money to keep it going.

But if a black football player never made it as far as any of the big colleges up north, the Steelers' scouts knew little about him. Every year at the banquet, Dan and his father met top players from the black colleges and heard their names for the first time. Ever since the first year for the banquet in 1964, Nunn had courted the Rooneys' support for his event, and the Steelers had responded by attending, and eventually, helping to sponsor the banquet. They had contributed at first just to be good neighbors, to support a football event in their home town. But the more time Dan spent with Nunn listening to the exploits of the black college game, the more he felt uncomfortable about what they didn't know.

Working at the team's offices inside the Roosevelt Hotel in late 1967, Dan sat at his desk in late December. The hotel once rated among the city's nicest but now sat in an area that had fallen on hard times, across the street from the opulent, but recently abandoned, Penn Theater. Moviegoers had gasped at the theater's marble staircases, bronze chandeliers and imported silk damask draperies in the 1920s, but owners walked away from the theater by the 1960s, unable to afford keep up the building as color television kept more people at home.[499] The Steelers' offices in the hotel seemed like something out of a movie on their own.[500] Art Sr., the "Chief" and head of the clan, had covered the walls with photographs and memorabilia from the football team as well as boxers he had promoted and baseball teams he had supported over the years. The office sat next to the hotel's men's room and the place had the bawdy feel of a boys' club, with men walking through the door tugging at their pants' fly as team officials sitting inside called out, "Next door, next door!"

Dan opened the *Courier*'s end-of-the-year edition and turned to the sports pages. He looked at Nunn's latest column and again saw the unfamiliar names and faces of the paper's 22 black college All-America players. Rooney wondered to himself why he didn't know any of them.[501] He also remembered that the previous banquet had attracted New York Giants' assistant coach Emlen Tunnell.[502] Other teams were starting to ask similar questions.

Rooney stood up and walked into his father's office, showed him the paper and said he had an idea. The team should try to hire the *Courier*'s sports editor.

"Well, who is he?" the Chief wanted to know.[503]

"He's Bill Nunn Sr.'s son," Dan answered back, knowing his father remembered the *Courier* editor from the boxing circuit and decades spent hanging out in the city's Hill District. Dan continued, explaining how it had been Nunn's son who had

Steelers scout Bill Nunn Jr., Art Rooney Jr., player personnel chief, Jack Butler, director of the BLESTO scouting combine, and Dick Haley, director of player personnel, at Steelers training camp in Latrobe. Photo courtesy of the Steelers.

Bill Nunn Jr. with stopwatch in hand evaluates players for the Pittsburgh Steelers in 1972. Courtesy of the Steelers.

put on the black college All-America banquets and who put out an annual list of the best black college football players.

"I think we ought to hire him," Dan said. "I really want to hire him."

Art Sr. looked back at his oldest son and trusted his instincts.

"Well, you do what you think's right," he answered.

Dan Rooney walked into the lobby of the Steelers' offices where a group of sports reporters were hanging out. He found Ric Roberts, a sports writer for the *Courier*, and asked him why Nunn never came around the team's offices himself.

Roberts shrugged his shoulders, saying he didn't know but he would find out. A few days later, he returned and told Rooney he wouldn't have to worry about ever seeing the *Courier*'s sports editor at the Roosevelt Hotel. His boss said he didn't come around because he didn't like the way the Steelers did business.

Dan was shocked. He thought the team had been more than fair to black players and the local black weekly. He picked up the phone and called Nunn at his desk. The men knew each other as acquaintances. Rooney asked Nunn to please come downtown to meet with him. Nunn hesitated but agreed to meet before hanging up.

When Nunn walked through the front door of the Steelers' offices, Dan Rooney looked up and called out to him.

"How come we never see you down here?" he wanted to know.[504]

Nunn felt like he had been waiting nearly 20 years for someone to ask him that question.

"There have been many times when I felt getting into the press box, and different things, that because I was the black newspaper, I wasn't particularly welcome," Nunn said. "Plus, I turn out an All-America football team every year, and nobody from the Steelers has ever contacted me. I heard from the Los Angeles Rams about 'Deacon' Dan Towler, and I even heard from the New York Giants about Roosevelt Brown. To tell you the truth, nobody from the Steelers ever called me. I don't think you'll ever be a winner."[505]

Rooney sat quietly and let Nunn finish. The admonition was overdue, but he hoped it would not be the final word. When the room fell silent again, Rooney didn't bother to say the sports editor was wrong.

"We'd like you to work for us," Rooney said.[506]

"Well, I've got this other job," Nunn answered back.

"You can start working with us as part-time," Rooney replied. "You know, you put the banquet on. We'll do that, and you tell us about the All-Americans, which you're already doing a little bit. But now you could start filing reports, telling us who can play, who can't. We'll do it right."

Nunn seemed surprised. He had believed the Steelers deliberately spurned the *Courier* and his All-America picks. Rooney knew the truth: The team didn't even know the players or how good they might be.

After a few minutes, Nunn said, "Okay." He would start sharing his knowledge with the Steelers on the side. He left the Roosevelt Hotel and headed back to the *Courier*, promising he would return to the team's offices later that evening after the newspaper was put to bed.

If he was going to work even a little bit as a part-time Steelers scout, Nunn also had to meet Dan's younger brother Art Rooney Jr. He headed up the team's scouting efforts and saw himself as the head of personnel. The moment Nunn left the team's headquarters, Dan walked over to his brother's office to give him the news about their latest hire.

Art Jr. already knew about Nunn and his *Courier* All-Americans. Even if the sports editor didn't believe it, the Steelers' scouts were aware of the list and saw it as a ready-made scouting report. Nunn would have had an easier time buying what the team did with the list, which was not much. The team's scouts really didn't understand much about the black colleges and certainly didn't feel comfortable just wandering around an all-black southern campus in search of players.

Dan walked into his brother's office and said, "You've got to hire Nunn as a part-timer."

Immediately, Art Jr. felt himself growing angry. He wanted to be in charge of the personnel department. He didn't mind the team hiring a black scout – but he wanted it to be his black scout.

But with Dan and their father in agreement over Nunn, Art Jr. had no choice but to wait around for the reporter to come back from working at the newspaper. That wouldn't be until after 7 p.m., so Art Jr. walked over to the hotel's still-fancy dining room with pastoral murals on the walls and white cloths on every table[507] to have a rib dinner. At least if he had to stick around late, he would get a decent meal out of it.

When Art Jr. returned to his offices after dinner, Nunn showed up a little while later. From the start, Art Jr. felt insecure, as if the reporter was looking at him and thinking, "Look at this guy: His old man gave him his job."

In his own mind, the son of the Steelers' owner could not help sizing up his new scout either. "Look at this black guy," Art Jr. thought to himself.[508] "He's trying to get a fix on a job, and I want to run this place."

But the men started talking. Over the next half-hour, it seemed they agreed on everything. Sure there were a lot of stiffs and do-nothings among athletes – white and black. But Art Jr. started realizing too just how much prejudice had colored the eyes of pro scouts. He could hear the outdated conventional wisdom again in his ears: Blacks could be good receivers and defensive backs but the closer you moved to the ball, like quarterback or center, they couldn't play as well. As the men sat there, Art Jr. realized more and more how silly those notions about race really were. He found himself agreeing with Nunn, that it was a disadvantage to overlook these guys based on some backwards thoughts about skin color.

Then a crazy idea started forming in Art Jr.'s mind: What if others in the league stayed prejudiced – except for himself, the Steelers' scouts and the team's coaches? Sitting there listening to Nunn talk about how the NFL had overlooked all of these black college players, Rooney found himself getting excited. Any team that stopped looking first at the color of black players' skin would beat the hell out of the competition. Finally he smiled and opened his mouth.

"Being prejudiced is a pretty good thing," Rooney blurted out, "if it's the other guys who are cutting their own throats."

Nunn had to wonder what kind of a decision he had made.

Some problems with the Steelers scouting system seemed obvious as soon as Nunn started. The Rooneys had been right: The scouts knew about the *Courier*'s All-Americans and many realized that the nation's small black colleges probably had at least pockets of talented players. That much had been obvious since men such as Tank Younger and Roosevelt Brown had started playing. They knew too that the *Courier* took much of the guess work out of the question by coming up each year with a list of the best players among those colleges. The problem was the remnants of segregation. Teams' white recruiters didn't know what to do with the information. Coming out of a period of deep division, many scouts felt uncomfortable walking onto an all-black campus and they didn't know what to do, how to act or who to talk with.

Nunn, of course, had grown up on these campuses and had known some of the school's athletic directors and coaches literally for decades. Thanks to his father's insistence, he had attended a black college and come of age among some of the nation's top black athletes – men who had first challenged the color barriers in basketball and football. Nunn had an advantage because he could see into two worlds when many of his competitors remained blind to one.

Even then, Nunn's eyes started opening in unexpected ways too. His job had changed. As a part-time scout for the Steelers, he not only had to use his subjective measurements to evaluate players based on desire and hard work. He had to write up detailed reports explaining each man's objective abilities. As he started measuring players' speed, size and athletic ability, Nunn started feeling even more confident that the NFL could find talent among these men.

Nunn recalled. "Naturally one of the things that was part of it was segregation. … A lot of the guys were all white guys looking for talent. A lot of them weren't going into the black schools. They weren't even comfortable going in to look at them."[509]

The Rooneys wanted more from Nunn than just his contacts on black campuses. Shortly after Nunn started, Dan Rooney called him back into his office at the Roosevelt Hotel.

"Look," Dan said, "I'm not hiring you as the black guy who's just going to tell us that. I want you to cover everybody?"

Nunn had not expected that. "Really?" he answered.

"Yeah," Dan replied. "I want you to cover everybody. I want you to go to the Big Ten. Your first assignment is to go to a school in the Big Ten."

The Steelers bought Nunn a ticket to Chicago and sent him to Northwestern University in the northern suburbs. Nunn came back with a new stack of reports – with the same sorts of insights and detailed information about players. Now he covered everybody.

More than that, Nunn started inserting himself among the team's upper management. If he saw something that seemed wrong, he spoke up and suggested another or better approach.

"Nunn started to really be part of our echelon," Dan Rooney said.[510] "He started to be part of our management team. He would tell us if we were doing things right – or if we were doing things wrong. I'm talking management."

Nunn started to believe the Rooneys really didn't care that much about a player's color – but they kept looking at it.

When he first walked into the team's evaluation room for the 1968 draft, Nunn checked out the draft board and each black player had a little black dot next to his name. The process had been a carryover from the NFL Scouting Combine where the league identified black players with a separate set of numbers from white ones. An even number like 110 was a white player, for example, while 111 meant the guy was black. The league didn't make that kind of distinction in any other way, for Jews or Italians or any other race or nationality.

Nunn spoke up: If the Steelers really wanted to be colorblind, to find the best men regardless of skin color, the team had to lose the dots. The Rooneys agreed – and stopped marking the names of black players.

The 1968 common draft ended up not being a deep one for the National and American football leagues, which had agreed to a merger plan two years earlier. Teams drafted three future Hall of Famers with the first eight picks, including Larry Csonka, a Syracuse University running back who went to Miami.[511] The Steelers picked tenth, choosing an offensive tackle who stayed with the team a year. In the 16th round, the team made its most notable pick, taking Notre Dame running back Rocky Bleier.[512]

Pittsburgh did not end up with any small black college players either. But the Rooneys had seen enough from Nunn to know that they wanted him fulltime, if he was willing.

When Dan Rooney tried to hire Nunn the first time, the sports editor said he needed at least a year to help the *Courier* find his replacement.

"A year?" Dan said.[513]

"I want to be fair," Nunn replied. "I've been with them a long time."

But in the 12 months since that first conversation, Nunn couldn't help feeling like he might have blown the entire offer. He realized helping out with the Steelers that the Rooneys were serious about changing their outlook – and he wanted to be working with the team fulltime.

Now when Dan repeated the offer, Nunn didn't hesitate. Best of all, the Steelers allowed Nunn to keep choosing the *Courier*'s black college All-America team too. The hardest part would be picking players for the newspaper without tipping his hand about the ones the Steelers hoped to draft.

The *Courier* celebrated Nunn's career change too. By then, with his father long-since dead, Nunn had taken up leadership roles throughout the organization. He had been with the paper more than two decades, working primarily as sports editor but also serving as managing editor of the national edition. He had received awards from the Newspaper Guild of Pittsburgh, and the Pigskin Club of Washington had named Nunn its columnist of the year. Most significantly for the newspaper, Nunn had broken down race barriers that had kept professional sports teams from taking the *Courier* seriously. When he started at the paper, Nunn could not even sit in the press box at Pittsburgh's Forbes Field ballpark – and now the Steelers wanted him to work in the team's front office.

"We plan to make full use of Nunn's talents," Dan Rooney told the *Courier*.[514]

The Steelers hired a new head coach named Chuck Noll in early 1969, and he arrived in Pittsburgh on the day before the draft, carrying only his suitcase. Noll had come up as a player through Paul Brown's system with the Cleveland Browns, attending law school at night. As a coach, Noll shared his mentor's vision for determining how a man played football by his abilities and not the color of his skin.

When Noll arrived in Pittsburgh, the Steelers had the fourth draft pick overall and the team's scouts had their eyes on Terry Hanratty, a local boy who had gone on to play quarterback at Notre Dame.[515] But Noll had been scouting a black defensive tackle out of North Texas State, a smaller school, but not a historically black one. North Texas had accepted its first black students and players in the mid-1950s.[516] At six-foot-four-inches and 275 pounds, Joe Greene was not going to hide in the draft for long. He had been named to the UPI, Associated Press and Sporting News All-America teams, and he had played in several college all-star games. Beyond that, Greene had a reputation for being a ferocious player who hated to lose and a talented athlete with a mind for the game.

The Buffalo Bills had the first pick overall and the team chose that year's Heisman trophy winner, a running back from the University of Southern California named Orenthal James "O.J." Simpson. After two more picks, the Steelers had a turn. Noll had been in town only for days but already knew he wanted to build his team on defense: "In order to win a game, you have to first not lose it."[517] He had been personally tracking Greene for three years and insisted the Steelers take him.

The draft pick baffled the local sports writers in Pittsburgh as they turned to each other, asking, "Who's he?"[518] The Steelers shared scouting responsibilities with a group of other professional teams called BLESTO V – an acronym for the Bears, Lions, Eagles, Steelers and Vikings Talent Organization.[519] The group was headed by Jack Butler, a former Steelers cornerback who had a half-of-fame career.

The sports writers had followed BLESTO closely, and they had expected the Steelers to take Hanratty, the hometown favorite. The Notre Dame quarterback had visited Pittsburgh the week before, a team doctor had cleared him to play, and the Rooney brothers, Dan and Art Jr., had taken him to lunch.[520] Hanratty was sitting in his Walsh Hall dorm room when he got the call that the Steelers had taken Greene in the first round.

"I guess you can't believe any rumors you hear," he said.[521]

As it turned out, the Steelers had wanted Hanratty. The team picked him in the second round, with the 30th pick overall. At the end of the first day, the Steelers figured they had been lucky to get the man the new coach wanted – and the quarterback the team owners liked too.

"Let's face it," Butler told newspaper reporters at the end of the day, "the Steelers have come up with a great draft."[522]

Noll, however, was not done. He had big expectations for the late rounds on the second day of the draft. After all, he had been taken in the 21st round by the Browns in 1953.

Sitting in the Steelers' draft room, Nunn took satisfaction from seeing some of his *Courier* All-America picks being chosen in the early rounds: The Kansas City Chiefs took Jim Marsalis, a Tennessee State University cornerback, with the 23rd pick overall, and the New Orleans Saints chose a Southern University defensive end at the start of the second round. In all, teams took five of Nunn's defensive All-Americans in the first four rounds. Nunn believed at least a couple would turn out to be stars.

But for the Steelers' new fulltime scout, the real satisfaction came from no one else knowing who he really wanted. Nunn had a couple of favorites whose names had not appeared as *Courier* All-Americans. Those men would not be feted at the *Courier*'s Royal Crown Cola banquet at the Pittsburgh Hilton – but with any luck, Nunn would give them a chance to play in the NFL.

Two years earlier, Nunn had started hearing about a defensive end at Arkansas Agricultural, Mechanical & Normal College, a small black school with just 3,000 students in the

Southwestern Athletic Conference. L.C. Greenwood stood 6-foot-8-inches tall and weighed 216 pounds as a third-year starter.[523] Despite his size, Greenwood had been a late bloomer. The player did not realize NFL teams might even be interested in him until his senior season when his teammates and coaches started talking about his monstrous presence and numbers. Nunn had hoped to keep expectations low. By then, Nunn had started picking the *Courier* All-Americans with help from coaches, other professional scouts and sports writers. But knowing other teams would be watching his moves, Nunn did not even go see Greenwood in person. Instead, he sent Art Rooney Jr.

Sitting at his locker after a game, Greenwood marveled at the bruises on his body and the wraps covering other places where he had been scraped and injured.[524] If anyone doubted the brutality of football, they had only to look at the many ordinary injuries Greenwood had suffered by hurling himself for 60 minutes at high speed into other men doing the same. Just then, a coach walked over to Greenwood's locker to let him know an NFL scout had attended the game and wanted to meet him. Concerned about looking too beaten up, Greenwood put his gear and uniform back on so the scout would not see the bandages and bruises.

The player didn't need to worry about how he looked after the game. Art Jr. had watched the game. And he had seen right away that everything Nunn had heard about Greenwood was true.

Finally by the tenth round of the draft, Nunn and Art Jr. felt the Steelers could not wait any longer. By then, teams had taken 11 of Nunn's *Courier* black college All-Americans off of the board.[525]

With the 238th pick overall, the Steelers chose Greenwood. Noll had wanted to start with defense, and over two days, his new team had built half of what would become its "Steel Curtain" front-four defensive line. Greene had been well-known and heavily scouted, but Greenwood had slipped under the radar to all but the Steelers' newest fulltime scout.

Inside the Steelers' draft room at Three Rivers Stadium (from left to right) Bill Nunn, Jr., Dick Haley, director of player personnel, V. Tim Rooney, a nephew of Art Rooney Sr., and Art Rooney Jr. , vice president. Photo courtesy of the Pittsburgh Steelers.

Bill Nunn, Jr. seated next to Art Rooney, Jr. in the Steelers' draft room. Photo courtesy of the Pittsburgh Steelers.

Greenwood met Nunn for the first time after the draft when the scout arrived in Pine Bluff, Arkansas.[526] The player had been so far removed from the *Courier*'s selection process, he did not even know Nunn's name.

The two men met at the Holiday Inn in town, and Nunn showed up with an attaché case. When they found a place to sit and talk, Nunn set the case on a small table between their two chairs. After a while, Nunn opened the lid to reveal stacks of cash inside.

Once he had realized NFL teams might want him, Greenwood had dreamed of making big money. It was widely known by then that the Bills had agreed to pay Simpson, the first pick overall, $600,000. Greene, the Steelers' first pick, had expected a large payday too. "I can't say what I'll ask," Greene told reporters after the draft, "but it's going to take a $600,000 man to stop O.J."[527]

Now Greenwood saw stacks of bills in front of him. It would be his signing bonus, Nunn said, if Greenwood agreed right then to a contract.

"How much money?" Greenwood asked.

Nunn replied, "$1,500."

Greenwood laughed out loud, and the first round of negotiations ended abruptly. Nunn had been able to pull off one sleight of hand to draft Greenwood but not another to sign him. In the end, it did not matter. Greenwood eventually agreed to terms with the Steelers in time for training camp.

Nunn had been the first representative from the Steelers to meet Greene too.

Greene was pleased to have been drafted so high – but he was not happy about going to Pittsburgh. The Steelers had won only two games the previous season and did not seem on the cusp of changing direction.

Coming home after classes to his apartment in Denton, Texas, Greene walked up to his front door and found someone sitting on the couch in his living room. The door had been unlocked, so the man let himself inside. Greene burst in and looked ready to beat up the intruder when he jumped to his feet.

"Bill Nunn," he said, "Pittsburgh Steelers."

Greene relaxed and shook the man's extended hand. Welcome to the NFL. The men ended up talking for a half-hour, finding an immediate rapport.

"We pretty much hit it off after that," Greene recalled.[528] "That was a good meeting, but a strange one."

Nunn and Noll, the new coach, barely had time to talk before they started making their first draft picks together. But over the following weeks and months as they came to know the players they had chosen, the scout and coach came to understand each other too. Nunn had seen other Steelers coaches draft young black men and then not use them.

Noll immediately seemed different for many reasons. He had gone to law school and had an affinity for classical music and literature. The Steelers had started holding training camp at St. Vincent College in Latrobe, a small town in the foothills of the Allegheny Mountains to the east of the city, in 1966. When the Steelers hired Nunn as a scout, he also took on the job of running the camp – assigning dorm rooms, making sure the facilities were ready, coordinating meals and preparing the "after-five club," a room where newspaper reporters and coaches could come in to get beers and liquor at the end of the day.[529] Most guys would drink whatever was available but Noll wanted the "fancy" beers that were harder to find.

Nunn recalled how Buddy Parker had treated the black quarterback Roy Curry, refusing to let him play the position. Similar practices had been common throughout the NFL. Coaches would bring in a black player, inundate him with complicated information and then criticize him for not understanding or acclimating right away. Other teams were scouting black players, Nunn thought to himself, but few knew what to do with them.

"Look," Noll told the scout, "you know athletes. You find me athletes. It's our job as coaches to give them an opportunity and let them make it."[530]

Now at camp, Nunn saw the coach making good on that promise. Both Greene and Greenwood would get a chance to line up on defense together.

Noll had set a tone that would carry over everything.

"The key was to form an attitude that you were looking for the best players," Nunn recalled years later.[531] "Whoever you came up with, you had to have an organization that's willing to go along with it. So to me, the key is the organization. And to me, the Steelers organization was the Rooneys, and the guy who set the tone, as far as I was concerned, was Chuck Noll. … Noll was a unique guy, colorblind and generally a good person."

The new-look Steelers started the 1969 season under sunny skies and 56-degree temperatures. It would be the team's last season-opener at the old Pitt Stadium on the University of Pittsburgh campus in Oakland. Construction already had started on the team's new, modern facility, a concrete bowl on the North Shore, across the Allegheny River from the city's Downtown business district.

As they took the field, the Steelers made history. For the first time in professional football, four black men would make up a team's entire defensive front line – with Greene and Greenwood joining veterans Ben McGee and Chuck Hinton, both former *Courier* All-Americans.[532] The Steelers had drafted McGee in 1964 and traded for Hinton the same season.

Playing before 51,360 fans, the Steelers traded field goals with the Detroit Lions for three quarters until the visitors scored a go-ahead touchdown. In the game's final minutes, the Steelers answered with a score of their own to win 16-13.[533] It would be the team's only taste of victory all season.

Noll's Steelers lost the next 12 games. In the season finale, the Steelers traveled to New Orleans and surged ahead of the Saints until the final minute of the game. The Saints drove to the Steelers' three yard line. On the next play, running back Andy Livingston made a leg-churning dive to gracefully clear the Steelers' line into the end zone, preserving the losing streak with just 53 seconds left on the clock. The play capped the Steelers' worst record ever, in 37 seasons.

"It would have been a gross miscarriage of justice had the game ended other than it did," Pittsburgh Press sports reporter Pat Livingston wrote for the next day's newspaper.[534]

The Steelers' 1-13 losing record meant the team tied with only the Chicago Bears for the league's worst record – and for the first pick in the 1970 draft. The Bears' only victory had come against Pittsburgh, but ties in those days were settled by a coin toss rather than a head-to-head record.

Two days before the Super Bowl in New Orleans, NFL Commissioner Pete Rozelle stood inside a hotel ballroom with a group of sports reporters, Dan Rooney and Ed McCaskey, the Bears' treasurer who had married the daughter of team owner George Halas. Rozelle asked Rooney to call the toss, but the Steelers' owner pointed to McCaskey, deferring over of a superstition about always letting the other guy choose. McCaskey called, "Heads."[535]

Rozelle flipped the 1921 silver dollar about a foot into the air and let it fall flat on the floor. "Tails it is," the commissioner yelled out.

It had been months since the Steelers had won anything. "Sure, I'm happy," Rooney told the reporters.

They wanted to know: Who would the Steelers take?

"We have not finalized any of our draft choices," Rooney demurred. "Our thinking is to draft what is best for our team."

Noll had just returned from watching the Senior Bowl in time to observe the coin flip. The coach already had made up his mind about the team's first pick, but he did not say anything.

Nunn had stayed back in Pittsburgh to host the *Courier*'s 22 black college All-Americans at the Hilton Hotel. Like Noll, he had made up his mind about who the Steelers should select later in the draft. But he wasn't talking either.

Over just a few years, the *Courier* banquets had developed their own traditions with the top college players coming to Pittsburgh for swag – trophies, watches, blazers embroidered with an All-America crest. The festivities started with an invocation by a local pastor at 7:42 p.m. and ended just before

11 p.m.[536] In between, Mississippi's Alcorn Agricultural and Mechanical College won a second straight national championship and its coach Marino Casem received the coach-of-the-year honors.

In a new twist, the dinner honored a Miss All-America Football Queen chosen from among the black college homecoming queens. Lonnie H. Wesley, a 22-year-old senior at Florida A&M University, won the title along with a tiara, a Swinger portable record player, a 10-day, chaperoned Trans World Airlines-sponsored trip to Hawaii and $50 a day in spending money from the Clairol Company. She had arrived in Pittsburgh with a chaperone as well, Mrs. A. Cooper, dean of women at the university, who followed her around from the airport to the dais. It had been a highlight of the evening when the ballroom lights darkened and a spotlight introduced Wesley to the crowd. Hundreds of clapping hands thundered their applause and then the room fell to a hush as the new Miss All-America spoke: "It is wonderful," she said with tears welling in her eyes, "that you have made it possible for a black girl to share in the glory of this wonderful event."

Nunn was sitting in the audience when he heard his name being called too. Royal Crown Cola had decided to surprise him and *Courier* sports editor Ric Roberts with prizes. Each man received a plaque honoring his contributions to sports. Nunn had never been one to grab the spotlight, preferring instead to express himself through the printed words on the page. Even as he stood before a room filled with men he had hand-picked as All-Americans, including a few who had gone onto successful professional careers, Nunn smiled but did not linger in the spotlight. He looked almost embarrassed to be singled out.

After the dinner, the guests — players, coaches, Miss All-America and a few other women — stayed at the Hilton for an after-party, sponsored by the Gulf Oil Company. Nunn glowed with pride over the recognition he had received and his mind drifted back, as always, to the picks the Steelers would soon make. The team had been lucky enough the year before to land a black college player in the 10th round and turn him into a starter. Nunn hoped they might pull off the same magic again. The Steelers might take one of the All-Americans in the room in the early rounds, but Nunn believed too they might once again have success with at least a couple of players who had not made the list. Hidden gems, like Greenwood.

Nunn always felt bad about leaving men off the list. With just 22 starters, and another 22 players on the "second team," many other deserving young men did not make it – even ones who might be able to play in the NFL. But he wasn't the only one looking for talent in the black colleges. Other teams had discovered athletes there too: The Kansas City Chiefs won the AFL championship that year with a third of the team's players coming from black colleges.[537] Five of the men had been *Courier* All-Americans. The newspaper that night had honored Chief's scout Lloyd Wells, who had been the first black fulltime professional scout.

More than ever, Nunn realized, the challenge had become finding talented young men no one else noticed. He also knew with confidence that the pool of talent in the black schools would be deep enough to hide many athletes who could play in the pro ranks. That had been true for years, and it remained so even now with a few teams looking.

By the time the draft started weeks later in late January, the Kansas City Chiefs had stunned the world again. Even after the AFL's Jets defeated the NFL's top team in 1969, few people believed the American league could field a superior team. The Chiefs dominated Super Bowl IV – the fourth, and final, AFL-NFL World Championship Game. The leagues would official merge before the start of the next season, and the AFL's strong showing removed some of the pain the Rooney family felt over the Steelers moving – with the Browns and Colts – into the NFL's newly formed American Football Conference.

After watching the Senior Bowl in Mobile, Alabama, Noll felt certain about the team's first overall draft pick. Terry Bradshaw, a quarterback from Louisiana Tech University, could stand in the pocket with an accurate arm, at 6-foot-3-inches and 215 pounds – and he was mobile enough to move around if needed. Bradshaw had cracked two ribs and torn his hamstring muscle in the Senior Bowl. The Steelers had received multiple offers to trade the top pick too. None of that dissuaded Noll.

"Terry convinced me that he was the most valuable piece of property in the college ranks," Noll told reporters who gathered at the Roosevelt Hotel after the Steelers made the team's first pick.[538]

In the second round, the Steelers took Ronnie Shanklin, a wide receiver from North Texas State who had played there with Greene and who came with his highest recommendations.

Now the Steelers executives turned to Nunn. For days, he and Noll had been arguing about whether the athlete from Southern University in Texas could play cornerback or safety. At 6-foot-4-inches, the player seemed too big to cover deep, Nunn feared. But Noll reasoned that the man's size could be an advantage: He could bump receivers at the line, throw them off their routes and then cover down the field.

Both men agreed Melvin Blount should join the Steelers. Nunn actually had named him a *Courier* All-American, identifying him as one of four defensive backs who could cover. "Each excelled at pass interceptions and hard-nosed tackling," Nunn wrote.[539]

The Steelers knew Blount would not last long in the draft, and chose him with the team's third pick. Blount became just the second *Courier* All-American drafted and signed by the Steelers; McGee had been the first, and two others had come to the team through trades.

Later in the draft, the Steelers took three more black college players: Bert Askson, a defensive end from Texas Southern, who made the team briefly, and two others who did not make it at all.

Noll had been right about Blount. With his size at corner, Blount redefined the position over a hall-of-fame career.

Still, it took a while for the team to feel his impact. The Steelers lost three games to start the 1970 season and began play in the new AFC Central Division. The team finished with a 5-9 record – four more wins than the year before, and bad enough to give the team the eighth pick in the 1971 draft.

❖❖❖

Just when it seemed the *Courier's* All-American banquets had become routine and predictable, Nunn found yet another new spark. As he looked out across the Hilton ballroom at the start of 1971, more than 600 people rose from their seats to applaud noisily as the latest crop of All-Americans paraded into the room, walked past a table laden with plaques and watches and headed to a dais near the front. Then as everyone settled into their seats, the emcee introduced the evening's guest speaker and the place erupted again – even louder than before.

Nunn had covered boxing since starting as a sports writer, and he had maintained strong contacts with the fighters and their promoters. On a lark, Nunn had reached out to see whether former heavyweight champion Cassius Clay could attend the banquet. Clay had taken to calling himself Muhammad Ali after converting to Islam, and he had gotten into legal trouble by conscientiously objecting to the military draft over the Vietnam War, citing his religious opposition. An all-white jury in New York had convicted him, leading a judge to sentence him to five years in prison – pending appeal. In the process, Ali was stripped of his boxing title.

Ali needed to change the public narrative, and Nunn knew it. The U.S. Supreme Court had just agreed to hear Ali's appeal, clearing him to box in the meantime. He and Joe Frazier were scheduled to fight two months later at New York's Madison Square Garden in a match expected to bring in $20 million and leave each fighter with at least $2 million. An appearance in front of Nunn's straight-laced black college All-Americans would enhance Ali's public image.

As the ballroom doors opened in the back of the room, Ali strode across the plush red carpet, smiling broadly in a pinstriped suit and necktie.[540] The *Courier* had hinted for weeks that Ali might attend the event, helping draw the capacity crowd. The boxer planned to stay only a few minutes so he would not overshadow the college athletes, but he shook hands with people in the crowd as he walked toward the podium where the emcee handed him a microphone.

The boxer looked out at the audience and praised the young football players at the head table for the hard work they had put in to be honored. He smiled toward the athletes and challenged any one of them who felt he was "bad" enough to come over and fight, but none did, smiling back and shaking their heads.

Then, shifting direction, Ali recited a lyrical poem about his upcoming bout. It ended with the promise to knock Frazier "so high that he will be changed into a black satellite" as Ali pointed his right hand toward the ceiling.

The crowd cheered loudly again as Ali walked away from the podium to meet each All-American, signing autographs and chatting.

From his seat, Nunn watched the boxer and knew that the *Courier*'s annual event had reached a new high. It would be hard to top this moment in future years. But Nunn also knew that the newspaper had assembled probably its strongest ever black college All-American team. Professional teams were recruiting more black college players than ever, and it seemed the young men had responded to the opportunity by working even harder. Just seven years earlier, Nunn had started the banquet to give his All-Americans more exposure. Now, it seemed, all of professional football was watching. Nunn believed that at least five of the men chosen for the banquet would be chosen in the first round of the NFL draft in a few days, and he hoped the Steelers would get one of them.[541] It would be an unprecedented showing for the black colleges.

Yet, Nunn knew too that few other scouts could see the whole picture. Most teams would cherry pick the best players off the All-America list, but plenty of other talented athletes remained. Men stayed hidden among the ranks of the 51 competing black colleges – men who could play in the NFL if given the chance.

As Ali walked out of the ballroom, the event unfolded with its traditional accolades. Hinton, the Steelers' defensive lineman, received the Willie Gallimore-John Farrington Memorial Award for a former All-American playing professionally. And Frank Lewis, a combination running back and receiver from Grambling College, made the list for a second time and received a prize as the "most outstanding back of the year."[542]

As Nunn introduced the All-Americans and called out Lewis's name, he hoped no one in the audience could read his mind.

❖❖❖

Grambling College sits less than five miles from Louisiana Tech University, separated from each other by only pine forests growing in sandy soil and groups of one-story homes scattered along narrow macadam roads. Each school has red-brick buildings, strong academic traditions and a prominent football stadium. And at the start of the 1970s, the two places produced back-to-back first-round draft picks for the Pittsburgh Steelers.

But until they came north, quarterback Terry Bradshaw and receiver Frank Lewis never had played on the same field for a college game, a practice or even a pick-up game of toss.[543] It had been another vestige of the segregated Deep South that the two men had lived so close, each playing the game of football at an extremely high level, and yet they never even had met, living in separate worlds because of the color of their skin.

As a child growing up in Houma, Louisiana, 300 miles away from Grambling, Lewis had dreamed of one day having his name appear as an All-American in the *Pittsburgh Courier*. Making the newspaper's list was an important benchmark, he knew. And after starting at Grambling, Lewis twice made the list and traveled to the banquet at the Pittsburgh Hilton.

Playing at Grambling had been another early goal for Lewis. So many professional football players were coming out of the school by the time Lewis attended that it seemed like the most logical way for a young black athlete to play as a professional. It had been 22 years since Tank Younger had stood with Coach Eddie Robinson at the train station in Grambling, wondering whether he had whatever it would take to play in the NFL for the Los Angeles Rams. Robinson had warned the running back then that he would set the standard, either way, for generations of young men coming behind him. The premonition had come true: Younger's success had allowed more black college players to follow him into professional ranks, and by the late 1960s, Grambling had become a proven path. Ernie Ladd, the "Big Cat," had graduated from Grambling a decade before Lewis in 1961, and he had gone on to play with the San Diego Chargers, the Houston Oilers and the Chiefs. Two years before Lewis came out of school, Grambling's quarterback James "Shack" Harris went to the Buffalo Bills in the eighth round, and that fall he became the first professional black quarterback to start a season.[544] Charlie Joiner, a wide receiver who also graduated in 1969, had gone to the Oilers and started a hall-of-fame career. Just as Younger had done, those men came back to Grambling's campus each spring to work out and maintain a high standard for the younger players. They brought their professional teammates back to campus to work out too. Lewis had no fear about going to the NFL. He expected it.

"We saw guys coming back on campus that was actually playing in the league," Lewis recalled years later.[545] "Every spring they were out there. The atmosphere of professional football was no big thing at all if you was playing on the Grambling team. That was something you knew. We had pro scouts watching practice all the time and things like that. It was an atmosphere of professional football even though it was a small college."

After taking Lewis in the first round in 1971, the Steelers drafted linebacker Jack Ham from Penn State University in the second round, offensive guard Gerry "Moon" Mullins from the University of Southern California and defensive end Dwight White from East Texas State University in the fourth. The Steelers used an eighth round pick on Ernie Holmes, a *Courier* All-American defensive tackle from Texas Southern.

Even after the draft ended, the Steelers were not done. Nunn knew about Glen Edwards, a safety from Florida A&M. Nunn had not listed the player among the All-Americans, and Edwards had remained a secret. The Steelers signed him as an undrafted free agent and he immediately found a place in the team's defensive backfield.

When the draft ended, the Steelers scouts thought they had done pretty well. After a few years, time proved they had done better than that. More than a dozen players the Steelers took in 1971 spent at least two years in the league, and many had lengthy careers. After decades of losing, the Steelers had built the nucleus of a champion.[546] But would it be enough to have an immediate impact?

Running the Steelers' training camp each summer, Nunn noticed another old practice that bothered him. Given the chance to pick their own roommates, rookies invariably ended up separating by race – whites with whites, and blacks with blacks. It always had been that way throughout the league, dating back to when the Los Angeles Rams hired Woody Strode so the team's star, Kenny Washington, would have a black roommate when they traveled. But the habit underscored divisions within the team, and Nunn felt the Steelers needed stronger unity to become winners.

"I made it a point," Nunn said. [547] "Hey rookies, 'Alphabetically, regardless.' You have to take it kind of deep."

At the worst, players managed to work out any differences: No one wanted to get cut from the Steelers for not being able to stay with his roommate. But at other times, the pairings clicked and players started forming a bond that lasted. Even after players could choose their roommates, some ended up staying together, regardless of color.

When Jon Kolb, a left tackle from Oklahoma State University, showed up for his first training camp in 1969, he roomed with quarterback Terry Hanratty. K next to H. But on the field that summer, Kolb started lining up next to Sam Davis, a left guard that Nunn had discovered two years earlier as an undrafted free agent from a small black school in South Carolina, Allen University. The men realized they had a lot in common because of their job and work habits – and that outweighed any differences about skin color. It really had never been an issue for Kolb anyway.

"I was blessed," Kolb recalled[548], "growing up in an Oklahoma town that had black kids, white kids, Indian kids, Mexican kids. We were always kind of just mixed together."

Working the left side of the line and rooming together all the time, Kolb and Davis became so familiar to each other that when they became starters next to each other on the offensive line in 1971, they no longer even used words to communicate the signals as they walked from the huddle to the line. Instead they used certain types of grunts with each other, confident that the other understood what was expected.

Nunn, with his expectations about overcoming issues of skin color, had fostered that kind of relationship, Kolb came to realize. While Noll, as the head coach, often had to keep himself separate from the players, Nunn made time to sit among the men, sharing stories and encouraging them to tell their own. Some of the players, like Davis who had gone unnoticed at a small black college, knew they had a shot at the NFL only because Nunn had recognized something in them that everyone else had overlooked. The message was clear: The players were there for a purpose – one that transcended divisions and that carried off the field.[549]

"Nunn could just recognize talent," Kolb said. "Bill Nunn really was responsible for opening it up so that players that would not have otherwise found their way to the NFL had that possibility, and he made the game better."

The fall of 1971 marked another season of change. At the University of Alabama, Coach Paul "Bear" Bryant had kept the Crimson Tide all-white under public pressure. But as the state's public high schools integrated under federal court order, Bryant started seeing talented black players who could help his team.

The year before, Alabama opened its football season with an out-of-conference game against the University of Southern California before 72,175 fans at Birmingham's Legion Field. Already, Alabama quietly had started to change:[550] Bryant, as the school's athletic director, had approved the signing of the school's first black scholarship athlete, Wendell Hudson, to the basketball team; Bryant also had recruited a black freshman football player, Wilbur Jackson, who attended the USC game but was ineligible to play.

But that night, as it always had before, the Crimson Tide fielded an all-white team. Whether Bryant had set up the game to make the case that Alabama football needed to integrate or not, the outcome gave him the evidence he needed: The Trojans' black fullback Sam Cunningham ran for 135 yards, and USC won the game 42-21.

Even the most racist fans could see how segregation had hurt the team's chances.

"It wasn't that they were that anxious to have blacks," Nunn said when he looked back years later[551], "but they either had to have them or they lost."

Before the following season, Bryant heard from Southern California's coach about John Mitchell Jr., a 6-foot-3-inch, 230-pound defensive end playing at Eastern Arizona Junior College. Mitchell had grown up in Alabama and had attended an all-black high school. He had graduated with more academic scholarship offers than athletic ones but he wanted to go where he could play football. He chose Eastern Arizona because he had friends there.

Bryant offered Mitchell a transfer scholarship without even seeing him play one down. If he was good enough to play at USC, Bryant wanted him to come home and play for Alabama.

Growing up watching the Crimson Tide win national championships, boys across Alabama – white and black – dreamed of playing for the university, even before an integrated team was possible, Mitchell recalled.[552] He knew that if he went to the school, he could earn a strong education and the experience would forever open doors in his life.

But he also felt a strong pull to attend Southern California. When he had gone there to visit, alumnus O.J. Simpson had come back to campus from the Buffalo Bills to show him around.

Mitchell's parents in Mobile helped seal the decision: They wanted to see their son play close to home, and his mother spoke up.

"Son, you'll have problems wherever you go, whether it's Alabama or Southern Cal," she said.[553] "You might as well face up to them some time."

Mitchell started the first game of the 1971 season, a 17-10 victory over Southern California in Los Angeles. Alabama ended up going undefeated during the regular season and playing in the national championship, losing to the University of Nebraska. Mitchell and Wilbur Jackson were the only black players on the team. When the Crimson Tide visited Ole Miss and Louisiana State University that fall, Mitchell looked around and saw he was the only black man on the field.

"I could hear some people say some things," Mitchell said years later, "but I didn't let that bother me."

Instead, he made close friends on the team. His white roommate from Albany, Georgia, came to accept him like a brother, and his roommate's family looked at Mitchell as a second son – even as it caused them grief back home. When Mitchell and his teammates went out on campus, some whites blanched at a black man entering restaurants and clubs with his teammates, until they found out he played on the football team too. He ended up going to places no other black student ever had gone.

In Mitchell's second season as a senior, Alabama had a few more black players but not many. Mitchell skipped the team meeting where players chose team captains, and he missed the moment when they elected him as the school's first black co-captain. Bryant was angry about one thing afterwards – that Mitchell had skipped the meeting.

"That was the biggest honor I ever had at Alabama," Mitchell recalled.

The Steelers finished the 1971 season with a losing record again – six wins and eight losses. The team had vied with Cleveland for the AFC Central Division title, with both teams tied at 5-5, when the Steelers lost three of the four final games. That left the team with the 13th overall pick in 1972.

Heading into the draft, Nunn had scouted a running back out of the University of Houston, Robert Newhouse, who had started his college career quietly but ended up setting records for most rushing yards in a season. Nunn felt Newhouse would fit into the Steelers offense. Noll, the head coach, had scouted another running back he liked from Penn State University, Franco Harris. That set up a lively debate among the team leadership about who to take in the first round.

Before the draft, Nunn also heard from one of his oldest friends, Joe Gilliam, his teammate from West Virginia State. Gilliam's son, Joe Jr., was graduating from Tennessee State University, where he had been the starting quarterback and a two-time *Courier* All-American. Fans had taken to calling him

"Jefferson Street" Joe for the nearby Nashville address where he had grown up.

"Is my son going to get drafted?" Gilliam wanted to know.[554]

The father had plenty of reason to be skeptical. He had come out of West Virginia State a generation earlier as a hot prospect with a shot at the NFL – but no team owner would allow him to tryout at quarterback. Then, he had been the quarterbacks coach for Roy Curry when the Steelers drafted him out of Mississippi's Jackson State University, and again, refused to let him play at quarterback, shifting him instead to wide receiver where he got hurt.

Nunn wanted to believe that Joe Jr. would get drafted in the early rounds but he couldn't be sure. He had the same skeptical fear that nipped at his friend. Nunn suggested that Joe Sr. talk with the Steelers executives, the Rooney brothers and Dick Haley, the Steelers' new director of player personnel.

Gilliam followed up and asked the question again. This time, the answer came back more definitively. The Steelers did not need a quarterback: They had just used the first overall pick two years earlier on Bradshaw, and the year before that, they had taken Hanratty in the second round. But plenty of teams needed a quarterback with a strong arm.

"He's going to get drafted," Dan Rooney told the father. "He's one of the best players there is. He has a great arm."

By the time the draft started, the Steelers executives and scouts had agreed on the team's first-round choice: Harris. Later, team insiders said the debate over the choice had been purely academic, to make sure they got the right guy. No one will ever know how close they came to taking Newhouse instead.

The pick seemed obvious afterward, as soon as Harris showed up for the team's first practice. He ran every route all the way to the goal line and he kept moving his quick feet all the time.

"The thing that impressed me about Franco," Nunn said[555] later, "was that coming out of Penn State, he wasn't the number-one back, but he showed a willingness to work."

Back in Tennessee, the Gilliams – father and son – waited for the phone call telling them where Joe Jr. would be going to play. But throughout the entire first day of the draft, the call never came. For whatever reason, it seemed, no one wanted him at quarterback. The attitude about black quarterbacks had shifted in some cities: Shack Harris already was starting for the Buffalo Bills. But the teams that needed a quarterback were not interested in Gilliam.

As the second day of picks started, Joe Sr. could not take the frustration and suspense any longer. He called back to Pittsburgh. Nunn felt just as badly. He was sitting in a corner of the draft room, sulking about the fact that Gilliam's name had not come off the board.[556] Dan Rooney took the call.

"You said that he was going to get drafted for sure," Joe Sr. said.[557] "Now he's not drafted, and it looks like…"

Rooney cut him off. "We'll draft him," he said.

The Steelers took Joe Gilliam Jr. in the 11th round with the 273rd overall pick.

✤✤✤

Joe Jr. had hoped to go higher, but he was pleased to come back to Pittsburgh. Just weeks earlier, he had been feted in the city at the Hilton, where the *Courier* had named him the collegiate back of the year.[558]

"Being selected *Courier* All-American twice, I feel as though some of the Pittsburghers might be familiar to me already," Gilliam said as reporters gathered around him when he arrived back in the city as a Steelers draft pick.[559]

Had racism played a role in him not going higher?

"Yes, I think color entered into the matter but there isn't anything I can do about that," Gilliam answered. "Right now I'm looking forward to competing for a job with the Steelers."

Would he be willing to play any other position? It was the same question that had haunted his father and kept him from playing in the NFL, the question that had turned Roy Curry into a wide receiver and cut his career short.

"I have only been taught the game at the quarterback's position," he said. "But I think if the Steelers properly evaluate me as a quarterback, they will not ask me to play any other position."

Unlike his predecessor Buddy Parker, Noll seemed willing to do the evaluation. He answered reporters' questions honestly, saying the Steelers had expected Gilliam to be long gone before the 11th round. When they saw an athlete of his caliber still on the board, they took him – even though the team had two quarterbacks already.

"Gilliam had one of the best throwing arms in the college ranks," Noll told the sports writers.

But how could he possibly make the team, especially as a third quarterback?

"We will give Joe a long look," Noll answered, "and there is a job to be won if he lives up to his ability."

If Gilliam felt fortunate the Steelers took a chance on him, it would soon be the other way around. Pittsburgh had been lucky no other team had used one of the 272 previous picks on "Jefferson Street" Joe.

Building a championship team requires front office executives to make many correct decisions – reaching the right stadium and television contracts to bring in enough revenue, creating an exciting atmosphere to sell enough tickets and merchandise, and assembling the right players through free agency and the draft, especially for teams that cannot afford to make financial mistakes.

Even then, perfection might not be enough. Luck, fate, mojo. Call it what they will, every winning team needs to have it. No one knows when a player will suffer a season-ending injury or a sudden inexplicable lack of self-confidence. No executive steps on the field once the whistle blows. And once the ball goes into the air, sometimes no one can predict where it will come down.

After seasons of losing, the Steelers started the 1972 season at home against a legitimate Super Bowl contender, the Oakland Raiders. Pittsburgh jumped off to an early lead with the Raiders' quarterback Kenny Stabler completing three of his first five passes – to Steelers defensive players for interceptions. George Blanda, the Slovak son of a coal miner from Youngwood in southwestern Pennsylvania, came in to replace Stabler but could not do any better. By the time Raiders' Coach John Madden went to his third quarterback, Daryle Lamonica, it was too late for a comeback even though he scored three touchdowns in the final 10 minutes. The Steelers won 34-28.

Asked if he felt second-guessed by fans who wondered why he waited so long to change quarterbacks, Madden sat in the visiting locker room with his feet propped up on a desk: "Bleep them." If fans couldn't tell, this wasn't the same old Pittsburgh football team.

"Pittsburgh's a much improved football team," Madden said[560], "and we gave them too much."

The hometown fans felt it too. More than 51,000 of them had come out for the opener, filling the concrete bowl of Three Rivers Stadium with chants of "Dee-Fense" as the game wound down.

Pittsburgh Press sports writer Phil Musick sat in the press box and sensed that something had changed.

"The longest prayer vigil in the history of football may have ended yesterday," he wrote.[561] "The long-suffering burg can get off its knees. There is tangible evidence that the football team it has worn like a hair shirt for four decades of a track record the Egyptian Air Force wouldn't envy may finally see the light."

In the Steelers locker room, defensive end Dwight White picked up on the confidence boost.

"I won't say we're the best," he said, "...but we can play with the best."

The Steelers lost three games all season, never by more than five points. The team won its first AFC Central division title and made the playoffs for just the second time in 40 years. The first opportunity had ended in 1947 with a loss to the Philadelphia Eagles.

This time, just two days before Christmas, Madden and the Oakland Raiders were returning to Three Rivers Stadium.

With 22 seconds left in the game, the Steelers trailed 7-6 and had the ball with a fourth-and-10 from the team's own 40-yard line.

On television, NBC announcer Curt Gowdy called it the last chance for the Steelers as Bradshaw took the snap, drifted back in the pocket and got chased backwards by three Raiders defenders.[562] Looking up, he threw a tight spiral towards running back John "Frenchy" Fuqua near the Raiders' 35-yard line.

Fuqua had attended Maryland's historically black Morgan State University but never appeared among Nunn's All-Americans; he came to Pittsburgh in a trade with the New York Giants, who drafted him in 1969. As the ball came toward Fuqua, Raiders safety Jack Tatum arrived at the same moment and the ball caromed high in the air before falling back down.[563]

Harris had been trailing the play and ran forward toward the ball, catching it off of his shoelaces as he streaked toward the end zone for a touchdown and the Steelers' win.

"You talk about Christmas miracles," Gowdy said during the replay on air, "here's the miracle of all miracles."

As Pittsburgh sportscaster Myron Cope prepared his commentary for the evening news, Steelers fan Sharon Levosky called WTAE-TV and said her friend Michael Ord had come up with a name for the play, "The Immaculate Reception."[564] Cope used the phrase on the air that night, and the name stuck. No one again ever doubted that the Steelers drafted the right running back the previous winter.

Pittsburgh went on the following week to lose the AFC Championship to the unbeaten Miami Dolphins. But after years of change – in the ways the team drafted players, practiced with them in training camp and prepared for games – the new philosophy finally had started to pay off.

Bill Nunn, Jr. (left) receives a surprise award from Charles J. Smith of the Royal Crown Cola Co. at the Courier *black college All-America banquet in 1970.* Courier *sports writer Ric Roberts looks on from behind Smith. Courtesy of the Nunn family and the* New Pittsburgh Courier.

Chapter 8. Champions

Sitting in his dorm room at Alabama A&M University, John Stallworth no longer wondered just whether he would have a shot at playing in the National Football League. After falling at least a step too slow when he ran the 40-yard dash for a group of professional scouts that morning, the senior wideout sat on his dorm room bed questioning whether he even belonged at the next level.[565]

He had done well at the small black college, moving from running back in high school to receiver with the Bulldogs. He even had been named an all-conference player in the Southern Intercollegiate Athletic Conference. But what did that really mean compared to athletes at bigger schools, at the places with coaches that never even looked his way in high school? He wasn't even at a well-known black school like Louisiana's Grambling College, turning out professional players every year. Only a couple of Bulldogs ever had made it that far. Running back Olliver Ross had been drafted the year before by the Denver Broncos – in the 16th round, as the 398th player overall. Stallworth's teammate Ronnie Coleman hoped to make it to the NFL as a running back too, but his prospects were even more uncertain. Stallworth had no other measuring stick than the 40-yard dash, and he had not measured up.

Just then, Stallworth heard a knock at the door. When he answered it, Bill Nunn Jr. stood in the hallway. Of all the scouts on campus that day, no one mattered more. Not only did Nunn represent the Pittsburgh Steelers, but he chose the top black college players for the *Pittsburgh Courier*'s All-American team too. If Stallworth made the newspaper's list of top players, he still had a chance to be noticed.

Standing in the hallway, tall and lean, wearing a white knit shirt with the Steelers' logo on a patch over his chest, Nunn looked like he had been restored. The mysterious, sudden illness that kept him in Normal, Alabama, when the other scouts moved onto the next city apparently had disappeared during the 5-minute sprint from the parking lot to the dormitory where Stallworth lived.

The scout had just one question: Would Stallworth like to go for a run?

This time, on a dry track in front of just one scout, Stallworth told himself he would do better. He would run faster. He had to run faster. This might be his last chance.

As he crossed the finish line, the college senior looked for some sign of improvement from the Steelers' scout. But Nunn remained quiet and his face betrayed nothing. He only looked up from his stopwatch and wrote something in his notebook.

Unlike the morning session when Stallworth had been too timid to talk with the scouts, he needed to know this time: How had he measured up? Still breathing hard, he walked over to Nunn.

"Was my time better?" Stallworth asked.

Nunn closed his notebook and answered, "Well, it was okay."[566]

Before leaving campus, Nunn circled back to the Bulldogs' athletic office. Even after other NFL teams started scouting the black colleges, Nunn still had an advantage: He had been going to these campuses for decades.

Alabama A&M wasn't a football powerhouse, but Nunn still knew head coach Louis Crews. And Crews certainly knew him – by reputation, of course, but also from years of experience. Crews had been at Alabama A&M since 1960, and it had taken him eight years to send his first player to the NFL. Before the Cincinnati Bengals had drafted William Kindricks out of Normal, Alabama, in the sixth round of the 1968 draft, Nunn had named the 265-pound guard to his All-America team and called him the nation's best defensive lineman at a black college.[567] It was the sort of praise that elevated a player's prospects – and that a head coach never forgot.

Nunn met with Crews and asked for all of the school's films on Stallworth. Alabama A&M's head coach had been as uncertain as his wideout after the morning workout. He was happy to give Nunn whatever he needed to take back to the Steelers.

The scout had his motives too. Nunn not only needed evidence to take back to Pittsburgh; he also wanted to make sure no one else would come looking for the film later. Nunn had realized after joining the Steelers that as soon as the *Courier* posted his All-American picks, other teams started circling back to black colleges taking a closer look at players who had not gotten much attention before. This time, Nunn hoped to cut off any competing attention.

Back in Pittsburgh, Nunn showed the Stallworth game film to Art Rooney Jr. and Dick Haley, the Steelers' director of player personnel. Those two men would play a big role in ranking that year's college players for the team's draft priorities.

Then head coach Chuck Noll watched the film. The wide receivers' coach saw it. The quarterbacks' coach. The other position coaches. Team founder and family patriarch Art Rooney Sr. saw the tape. His oldest son, Dan, still the unofficial team president, watched it. After several weeks, it seemed everyone in the facility down to Steven "Dirt" Dinardo, the cigar-chomping steward of Teamsters Local 250 who ran the Three Rivers Stadium grounds crew, had seen the film. That meant the only tape on Stallworth had been unavailable for other teams.

Art Jr. started to worry. If a college coach said to keep a film for a week, he meant it. Other teams would want to see the tape too, and most coaches wanted to give their athletes the best shot at getting drafted. They cared less about what team drafted the player. If a scout took advantage of the situation by keeping a highlight reel to himself, other teams couldn't see it – and the school might not invite him back the following season.

"Bill, we've had this thing a month now," Art Jr. finally said to Nunn one day.[568]

"Don't worry," Nunn replied. "Don't worry about it."

"Now you guys have to send this back," Art Jr. insisted. "This is a disgrace. This is a disgrace. Send it back."

Nunn eventually returned the game films on Stallworth – but by then the draft was just days away.

When Nunn named the *Courier* All-Americans for 1973, he didn't attempt to leave Stallworth off the list.

By then, other teams were onto that trick too. If Nunn ignored a man that everyone already had on their draft board, the Steelers must really want him. Other teams knew about Stallworth, and Nunn gave the player the attention he deserved, adding his name to the 22 black college All-Americans.

Still, he was just one, among many.

"Our other receiver was John Stallworth, a super catcher from Alabama A&M," Nunn wrote in the newspaper.[569] "Stallworth, rated as one of the greatest players ever at Alabama A&M, finished the year with 48 catches for 925 yards and seven touchdowns. He did all this in a season that covered nine games."

The Steelers caught one more break. After the 1973 season when organizers of the Senior Bowl put together their rosters of the nation's top college players, they invited Stallworth. But the coaches put him on the defensive side of the ball, in the backfield. The Steelers scouts couldn't believe it.

"We got so lucky," Art Jr. said. "They put him at defensive back. Can you imagine that? Can you imagine getting lucky like that? It was like we paid someone to do it."

When the NFL draft started in late January at the Americana Hotel in New York City, the Dallas Cowboys used the first pick overall on Edward "Too Tall" Jones, a defensive end from Tennessee State University. From the start, it was more proof that the black colleges had been discovered.

Noll realized what was happening. By then, he had fallen in love with the idea of having Stallworth on his team. Now he wanted to take the wide receiver in the first round.[570] Already, draft experts had declared the college crop that year to be a thin one, and Noll had told reporters that the Steelers might get only one meaningful pick.[571] He had said he expected all of the top players to go in the first two rounds.

Inside the team's Three Rivers Stadium offices, the Steelers scouts had tacked a sheet of white paper to a large piece of plywood, listing the names of about 10 potential first-round picks. The list had two tight ends, and they went early. Soon all ten names on the list had been crossed off.

"You sit there and have a kid picked that everyone agrees would make a good number one, and after a while, you start to sweat," Noll said later.[572]

Inside the draft room, the Steelers' scouts posted their second list of ten names.

The Steelers would draft the team's first player with the 21st pick, and Noll still wanted Stallworth. Nunn, Art Jr. and the others told him to wait. They could afford to sleep on the wide receiver a little longer. Yes, other teams were looking at the black colleges. But no other team had seen the wide receiver the way they had. Other scouts believed he was a step too slow, injury prone and perhaps even better suited to knocking balls away on defense rather than catching them.

When the pick finally came around after more than two hours of waiting, Noll and the scouts agreed they wanted a receiver. The team already had three top quarterbacks, and now they needed more targets. Grambling's Frank Lewis had been a solid receiver but he also had suffered injuries that kept him from being a regular starter.

The team used its first pick on Lynn Swann, a graceful receiver from the University of Southern California. The scouts believed he could outrun and out-jump any defensive back in the league.[573] Swann had run the 40-yard dash in 4.56 seconds. He had been a long-time starter at Southern California. And the scouts had a favorite image of him: At one of the all-star games, Swann had buried his helmet in a linebacker's stomach, hitting him so hard that he almost needed surgery.

"Swann's done it in big time competition," Noll said to reporters after the draft, making no mention of his desire for Stallworth.[574] "Swann's got great hands… great instincts for catching the ball. He goes for the football better than anyone I've seen."

As far anyone outside of the draft room knew, Noll had always wanted Swann with the team's first pick.

In the second round, the Steelers' head coach again wanted to pick Stallworth. He had seen three wide receivers come off the board already, including John Holland, one of Nunn's All-Americans who had gone to the Minnesota Vikings. The team needed to get Stallworth.

But again, Nunn and the scouts told the coach to wait. Be patient. Art Jr. had seen a linebacker at Kent State that he wanted to take. The player looked too tall and thin to be a linebacker, but Rooney had been unable to forget the image he had seen of Jack Lambert on campus. Kent State had moved practice that day from a muddy field to a gravel parking lot.[575] Lambert continued to throw himself hard at the players and the ground, walking back to the huddle after each play as he calmly picked rock chips from his knees and elbows before doing it all over again.

With the 46th pick overall, the Steelers chose Lambert.

Noll stewed in a corner of the draft room. The Steelers already had traded away the team's third-round choice to Oakland. They would watch other teams make 35 more picks before choosing again.

"Well, forget about it," Noll said to no one in particular.[576] "He won't be there."

❖❖❖

Three more wide receivers came off the board. The Chicago Bears took Wayne Wheeler from the University of Alabama. In the era that finally had dawned, with the Crimson Tide fielding black players for the first time in 1971, perhaps Stallworth could have played for Alabama. Perhaps he would have received the same high-profile college recognition as Wheeler. But that time had come too late for Stallworth. Wheeler came off the board, and Stallworth, from the small black college, did not.

Noll paced the draft room inside the stadium offices. Now many sheets of white paper with players' names and ratings hung behind the table where the scouts and coaches sat. With each choice, one more name came off the list.

With the 81st pick, one pick before the Steelers would get to choose again, the San Diego Chargers took a wide receiver. They selected Harrison Davis from the University of Virginia.

Noll could not believe it. He never expected Stallworth to still be there, after all those picks. A loud shout went up in the Steelers draft room as Art Jr., Nunn and the others finally relaxed. They had gambled big, and it had paid off. The Steelers chose Alabama A&M's wide receiver with the fourth pick of the fourth round, 82nd overall.

It was a moment the men in that room never would forget.

"I was so happy," Art Jr. recalled years later. "So happy because we predicted it, and in predicting it, we could have been 100 percent wrong. And here he was in the fourth round."

The Steelers had a second pick in the fourth round, choosing Jimmy Allen, a cornerback out of the University of California Los Angeles.

And then in the fifth round, with the 125th pick overall, Pittsburgh drafted a smallish center with an outsized ability to leverage heavier opponents – Mike Webster, from the University of Wisconsin.

The draft results were not immediately obvious. Legend has it that one Pittsburgh sports writer quipped: "What they did get was Swann, who seems to be a sure-pop to help; Lambert, who figures to be the number-5 linebacker if he pans out; and three question marks."

In reality, the Steelers scouts and coaches had just completed the most remarkable draft in NFL history – using the team's first five picks to choose four future hall-of-famers: Swann, Lambert, Stallworth and Webster. Even Allen went on to play eight years in the league.

Back in Normal, Alabama, Stallworth had gone all day without knowing anything about his future.

He had attended classes like always and then he had spent the rest of the day in his dormitory room, waiting for any word out of the NFL draft. Coach Crews had told Stallworth that he still might go high in the draft, certainly in the first of two days. Several teams had paid attention to the wide receiver, especially the Green Bay Packers and Miami Dolphins. After hearing that, Stallworth had dreamed of playing in the South Florida sun. But all day had passed and no one had called. The residence hall had just one telephone in the hallway, and Stallworth did not know if anyone even had the number.

Finally in the evening, after dinner, the phone rang. A sports writer from Pittsburgh was on the other end of the line, telling Stallworth he had been drafted by the Steelers in the fourth round. How did it feel?

Stallworth at once felt relieved and disappointed.[577] He had been drafted after all. But he hadn't been taken until the fourth round, and the Steelers had taken another receiver ahead of him. He hadn't even been the team's first choice. And yet he had been drafted. He would get a shot to play professional football after all. Now it would be up to him to prove that he belonged there.

Back in Pittsburgh, team officials went through the second day of the draft without much drama. The Steelers picked 16 more players, including Jim Wolf, a defensive end from Prairie View A&M University who had been among Nunn's second team All-Americans.

When the draft ended, Nunn still had names left on his list of potential players – men who had not been taken by the Steelers or anyone else. Free agents always remained after the draft ended, and teams would expend a little effort to sign these guys for training camp. Most often, they filled out rosters only for a few weeks over the summer. But occasionally, one would stand out and make the team. Even the best scouting operations still missed talented athletes, with more hunger than raw statistics revealed.

A few days later, Nunn received a phone call at the office from Willie Jeffries, the head coach at South Carolina State University. He wanted to talk about Donnie Shell, the Bulldogs' defensive back.

The Steelers scout already knew the name. Shell had been a *Courier* All-American. Nunn had called him "tough, fast and reckless."[578] Shell hit hard, covered down the field and came to play every day, he wrote.

Jeffries told Nunn that Shell had offers from two other teams. But the South Carolina State coach wanted Shell to come to Pittsburgh. After hearing Nunn talk about the Steelers' colorblind approach to players, Jeffries was convinced Shell would have the best chance of making an NFL roster with the Steelers.

Nunn got off the phone and worked out a deal to bring Shell to Steelers' training camp.

When the Steelers' rookies arrived at St. Vincent's College in Latrobe for the start of the 1974 training camp, they found a picket line manned by veteran players wearing long hair and mustaches, loafing around and talking.[579] The players were not threatening but they were not going to work either. The National Football League Players Association had a list of 57 grievances, headlined by the demand for improved free agency. Until then, a team that hired away a free agent player had to compensate his old team with money or draft picks. Only four players had moved to other clubs in the previous decade.

The newest Steelers faced a choice: They needed to cross the picket line and attend practice if they had any hope of making the team. Stallworth had arrived in Latrobe still worrying about his status.

"My thinking was, 'They took a guy number one,'" he recalled later.[580] "Most of the time, teams are going to keep their number-one draft choice. So I'm thinking, 'I'm a fourth-round draft choice, and no guarantees here.'"

Joe Gilliam Jr., the second-year quarterback out of Tennessee State University, worried for his job too. With starting quarterback Terry Bradshaw sitting on the picket line, Gilliam crossed into camp and started taking snaps with the first team. Joe Greene had emerged as the conscience of the Steelers: Nunn noted in the *Courier* that while the defensive lineman backed Bradshaw as the starting quarterback, he gave his blessings to Gilliam to report to camp.[581] As the first quarterback in camp, Gilliam took nearly all of the meaningful snaps, often throwing the ball down the field to the two new receivers – Swann and

Stallworth. All three got more attention than they normally would have received.

Stallworth could not let go of the fears that had seeped into his mind that morning when the NFL scouts came to Normal, Alabama. He still worried about not being good enough – and so he pushed himself harder, even after the team won its first four preseason games. The following week, Stallworth collapsed at practice and ended up going to the hospital needing intravenous fluids.

When Stallworth returned to campus, wide receivers coach Lionel Taylor pulled him aside. The team still had two more preseason games and the coaches had not finished making all of their cuts.

"You made the team," Taylor told him.[582] "Just relax. Do what you know to do, and it should be fine."

Later that night after the evening meeting, Noll walked over to the rookie wide receiver and told him to calm down.

"I want you to relax," the coach said. "You need to get enough bodily fluids in you."

Then he suggested that Stallworth join some of the other players at the local bar for a few beers. Never a big drinker, Stallworth was surprised by the advice – but he got the message.

The Steelers won all six preseason games, and Gilliam got the chance to start the season at quarterback even though the veterans had returned.

In the first game of the regular season, the Steelers beat the Baltimore Colts at home 30-0. Swann scored a touchdown on a 54-yard pass from Gilliam, and Stallworth had two receptions for 25 yards. On defense, Lambert played at middle linebacker and contributed to the shutout.

Taylor, the receiver's coach, sought out Stallworth again: It seemed, he said, like the Steelers had gotten three first-round draft picks with the team's first three picks over four rounds of the draft.[583]

Gilliam stayed under center for six games, including four wins and a tie against the Denver Broncos. The only loss had come in week three against the Oakland Raiders. By the end of September, the *Courier* was touting Gilliam on the front page as the "best quarterback in football,"[584] and Nunn boasted in his column that even other players around the league were rooting for the black quarterback.

"If the Pittsburgh Steelers continue winning," he typed into his typewriter that week, "it will be surprising the number of players who will be rooting for the former Tennessee State University star to carry the Steelers to the Super Bowl."[585]

Behind the scenes, Noll was becoming frustrated with Gilliam even in victory. The quarterback was too reliant on the pass, despite the potential for a strong running game behind Franco Harris and Rocky Bleier.

The coach decided to replace Gilliam before week seven. And the old issues of race came rushing back.

The *Courier* argued that the black quarterback had been held to an unfair standard: "Isn't it funny how blacks have to perform twice as well as whites to hold a position in this country? One or two poor performances and you are out, baby."[586] White fans and the media "just can't stomach a black man leading the team while white quarterbacks sit on the bench," the paper wrote in an editorial about prejudice.[587]

Nunn initially noted that Jets quarterback Joe Namath was having a worse season than Gilliam but no one was calling for him to be replaced in New York.[588] But then weeks later, Nunn told his readers that the Steelers' decision had been strictly about perking up the team's offense.[589] He quoted his former teammate, Gilliam's father, too. This was not a repeat of the situation with Roy Curry a generation earlier when the Steelers' previous head coach simply wouldn't give the black player a chance at quarterback. "As a coach, I might not agree with all of Noll's decisions," Gilliam Sr. was quoted as saying in Nunn's column, "but I'm certain he is one of the fairest coaches in pro football."[590]

Not all of the vitriol came from the *Courier* and Gilliam's supporters. As the quarterback controversy played out, Gilliam received threatening hate mail from white fans too.[591]

"Noll played Bradshaw because he thought it time to go with his first-round draft pick," team president Dan Rooney said later. "Race was not an issue. Noll believed Terry could get the job done – it was that simple."[592]

After three more games, including a loss to the Cincinnati Bengals, Noll benched Bradshaw too and gave the ball to Terry Hanratty. The Steelers won the next game, but Noll brought back Bradshaw as the starter for the rest of the regular season, through three wins and one loss.

The Steelers finished with 10 wins, three losses and a tie – enough for first place again in the AFC Central Division.

In a game that pitted a top NFL defense against a leading offense, the Steelers defeated the Buffalo Bills and running back O.J. Simpson in the first round of the playoffs. The same week, the Oakland Raiders played the Miami Dolphins in a game that many expected would decide the eventual Super Bowl winner. Oakland won – and got to host the Steelers the following week.

Heading into that game, Noll found himself getting irked about the Raiders saying they already had played and beaten the AFC's best team in Miami. Typically quiet even around his players, the Steelers' head coach called a team meeting at Three Rivers Stadium on the Monday after beating Buffalo. Normally he could come off as cool, detached and businesslike – but now he was fired up.

"You know, the coach of the Raiders said the two best teams in football (Oakland and Miami) played yesterday, and that was the Super Bowl," Noll told his players.[593] "Well, the Super Bowl is three weeks from now, and the best team in pro football is sitting right here in this room."

Greene, the Steelers' lineman, felt like he just about levitated out of his seat as he listened to Noll.

The following Sunday in Oakland, the two teams traded field goals in the first quarter and then Stallworth had a chance to break the game open near the end of the first half. Running out of room in the end zone, he fought off a defender with his right hand and caught the ball with the left, tiptoeing along the line to stay in bounds. The referees, in the days before instant replay, said he had not maintained control of the ball and waved off the touchdown.

In the end, the Steelers won the game 17-10, after a late Steelers interception. With the ball on the Raiders' 9-yard line, Bradshaw found Swann in the end zone. Pittsburgh, a team that had until recently struggled to win even one playoff game, was heading to Super Bowl IX in New Orleans.

On the Friday night before the Super Bowl, Nunn arrived at the Marriott Inn in New Orleans for a party that almost never happened.

Royal Crown Cola had been a founding sponsor of the *Courier*'s black college All-America banquets but backed out this year just weeks before the event. Nunn scrambled around and found another lead sponsor, Pittsburgh-based Gulf Oil Corporation. He made arrangements to have the party in New Orleans to coincide with the Super Bowl, but the planning started so late that few of the players were able to make it and even the plaques honoring them did not show up in time.

That year's All-Americans included a running back from Mississippi's Jackson State University named Walter Payton. He was appearing, as a senior, on the All-America team for the third time. Over four years, Payton had run for 3,563 yards and 66 touchdowns, scoring a total of 464 points.

Still, one prize remained above all of the others in the player's mind.

"Being selected to the *Courier* team again has to rate as the biggest thrill of my college career," Payton told Nunn.[594] "I'll treasure this award for the rest of my life."

The essence of the party remained too. More than 200 people turned out at the Marriott, many of them Pittsburghers in town already for the game Sunday. Mississippi's Alcorn State University was named the black college national champion, and Coach Marino Casem stood up to receive a 6-foot-tall trophy.

Two former All-Americans on the Steelers' roster, quarterback Joe Gilliam and cornerback Mel Blount, presented the trophies for the top offensive and defensive players of the year.[595] Continental Airlines sponsored a Man of the Year award and recognized Gilliam with the trophy.

It was no coincidence that so many Steelers were involved in the banquet, the *Courier* reminded its readers after the event. "Now that blacks are becoming more dominant in the NFL, every player chosen on the team generally goes in the first 10 rounds except for centers and quarterbacks," sports editor Ulish Carter wrote.[596] "The color barrier hasn't been broken in the NFL at center, and there are only two black quarterbacks in the NFL."

But thanks to Nunn, the paper wrote, Pittsburgh's team had found an advantage: "His contacts and knowledge of the players in these colleges gives the Steelers an inside track."

Nunn's influence could be seen all over the Steelers even before they arrived at Tulane University's dilapidated stadium for the game. The Super Bowl was supposed to be played at New Orleans' space-age Superdome but construction had not been completed in time, so the game was moved to Tulane for a third and final time. Only a decade earlier, the American Football League had canceled its all-star game in New Orleans after the players felt intense discrimination from the airport to the hotels to Bourbon Street and its clubs.

Now here came the Steelers, with blacks making up half of the overall roster. Even among those black players, half of them came from the black colleges. Many had come to the Steelers in the late rounds of the draft: left defensive end L.C. Greenwood from Arkansas AM& N had been the 238th pick overall in 1969; running back John "Frenchy" Fuqua from Morgan State College had gone 35 slots later that year to the New York Giants who traded him to Pittsburgh; right defensive tackle Ernie Holmes from Texas Southern University had been chosen 203rd in 1971; and backup quarterback Joe Gilliam Jr. from Tennessee State University had been the 273rd pick in 1972.

That list of players did not even include the Steelers who had come from small schools that were not black colleges. Left defensive tackle Joe Greene and wide receiver Ron Shanklin had come out of the University of North Texas, and right

Bill Nunn, Jr. in the summer of 1975. Photo courtesy of the Nunn family.

defensive end Dwight White had come from East Texas State University. Nicknamed the "Steel Curtain," the entire defensive line had come from small schools and black colleges: Greene had been an obvious first-round pick but none of the other three had gone higher than 104th in the draft.

Then there were the black college players who never even had been drafted. Nunn took special pride in looking onto the football field to see men on the Steelers who almost had been passed over. They had been given a chance, unlike the generations of black athletes before them who never even had someone look in their direction. The team preparing to take the field in New Orleans had four black free agents. Shell and Reggie Garrett had joined the Steelers as rookies that season. Sam Davis, an offensive lineman from tiny Allen University, had been with the team seven years and he would walk onto the field for the coin toss as the Steelers' offensive captain. Glen Edwards came to Pittsburgh from Florida A&M in 1971 and would be starting in the Super Bowl at free safety.

Standing in the tunnel beneath Tulane Stadium, the young Steelers felt intimidated at first, looking across the narrow hallway at the Minnesota Vikings lined up next to them.[597] These were men with thick beards who looked like real Vikings and who already had been to the Super Bowl twice before. Steelers cornerback J.T. Thomas felt a palpable fear among his teammates as they waited. Suddenly Edwards started bellowing out words – not encouragement but more of a guttural yell. Everyone on the Steelers looked at him and a vibration passed through the men, from Greene to Lambert and White. "We went crazy," Thomas recalled later. "It was on in the tunnel."

Dwight White had started out that week with stomach cramps, and he had ended up in the hospital with pneumonia. He hadn't eaten any solid food from Sunday through Wednesday and he had lost 18 pounds since arriving in New Orleans. He had woken up in a hospital bed the day before the game and he had arrived at Tulane Stadium uncertain about playing. But the doctors had cleared him to play and he had warmed up with the team, going through a couple of intense hitting drills lined up against Joe Greene. Everyone agreed he could start the game.

Even in New Orleans, the game had a feel of being played further north with a game-time temperature of just 46 degrees and a wind-chill factor of 22 degrees.[598] An estimated 10,000 people with tickets never showed up at the stadium. Nunn sat in the stands with his wife and daughter, unable to do any more for the team by that point than cheer them on and worry about whether they would win.

With two of the league's best defenses on the field, neither team scored through the first quarter, and the first points did not come off of an offensive play. Deep in his own end of the field, Vikings quarterback Fran Tarkenton turned to hand off the ball to the team's running back but the ball came loose and rolled across the turf. Tarkenton landed on the ball to prevent the Steelers from scoring a touchdown just as White had smashed through the line and landed on top of the quarterback in the end zone for a two-point safety. Fittingly, the Steelers defense had scored first.

With less than two minutes left in the first half, the Vikings had regained their composure and were driving for a score. Tarkenton threw a perfect pass toward his receiver at the 5-yard line, but Glen Edwards arrived at the same moment as the ball and it flew up in the air. Cornerback Mel Blount grabbed the ball for a Steelers interception. Two former black college All-Americans had just prevented the Vikings from reaching the end zone.

Even halftime had a black college influence. In an effort to make sure the Super Bowl in New Orleans felt welcoming to everyone, the league had arranged for the Grambling College marching band to appear, and its members played a Duke Ellington tribute.

When the second half started, the Steelers struck first on a nine-yard touchdown run by Franco Harris, the black running back out of Penn State University. Those yards were among the Super Bowl-record 158 yards he would cover in the game.

Minnesota still struggled to move the ball. Later in the third quarter, Tarkenton dropped back to pass, let go of the ball and watched as Greenwood batted it up into the air. The quarterback grabbed the ball back, scrambled and then let go a second pass for 41 yards down the field. It had been a bizarre play and the referees ruled correctly that the second pass had been an illegal one. With his speed and long wingspan, Greenwood had broken up the Vikings' passing game, batting away three passes throughout the day. Moments later on the same drive, White broke up another Tarkenton pass, batting it up in the air so Greene could pluck it away for an interception. Then early in the fourth quarter, Minnesota was driving again toward the Steelers' end zone when Greene forced and recovered a fumble.

The Steelers' offense was not having much more success than the Vikings, and Minnesota was not done. Its defense scored a touchdown on a blocked punt, leaving the score at 9-6 after a blocked extra point attempt.

Pittsburgh got the ball back and Bradshaw finally started moving the offense. He hit tight end Larry Brown, a black player from Kansas University, for a 30-yard reception on the drive. Then with the Steelers lined up on the 4-yard line, Bradshaw looked to the sidelines for a play. Gilliam, who had started the season as the Steelers quarterback, had watched the game as a backup. He had seen a weakness in the Vikings' defense and he had walked over to tell Noll after the previous play. The coach sent in the signal and Bradshaw rifled a pass to Brown in the end zone for the game-deciding touchdown.

The players understood the importance of the victory to Pittsburgh, joking that they would return home to find that fans had burned the city to the ground in celebration. They were not far off: About 20,000 people spilled into Pittsburgh's downtown area as the game ended at 6:10 p.m., setting off firecrackers and Roman candles, climbing on top of a billboard and a public bus, and opening a fire hydrant in the freezing weather. Police arrested 233 people, mostly for intoxication, and 69 people were injured, including 10 officers.[599]

"You could see it in their eyes on the field," Noll said after the game about his players.[600] "They wouldn't let themselves be denied."

From his seat in Tulane Stadium, Nunn cheered with the fans and smiled broadly, enjoying the moment. He knew that his men, the players who might have otherwise gone unnoticed at small black colleges, had contributed in major ways to the Steelers' victory. He could hear the echoes too, of all the men who had come before.

The Steelers' championship validated what Nunn and black college athletic directors, presidents and fans had believed for generations: Given a chance, their athletes could compete with the best in the world. Sam Davis, Glen Edwards, L.C. Greenwood, Mel Blount, Ernie Holmes, Frank Lewis, John Stallworth. These men played not only for themselves but for the countless black men who perhaps could have stood with them – if they had been given an opportunity to try out for a professional football team.

The moment also belonged to Charles Follis, the first black professional player back in 1904. It represented a victory for Ray Kemp, a starter for the Steelers when the team formed in 1933 but who had to leave the following year when the NFL purged its ranks of color during the Great Depression. The Steelers victory would be a celebration for Kenny Washington and Woody Strode, the first blacks who came back to the NFL past their prime years when the Rams moved to Los Angeles and the nation's black newspapers insisted the team re-integrate the league. The ghosts of Marion Motley, Bill Willis, Buddy Young, Tank Younger and so many other early black football pioneers ran onto the field with the Steelers' players when Joe Greene, Franco Harris and Lynn Swann lifted their coach into the air in victory.

Nunn never rushed into the limelight with them. He felt intense pride in the moment, knowing the impact that the *Courier* had on the Steelers forming this championship team. But he deflected praise. Nunn remembered his father, the newspaper's managing editor who had first come up with the idea for a black-college All-America team. Ches Washington and Wendell Smith had made the picks before Nunn, setting the standard for what a black college All-American should represent – even in the days when everyone knew those top players never would play anywhere again. Pops Turner, Big Ben Stevenson, Tick Smith and Harry "Wu Fang" Ward had all appeared on that first *Courier* All-America team in 1925. They had been born too soon.[601]

When the Steelers returned home to Pittsburgh, Nunn posed for a photograph with the Lombardi trophy. And when the team handed out championship rings, Nunn wore his with pride. He celebrated in a modest way.

The following season, the Steelers came back and won the Super Bowl again. The championship game only had been around for a decade but already the Green Bay Packers, Miami Dolphins and Pittsburgh had won the top game in consecutive seasons. The second victory solidified the Steelers' place among the league's top teams.

Super Bowl X took place at the Orange Bowl in Miami, the site of the Orange Blossom Classic, which often had served as the unofficial black college championship. As the NFL sought warm-weather cities for its championship game, the league also was forced to confront the ghosts of segregation. For this game, in early 1976, the focus would be on the nation's overall history: The Steelers and NFC champion Dallas Cowboys wore bicentennial patches on their jerseys to celebration the United States' 200th anniversary.

The game had started to arrive as a national phenomenon too. More than 80,000 fans attended the game in person and an estimated 57 million watched at home.

Two weeks earlier in the Steelers' AFC championship victory over the Oakland Raiders, receiver Swann was hit so hard that he suffered a concussion and had to be helped staggering off the field by Coach Noll. Swann had ended up in the hospital for two days with what the coach called a "very large headache."[602] Stallworth had stepped up in that game, throwing a key block on a 25-yard touchdown run by Harris and then later catching the game-winning touchdown in the end zone.

Many people thought Swann would not come back to play in the Super Bowl, including Cowboys safety Cliff "Captain Crush" Harris, who essentially dared the Steelers' receiver to show up for the game. "I'm not going to hurt anyone intentionally," he told reporters before the game.[603] "But getting hit again while he's running a pass route must be in the back of Swann's mind. I know it would be in the back of my mind."

In an era before concussion protocols and evidence about long-term effects, Swann read the comments and reacted: "He was trying to intimidate me. He said I'd be afraid out there. He needn't worry. He doesn't know Lynn Swann. He can't scare me or the team. I said to myself, 'The hell with it, I'm gonna play.'"

Swann caught four passes for 161 yards, including the game-winner on a 64-yard touchdown pass with just over four minutes left in the game. Bradshaw, who also had suffered a concussion in the AFC championship, had to leave the Super Bowl after the touchdown pass because he got hit in the head again.

With the game clock expiring and the Cowboys attempting a touchdown to win the game, Dallas quarterback Roger Staubach passed into the end zone where the ball was tipped into the hands of Glen Edwards, the Steelers' undrafted safety out of Florida A&M, as time expired.

For the second year in a row, the game had turned on plays by men who might not otherwise even be playing in the NFL if Nunn had not discovered them, and if the rest of the Steelers' organization had not given them a fair chance. Nunn looked at the Super Bowl victories as evidence of the Steelers' even-handed approach to scouting and evaluating players. The Rooneys had a colorblind outlook about bringing players into training camp, and Coach Noll always seemed to be rooting for the underdog.

"It's not that other teams weren't looking," Nunn recalled.[604] "It's what you do with them when they come in."

Nunn wasn't finished, despite the repeated successes of black college players in the NFL. As he looked around the league, he still saw discrimination. And now, with the league watching and listening, Nunn used his occasional column in the *Courier* to call for change.

Before the start of the following training camp, Nunn pointed out that while many teams had successful black players, few had hired black coaches. Of more than 200 head coaches, coordinators and assistants throughout the league, teams had hired only 11 blacks. The Steelers had just one, receivers coach Lionel Taylor, the longest-serving coach on the team and Coach Noll's roommate when the team traveled.

As a wide receiver with the Denver Broncos, Taylor previously had led the newly formed American Football League in receptions for five of its first six years. Nunn figured if anyone deserved a chance to move up in the coaching ranks after Super Bowls IX and X, Lionel had the best chance. Clacking the words into his typewriter between drags on a cigarette, Nunn sat in his office wearing a white polo shirt with the Steelers' logo and a championship ring on his finger.

"Strange," he wrote[605], "that in a league where so many blacks excel as players, there are so few who qualify as being capable of teaching the sport as coaches."

Within a year, Taylor left the Steelers to join the Los Angeles Rams, and he soon moved up to offensive coordinator. He eventually became a head coach – but at Texas Southern University, rather than in the NFL.

Nunn did more than just write columns too. He looked to create changes by joining men such as Tank Younger, the first black college player in the NFL, and John Wooten, a black offensive lineman drafted by the Cleveland Browns in 1959. Wooten later went on to work as director of pro scouting for the Dallas Cowboys and in other scouting jobs with the Philadelphia Eagles and Baltimore Ravens.

Together, the men asked longtime Commissioner Pete Rozelle for help moving more blacks into coaching and front office positions. He answered that the league could not force teams to hire anyone. Instead, the NFL created a minority coaching fellowship in which black coaches could join professional teams during training camps and offseason workouts to observe and learn.

"I can't even start to tell you how we fought to try to make this happen," Wooten said.[606] "I can remember going to meetings … asking him, 'What can we do? How can we do it to get black coaches and more black people in the front office?'"

❖❖❖

The *Courier* had taken its All-America banquet on the road for five years to cities such Memphis, Houston and New Orleans. But the event ended up nearly getting canceled, and Nunn brought it back to the Pittsburgh Hilton in 1977.

In an unexpected twist, as the NFL started paying more attention to the black college players, the *Courier* and its list lost some of its luster. Players still wanted to see their name in the newspaper, but they saw the recognition as a step on the way to the league and getting paid – rather than as a triumph on its own. Often, too, the best players ended up facing conflicts the same weekend as the banquet, having to play in one of the college all-star games where scouts evaluated talent.

By coming back to Pittsburgh, Nunn saw a chance to return the dinner to its roots – when black college players from around the country came into the city for a weekend of dinners and parties. Walter Payton, the former *Courier* All-American, returned as a Chicago Bears star running back to receive an award as the top National Football Conference player of the year. He had led the league in rushing until the final week when he got injured and O.J. Simpson passed him.

Art Rooney Sr., with a cigar in his left hand and his sons sitting at his table, listened as Steelers' defensive tackle Ernie Holmes received an award as the top player in the American Football Conference. He stood at the Hilton podium in front of a large sign in the shape of a football, and he recalled being cut by the Steelers in his first season out of Texas Southern. He came back the next year, made the team and then became one-fourth of what already was being called the greatest defensive front line in NFL history.

Nineteen of the 22 All-Americans made it to Pittsburgh too, and Nunn posed with them for a photo. Grambling State University quarterback Doug Williams received a trophy as the black college offensive player of the year.

"Mark it down," Nunn wrote to *Courier* readers the following week.[607] "…That's the kind of night it was. Super athletes. A feeling of brotherhood and a sense of total togetherness."

Bill Nunn Jr. named his final *Courier* black college All-America team two years later. For at least a decade, he had been receiving input from coaches, NFL scouts and sports writers. As he spent more time working for the Steelers, Nunn came to rely on these other sources both for their ability to see more of the games and players – but also as a way to deflect criticism when the Steelers drafted a player who had not been named to the newspaper's all-star team.

The previous season had proven that Nunn's picks still deserved the attention. Nine of the 22 All-Americans immediately had started playing in the NFL, including Williams, the Grambling quarterback who became the Tampa Bay Buccaneers' first-round draft choice and starter.

Nunn realized it would be hard to top that record, and he decided to dedicate himself fulltime to the Steelers. This would be his final *Courier* black college All-America team.

That December as Nunn counted up the ballots from the people helping him choose the All-Americans, the Steelers seemed poised for another run into the playoffs. After winning two Super Bowls, the Steelers had come close but failed to make it back to the championship game for two seasons. This year, the team had just finished the regular season as the top team in the AFC and its defense had given up the fewest points in the league. Tony Dungy, a safety drafted by the Steelers in 1977, led the team with six interceptions.

As he typed, Nunn allowed himself a little bit of reflection over the three decades since he started traveling the country 15,000 miles each fall to watch the best black college football games in an attempt to choose the 22 best players from more than 50 schools. In that time, he had discovered the first black college athletes to play as professionals and men who had risen up from the shadows to distinguish themselves with hall-of-fame careers. For more than 30 years, that tradition had continued, with Nunn sitting at his typewriter and putting down their names in ink.

"They begin in August under a hot blistering sun," Nunn wrote for a final time.[608] "Thousands of college football players across the nation don the pads in search of the glory that will belong to the victors and those who have excelled for their various alma maters.

"For many there is frustration. Others can look back later and embellish on careers that were steeped in mediocrity. But for a handful, there is the pride of knowing they were the best in a particular year. To those few men go the plaudits of the multitudes."

The men on Nunn's list that year included fullback Timmy Newsome from North Carolina's Winston Salem State University, who went on to play nine seasons for the Dallas Cowboys, and Charles Johnson, a Grambling defensive back who ended up with the San Francisco 49ers.

By the time Nunn's final All-Americans arrived in Pittsburgh for their banquet a month later, the Steelers had won a third Super Bowl – again beating the Dallas Cowboys in Miami's Orange Bowl. With the 35-31 outcome not settled until the final seconds, many football fans ranked it among the best championship games ever. Dallas had been the previous year's champion, and both teams were vying to be the first to win three Super Bowls.

The game also proved to be a showcase for former *Courier* All-Americans. The newspaper previewed its annual banquet by noting that ten former black college players had figured prominently into the Super Bowl outcome.[609]

John Stallworth scored the Steelers' first two touchdowns, including a 10-yard pass that he turned into a 75-yard score.

Sam Davis, the undrafted veteran lineman from Allen University, had contained the NFL's defensive player of the year long enough to give quarterback Terry Bradshaw time to "count the Orange Bowl crowd" while throwing passes, the paper said.

L.C. Greenwood had slowed down Dallas running back Tony Dorsett, while Mel "Supe" Blount and Donnie Shell had prevented Dallas from breaking a big score down the field.

Two weeks later, the *Courier* hosted its banquet in Pittsburgh and honored Doug Williams, a former three-time black college All-American from Grambling, with its rookie offensive player award. The college players arrived too, many wearing the wide, disco-inspired collars of the day. Chester Washington, the sports writer who had worked with Nunn's father on the first *Courier* All-American list in 1925, flew in from Los Angeles for the dinner.

No one mentioned this would be Nunn's final group of All-Americans.

Twenty-two players won four Super Bowls with the Steelers during the 1970s. Half of the men were black, and five had come to Pittsburgh from historically black colleges – Mel Blount, Sam Davis, L.C. Greenwood, Donnie Shell and John Stallworth.

Super Bowl XIV took place in Los Angeles, where the league had reintegrated three-and-a-half decades earlier. The game, however, was played at the Rose Bowl, and not the Coliseum, whose commission members had forced the NFL to reintegrate. Nearly 104,000 fans packed into the building.

For a time, it appeared the hometown Los Angeles Rams would pull off an upset over the heavily favored Steelers, carrying a 19-17 lead into the game's final quarter.[610]

But in a moment that would serve as the lasting image of the championship, especially when it appeared on the cover of *Sports Illustrated* the following week, Stallworth streaked down the field, looking over his shoulder at the Rams' 32-yard line to catch Terry Bradshaw's pass over the reaching arms of a Los Angeles defender. Stallworth continued into the end zone for a 73-yard touchdown that put the Steelers ahead for good.

The player who was too skinny to play football in high school, who was too dark-skinned to play at the University of Alabama, who wondered after his pro tryout whether he could play at the NFL level had just secured the Steelers' record fourth Super Bowl in six seasons.

Later that evening at the team hotel, Stallworth sat at a table in the lobby with his wife as Bill Nunn Jr. walked over with Chuck Noll. By then the Steelers were accustomed to winning, but they also knew perhaps better than anyone how much hard work and luck it took to finish on top. The players

Steelers receiver Lynn Swann celebrates in Super Bowl XIV after scoring a 47-yard touchdown in the third quarter. Swann and John Stallworth combined for 200 yards on 8 receptions and two touchdowns in the Steelers' 31-19 victory over the Los Angeles Rams. Photo by William T. Larkin, used with the permission of the Pittsburgh Tribune-Review.

had learned, even after winning four Super Bowls, to still savor the moment.

While Noll and Stallworth talked, Nunn stood quietly nearby, just smiling. It wasn't a big grin or a brash celebration but simply recognition of the moment – that Stallworth, the player who had nearly gone unnoticed, had accomplished so much for himself, for his team and for so many other black college players. The memory of Nunn's smiling face stayed with Stallworth long after that night.

"He was proud of me," Stallworth said.[611] "He was proud of the black college that I came from, and what he had done for making that happen, and for the Steelers. There's a look on his face, and it was special to me. I treasure that because it made me feel good about who I was, and who I was to that team. And also a sense that Bill played a part in that."

Before the players left Southern California, Nunn had one more goal in mind before the team returned home and everyone scattered. He pulled together a few of the men, starting with Sam Davis, who had played well in the Super Bowl despite a sore hamstring. Nunn talked with Joe Greene and Dwight White, two of the men who made up half of the team's "Steel Curtain" defensive front. And he talked with Franco Harris, the star running back. The players all agreed.

During the week before the game, Nunn had run into an old friend, Benjamin Hooks, a Baptist minister and attorney who also headed up the National Association for the Advancement of Colored People. Their talk reminded Nunn about all of the gains that black players had accomplished during his career. They had gone from being unofficially banned from the league to now making up half of the roster of a four-time Super Bowl champion.

"I started thinking about it," Nunn recalled years later.[612] "It would be a heck of a thing for them to show the young kids that these guys were interested in the causes."

Nunn asked each of the 24 black men on the team to take $500 from their own Super Bowl victory bonus and use the money to purchase a lifetime membership in the NAACP.

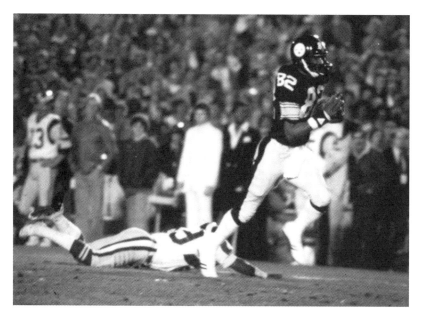

Steelers wide receiver John Stallworth's 73-yard touchdown catch in Super Bowl XIV became the signature moment of the game and sealed the victory over the Los Angeles Rams. Photo courtesy of the Pittsburgh Steelers.

Bill Nunn Jr. poses with the Steelers' four Vince Lombardi trophies from Super Bowls IX, X, XIII and XIV in 1980 at Three Rivers Stadium. Photo courtesy of the Pittsburgh Steelers.

"I approached each of them individually about it and without hesitation, each of them said, 'Yes,'" Nunn told a reporter before the team plane left for Pittsburgh.[613]

"The main doggone thing," he later said about the moment, "is that they took the money out of their bonus."

For Stallworth, the decision to support Nunn's idea had been easy. He did not live in Pittsburgh during the offseason but he knew things in the community had started turning gray. Steel workers were losing jobs that never would come back to the river valleys of Western Pennsylvania. The Hill District community where the *Courier* was based had turned for the worse too, especially after a redevelopment plan to tear down homes and businesses to build an arena.

"We were part of this community and we were role models in this community," Stallworth said years later.[614] "It wasn't a pretty thing in Pittsburgh. For the most part, there was a lot of depression, a lot of things going down. It was a way to lend some pride, to show that the players on the team identified with what was going on in the community. Be a source of motivation to folks. The Steelers are doing well, but yeah, the whole community can take pride in that."

More than anything, it just seemed like a good idea, Greene said. He immediately agreed when Nunn asked him to give.

By then, after four Super Bowl victories, the players realized that people not just in Pittsburgh but across the country closely followed whatever they did. Greene had been featured in a heartwarming ad that played off his nickname "Mean Joe," showing him tossing his jersey to a fan who gave him a Coke after a game. The ad had debuted in October and played on television several times during the championship.

They never talked openly about it, but the team's black players felt a brotherhood and a sense of responsibility, Greene said.

"I felt that my performance did have an effect on all black players," Greene recalled.[615] "That's what we felt. I think that's what we all felt, that at the time, we had a responsibility as black players to be successful. That probably faded as time went on but I had a feeling that we all had a sense of that. Not something that was said verbally but it was just an inward feeling."

By the time the team touched down in Pittsburgh, Nunn was able to deliver a $12,000 gift to the NAACP.

A bronze plaque honoring Bill Nunn Jr. hangs outside the Pittsburgh Steelers' draft room, which has been named for him, at the team's South Side offices. Photo by Andrew Conte.

Epilogue

On the night when boxer Ezzard Charles defeated Joe Louis in 1950, Bill Nunn Jr. sat ringside in Yankee Stadium next to another legend of that sport, Sugar Ray Robinson. Louis would jab and jab again, but then fail to follow through with his powerful right fist. And each time, Sugar Ray sitting in his seat would implore the Brown Bomber to "throw it, throw it." Then when Louis failed again to land his punch, Nunn would look to the man next to him and see the hurt in his eyes.

Louis had retired more than a year earlier but he returned to the ring in need of money, overweight and out of shape. He stood to make more than $100,000 from the bout, compared to Charles' take at $57,000. Louis was the bettors' favorite too, at 2-to-1 odds. But the Brown Bomber took a beating for his paycheck and lost by unanimous decision.

It had been hard for everyone who had grown up idolizing Louis to see him struggling this way against a lighter, faster opponent. This time, Louis would not regain his footing with one swing of his right arm the way he had against Billy Conn nearly a decade earlier.

"When I lost, I found it hard to face the truth," Louis told Nunn years after the fight. "What I had, I could never explain: It was always jab, hook, followed by a right. In the end it seemed as though my right hand was frozen. I knew what I was supposed to do but I never did it. At the time, I couldn't explain it. Now I know that my coordination was gone. Without that, you are no longer a great fighter."

Nunn was lucky that way: He never lost his punch.

He had retired, of course, in 1987, but Nunn kept coming to the office every day. Even at age 89. He and Steelers Chairman Dan Rooney had choreographed a dance that they performed after each draft. Nunn would come into Rooney's office and announce that he had decided to quit. He didn't want to get in the way. The younger scouts and managers could handle the job without him.

"I don't think I'll come in anymore," Nunn would say.

And each time, Rooney would ask him to keep coming around, at least for one more year. After Nunn grew too old to drive the 15 minutes from his house at the top of the Hill District down to the Steelers' offices on the site of a former steel mill on the city's Southside, the team would ask one of the younger assistants to pick up Nunn in the morning and take him home at the end of the day. His insights on young athletes remained that important. Nunn ended up as just one of five people[616] with championship rings from the Steelers' first six Super Bowl victories.

After the four Super Bowls in the 1970s, the Steelers looked mortal again for a time. The draft magic they experienced with Lynn Swann, Jack Lambert, John Stallworth and Mike Webster seemed to wear off. The scouts still hoped to pull off another steal like they had at Alabama A&M, and they came close a few times. Nunn thought he had fooled the league again in 1985 until the San Francisco 49ers moved up in the draft to snag a wide receiver named Jerry Rice out of Mississippi Valley State University, the small historically black school in Itta Bena, Mississippi, not far from where white hoodlums snatched 14-year-old Emmett Till out of his bed in the middle of the night in 1955 before beating him to death for flirting with a white woman. Nunn took pride in finding Rice – and in knowing that the game had evolved so far that another scout had found him there too.

In 1987, the Steelers discovered linebacker Greg Lloyd with the 150th pick out of Fort Valley State University, a historically black school in Georgia. He played 11 years in the NFL and was named to five Pro Bowl teams. The path from small black schools to the league had narrowed but not completely disappeared. Nunn's influence remained.

"He had the insight, the knowledge, the ability to go to these schools – and you had to dig them out," Joe Greene said.[617] "Bill had that ability to ask the right question – which is as important as the visual, looking at those guys – to ask the right questions of the coaches and the players, and to do your homework. He was very good at that."

After retiring as a player, Greene worked as an assistant coach with the Steelers, Miami Dolphins and Arizona Cardinals before returning to Pittsburgh as a scout, the special assistant for player personnel. Back at Steelers' headquarters, Greene often sat next to Nunn in meetings to learn from him. While watching film, Nunn explained what to watch and he could articulate his thoughts precisely.

"Because of his ability to write and use the English language, he had a way of writing reports that made it easier to follow," Greene said. "When you finished reading his reports, you knew if the guy could play and if he couldn't play. ... He didn't mince his words about that talent and that was the most important thing – knowing the talent and then not having a problem expressing himself about it."

The *Pittsburgh Courier* had transformed into the *New Pittsburgh Courier* when it was bought out by the owner of a rival black newspaper, the *Chicago Defender*, in 1966.[618] After Nunn stopped compiling the black college All-America team, sports writer Eddie Jefferies did it for at least one more year – although the names were not announced until February, and the reporter asked readers to be kind: "There's an old axiom that states in effect, anything worthwhile is worth waiting for."[619]

American Urban Radio Networks, a nationwide broadcast network based in Pittsburgh, started picking a black college All-America team in 1974 and maintained the tradition.

Former black college players took up the mantle, too, of recognizing the great men who had come out of the schools and the struggle they had endured, first to win access to the National Football League and then to win equality. Former NFL quarterbacks James "Shack" Harris and Doug Williams formed the Black College Hall of Fame in Atlanta in 2010. Their inaugural class of 11 inductees included Paul "Tank" Younger, the NFL's first black college player; Eddie Robinson, longtime coach at Grambling State University; Jake Gaither, Florida A&M's coach for 24 years; and Bill Nunn Jr.

Members of the Rooney family seemed never to forget that the first Steelers team had a black player, Ray Kemp, nor that their franchise had gone along with other league owners from 1933 until 1946 when no blacks played in the NFL. John Brewer, a historian of Pittsburgh's black community, credits the family members with doing everything in their power to make up for the slight in the decades since.

"I could never figure out why a person could dislike another person because of his color, whether he was red, yellow, black, or white, or whether he was a Jew or a Protestant or Catholic," Art Rooney Sr. said at the team's 50th anniversary banquet.[620] "I often thought of what God would think of us for thinking in such a manner."

Steelers head coach Chuck Noll hired the team's former safety Tony Dungy as a defensive assistant and then as the league's only black defensive coordinator in 1984. Dungy went on to become a head coach in Tampa Bay and Indianapolis.

The black coaching fellowship that Nunn had sought with John Wooten and Younger took off too. NFL head coaches Herm Edwards, Marvin Lewis, Lovie Smith and hundreds of other black coaches passed through the program, spending time with teams at training camp, learning systems and making the contacts to find a job.[621]

Then in the fall of 2002, two equal-opportunity lawyers, Johnnie Cochran Jr. and Cyrus Mehri, issued a report – "Black Coaches in the National Football League: Superior Performance, Inferior Opportunities" – that found black NFL coaches were held to a higher standard and denied a fair chance to compete for head coaching jobs.[622] A month later, Commissioner Paul Tagliabue formed a diversity committee to examine the league's hiring practices, and he asked Dan Rooney to chair it.

Within three months, the NFL adopted a rule requiring teams to interview at least one minority candidate whenever a head coaching position came open. Former black players who had been asking for help getting more blacks into those top jobs chose to name the requirement the "Rooney Rule."

"Rooney didn't call it this himself," Wooten said.[623] "We took that name of the Rooney Rule because of his commitment and his work to make this thing go – his diligence, openness, toughness and hardness – getting behind something that he truly believed in."

Around the same time, a group of black coaches, scouts and managers formed the Fritz Pollard Alliance, named for the league's first black coach just after the NFL formed. The group advocates for minorities in the league and works to create more opportunities for them to become leaders.

When Steelers' head coach Bill Cowher resigned three years after the league adopted the Rooney Rule, the team seemed to have his successor picked. The team also had satisfied the rule by interviewing two minority coaches, but Dan Rooney felt he still had one more interview to do. He called up Wooten, the chairman of the Fritz Pollard Alliance.

"He said to us, to me directly, 'You guys have been talking about this youngster up at Minnesota,'" Wooten recalled.[624] "'I'm gonna go up there and see him myself.'"

Rooney interviewed Mike Tomlin, who had been the Minnesota Vikings' defensive coordinator the previous season. His defense had ranked eighth in the NFL and had not allowed a 100-yard rusher the entire year.[625]

"(Rooney) came back, and he said, 'Hey, the more I talked with that young man, the more I realized I had to have him here in Pittsburgh,'" Wooten said. "That's why when you see that kind of thing, you knew you were right when you called it the Rooney Rule. That's what all of this is about."

Tomlin led the Steelers to the team's record sixth Super Bowl victory in his second season, and he took the team back to the championship game two years after that.

"Do we have mountains to climb?" Wooten said.[626] "Yes. But we're so far from where we were. When I came into this league in 1959, there wasn't a black coach anywhere. The only blacks you saw, other than the few players, were those that were sweeping up the floor, doing the laundry. That's what you saw. Now you look out across the field and not only do you see the players, but you see the coaches on the sideline, you see the game day officials."

Young people, regardless of color, need to understand that they stand on someone else's shoulders, Wooten said. Other people before them opened the doors, built the league and changed past practices that took away opportunities.

"You're not trying to drudge up the past from a point of negativity," Wooten said.[627] "You're trying to bring it up from a point of helping young people see how you must continually push forward, and what is right, and opportunities for everybody. How you have to respect everybody – women, children. Everybody has to be respected. Forget color. Just deal with the fact that this is a human being and therefore I'm gonna do what is right. That is to respect them and give them the same opportunity that everybody should enjoy."

Nunn was back at Steelers' headquarters in April 2014, two weeks before the draft, as General Manager Kevin Colbert worked with coaches and scouts to review player reports and devise strategies for who the team might take with both the 15th pick in the first round and also the 230th pick in the seventh.

Three walls of the draft room are metal and beneath the helmet logo of each NFL team, scouts hang magnets with the names and information of players that team might draft, through every round. The Steelers named the room for Bill Nunn and hung a bronze plaque by the door with his smiling face between images of the Lombardi trophy and the Steelers' logo.

Nunn sat in one of about 20 gray office chairs in the room. Most of the debate happened around a group of black conference tables across the room, but Nunn liked to sit at one of the two light-colored wooden tables closer to the door. They had come out of Art Rooney Sr.'s office at the Roosevelt Hotel, traveled to Three Rivers Stadium and then moved again to the team's practice facility on the Southside when it opened in 2001. The tables have been refinished but burn marks still show where the ashes fell from Art Jr.'s cigars and Nunn's cigarettes.

As Nunn sat there, the team still relied on his insights, even at age 89. He would listen to the scouts' reports, watch film with them and, only when they were ready, offer his own thoughts.

"He had an old-school, grassroots understanding of what we were doing and what we were looking for," Colbert said.[628]

Nunn had been a key link to the black colleges but the Steelers had come to rely on his unique ability to discover information about players and to notice an intangible desire in athletes of any color. A player's true worth does not always appear just in the statistics about running, jumping and lifting.

"He had the same ability to walk into Harvard and Ohio State or any of the big colleges in the nation," Colbert said. "He could unearth information because of his ability to talk with people."

Colbert's son Dan had gone from being a Steelers scouting intern to a college and pro scout while working with Nunn, and he was among the young men who would pick up Nunn from his house in the morning and take him home in the late afternoon.[629] The men called the drive back the "long goodbye."[630] Invariably, Nunn would start talking about Joe Louis, Josh Gibson and the Negro leagues, Lena Horne or some other person he had known across the years.

"You would get to the house and still sit there another ten to fifteen minutes," Stephen Meyer, a scouting assistant, said.[631]

Once after hearing Nunn talk so often about Roberto Clemente, the men convinced him to go with them to a small museum in Pittsburgh honoring the right fielder. The docent had been telling them about the 1960 World Series and how Clemente had stormed off after the game, upset about not being chosen the league's most valuable player. Nunn chuckled and the guide looked at him as if to say, "What? Were you there?" Nunn spoke up and told the story of how he had driven the ballplayer to the airport that night.

"He was much bigger than football because of his days with the *Courier* and his father's days with the *Courier*," Kevin Colbert said. "It was fascinating who he knew and what he had seen and done."

That April morning at the Steelers offices, the men had started analyzing players at 7:30 a.m. and they took a break around 9 a.m.[632] As they came back, Colbert stopped by Nunn's desk to chat for a moment and then headed to his place at the center of the room. He looked back a moment later, and Nunn had slumped in his chair, still holding a player report in his hand but now his glasses were askew. Colbert stopped the discussion as the scout next to Nunn nudged him and realized he needed help. They called for an ambulance and brought in the team trainers. Nunn was having a stroke.

A day or two before, Nunn had spent 40 minutes telling a reporter from the local newspaper not to bother trying to write about his life story. They had had the conversation several times but now the reporter needed information about Nunn's personal story, about how he had met Frances and how they had fallen in love. Nunn didn't want to hear any of it, mostly because he never liked being at the center of attention.

"I don't even want to be talking about all of that," he said.[633] "Everybody is born. Everybody dies. And all that stuff in between is, you know... There's so much of it that you don't even want to talk about."

Nunn died within two weeks, late on a Tuesday night. The Steelers issued statements the following day, praising Nunn for his lifetime commitment to sports but also his insistence on creating opportunities for other people.

Chairman Dan Rooney acknowledged that his friend had been an athlete, a pioneering journalist and a scout. Even in death, Nunn still was being remembered for the 1974 draft. He had an extraordinary instinct in identifying talent throughout his career, Rooney said.

"He put us ahead of so many other teams in the NFL by leading the efforts of drafting African-American football players at traditional black colleges," he said. "Very few people had a bigger impact in the history of our franchise."

Steelers head coach Mike Tomlin recalled Nunn not for his impact on opening the game to black players and coaches like himself – but for his insight, regardless of race.

"We lost a legendary man of many talents," Tomlin said. "His legacy will live on in the stories told, lessons taught and wisdom shared with those of us who remain."

The story of Nunn's death filled the front pages of Pittsburgh's two daily newspapers on Thursday morning. That night the NFL held its 79th annual draft.

Inside the Steelers' draft room with Nunn's name on the door, the scouts and coaches rearranged the furniture.

They wanted to use the old tables – the ones with the burn marks in the wood, the ones that Nunn and the team had used for the charmed draft of 1974. They left Nunn's chair open, out of respect, but also because so many felt his spirit with them as they debated what players to take.

Of the 31 players drafted by NFL teams in the first round, 26 were black. No one mentioned race as a factor in the picks.

All of the Steelers' first four picks – Ryan Shazier, a linebacker from Ohio State; Stephon Tuitt, a defensive tackle from Notre Dame; Dri Archer, a running back from Kent State; and Martavis Bryant, a wide receiver from Clemson – made the team and saw significant playing time the following season.

❖❖❖

Nunn's family waited until after the draft to bury him. His funeral took place at Grace Memorial Presbyterian Church, a yellow-brick building not far from where the *Pittsburgh Courier*'s office used to stand. The church had formed in 1868, as the first black Presbyterian congregation in the country.[634]

Down the street, a house across from a vacant lot held a banner saying, "You're in Steelers country." Another house on the block had a Steelers flag hanging from its roof porch. No one hung the signs for Nunn's funeral. Ever since the 1970s, Pittsburghers have flown the team's colors year-round, even in mid-May.

Former Steelers J.T. Thomas, Joe Greene, Mel Blount and John Stallworth sat in the overflow audience that filled the first floor of the church and spilled into the balcony.

Dan Rooney was too sick to attend the funeral, but his son Art Rooney II spoke for the family. He recalled how he and Nunn's son, Bill Nunn III, had been ball boys at Steelers training camp in Latrobe, starting in 1967 when they were in high school.

"I guess it's fair to say, being our boss was not the easiest part of his job," Rooney said to laughter.[635] "I'll leave it at that."

Even then in the summer of 1967, the boys, like everyone, felt the nation's mood shifting.

"Change was in the air at that point and we all could feel it," Rooney told the congregation. "Change was happening in our country. The Civil Rights movement was in full throat.

"Less obvious at the time, was that change was coming to the Pittsburgh Steelers. We started having players coming to camp from small southern schools, predominantly black colleges. Players like L.C. Greenwood from Arkansas AM&N, Ben McGee, Jackson State, Chuck Hinton, North Carolina College ... Mel Blount from Southern and Frank Lewis from Grambling, just to name a few."

Rooney recalled the 1974 draft and how Stallworth likely would have gone to another team in the first or second round – if anyone else had seen the player's college film.

"Obviously Bill helped build a foundation that we still stand on," Rooney said, pausing to clear his throat as he started to choke up, "and he helped provide opportunity to many, where in earlier times those opportunities didn't exist."

Bill Nunn III spoke next, and he recalled a day when he was in first grade and his father came home with two baseball gloves for their first game of catch. The son dropped the ball and then struggled to throw it back.

"It was kind of intimidating growing up under Bill Nunn Jr.," his son said.[636] "My dad was a legend in this neighborhood, in this city – a sports legend. So the first thing I heard as a young kid was, 'So you're gonna be like your dad, a great player and a sports hero?'

"I was like, 'I dunno know.' I had a feeling it might not be in the cards."

Years later when it became clear Bill Nunn III would not be an athlete, his father encouraged him to follow his own dreams. He wanted to be an actor and his parents helped him pursue that dream. Coming out of Morehouse College, an historically black school in Atlanta, Nunn landed his first major role in director Spike Lee's movie *School Daze* and then the following year famously played Radio Raheem, the feature character in Lee's *Do the Right Thing*, blaring music from a boom box until a police officer kills him, setting off a riot.[637] The role continues to resonate with viewers decades later.

"I can remember, about the time he found out I may not be an athlete like him," Nunn said at his father's funeral. "He told me he didn't want me to be like him. He wanted me to be me. And I bought that, and that freed me up a lot the rest of my life, and he stood by that."

When the service ended, a procession of about 30 cars cut through the city's eastern neighborhoods.

It followed a path from the church, through some of the Pittsburgh's wealthiest blocks and ultimately to Homewood, where Nunn grew up watching black boxers train in the backyards of the neighborhood bookies.

The pallbearers – all current or former Steelers scouts – carried the casket from the hearse to the gravesite to be lowered into the ground. Nunn's wife, Frances, stood in a black dress between their children and watched as a minister dropped flower petals on the closed casket.

Nunn was buried next to his parents and across a narrow, macadam path from *Pittsburgh Courier*'s founding publisher, Robert L. Vann.

The summer after Nunn died, the Steelers dedicated a favorite bench in his memory at training camp in Latrobe. It marked the place where he had sat in recent summers, watching practice and handing out wisdom and stories to Steelers coaches, players and scouts, friends and really anyone who stopped to talk.

Then, on conference championship weekend after the regular season ended, the NFL announced the creation of the Nunn-Wooten Scouting Fellowship.[638] The league asked every team to bring in two former players, regardless of color, to learn how to be professional scouts. Nearly 40 former players applied to enter the program in its first few months.[639]

Acknowledgements

I didn't know anything about Bill Nunn Jr. until Mark Hart, the Steelers' director of planning and development, started telling me about him over lunch one day. Mark suggested that it might make an interesting book. I'm grateful Mark had confidence in me to tell this story and that he introduced me to the idea while Nunn was still alive.

Nunn did not want to talk with me when we first started. He just didn't want the attention or to give the impression that he had done something special. Always, he directed the story toward others and I learned so much because of that. Thanks to him, I talked with people such as Earl Lloyd, Bob Wilson and L.C. Greenwood – all men who lived outsized lives and who died during the reporting on this project. When I called Lloyd's phone, he picked up right away. I introduced myself and asked if he had a moment to talk. "You better catch me while I'm hot," he answered. I'm glad I did.

Nunn ultimately started sharing his stories only when he understood my sincere interest in hearing them. I wish I had been able to hear even more before his sudden death. Fortunately, we already had spent hours together. But his passing caught me off guard (even though he was 89 years old). It took me back to the death of my grandfather, who used to sit for hours telling me stories about his life. I never fully understood my love of historical narratives until Nunn died and I realized how much I miss hearing his and my grandfather's voices.

The Nunn family lives near a blue water tower at the top of the Hill District. It's visible from my office on the North Side, from the Mt. Washington overlooks and from many unexpected places around Pittsburgh. Whenever I wondered whether I could finish this project, I would see that tower and be reminded that I had to tell Nunn's story. I waited several months after Nunn died before I reached out to his family, but when I talked with his wife and daughter, they opened up their home to me, filled in missing blanks and shared their family photos. They wanted me to get the story right. I hope this effort lives up to their expectations.

The Steelers, Nunn's other family, embraced this idea from the start. Ambassador Dan Rooney made time to talk with me from Ireland, even while he was busy visiting every county in that country. His autobiography, *Dan Rooney: My 75 years with the Pittsburgh Steelers and the NFL*, was a valuable resource and deserves a read by the team's many fans. (My dog, Angel, loved it too, chewing on it and literally dog-earing its corners). I'm grateful to the Steelers for making sources available, helping me connect with former players and providing images for this book. In particular, Burt Lauten, the team's communications coordinator, went out of his way to help.

My own family gave more than anyone for this book. The research and writing takes hours that I otherwise could be spending with them, and I'm grateful they realize how much this effort means to me. Still, I want to say for the record how they always will mean more. My wife, Tania, has believed in me from the start – and I mean really the start, from the moment we met, before I even knew I could write stories or that I wanted to tell them. My children, Noah and Claudia, are just starting their adventures and I hope reading Nunn's story helps them understand that anything is possible: Dream big, work hard and live with a full heart. My parents, George and Olive, always have supported me in whatever I wanted to do, and as I created this book, they encouraged me with their enthusiasm. Theirs is always a hard act to follow. My in-laws, Pam and Al Miller, have been like second parents and I appreciate their keen interest in this book's development.

Many friends buoyed me through the writing process, listening patiently as I shared each new discovery even as the months dragged on and they had to wonder if I ever would finish. I'm particularly indebted to Chris Cunningham, who met regularly to talk about writing; to Luis Fabregas, Jeremy Boren, Rob Rossi and Jim Wilhelm, whose enthusiasm for this project is second only to my own; to Frank Craig, Jim Cuddy and Sandy Tolliver at the Tribune-Review, for always giving me their confidence; and to the Dandy Gents, who have heard me tell Nunn's stories on runs and around campfires. I always will be grateful to Tom Doherty for seeing value in my words and giving me the chance to tell stories. Thank you to these, and many unmentioned others, who keep me going with their friendship and affection.

Finally, as I wrote this book, I was inspired by nephews' love of sports and stories. Thank you to their parents, Elizabeth and Iwan, and to them – Nikolai, Cameron, Andre and Johann.

Endnotes

INTRODUCTION

1   Stallworth, John, interview by Andrew Conte. Receiver, Pittsburgh Steelers (February 4, 2015).

2   Stallworth, John, interview by Andrew Conte. Receiver, Pittsburgh Steelers (February 4, 2015). "There weren't a whole lot of places to go," Stallworth recalled years later, looking back. "Certainly there were black athletes who had the ability to play college ball, whether that be at the highest division or some lesser division, but because there were not as many opportunities, not as many places to do that, they did not get an opportunity to go forward."

3   Stallworth, John, interview by Andrew Conte. Receiver, Pittsburgh Steelers (February 4, 2015). "I had no gauge," he said. "I had no measuring stick to say this is how I compare, this is how my motivation compares, this is how my ability to catch the football compares. The only measuring stick I had was a 40-yard dash."

CHAPTER 1

4   Nunn Jr., Bill, interview by Andrew Conte. (September 13, 2013).

5   Vondas, Jerry. "The Ward Boss Era: Retiring Politico Yearns For Days When 'The 32 Club' Ran The City." *The Pittsburgh Press*, March 26, 1982: A-17.

6   Nunn Jr., Bill, interview by Andrew Conte. (July 11, 2013).

7   Buni, Andrew. *Robert L. Vann of The Pittsburgh Courier: Politics and Black Journalism*. Pittsburgh, PA: University of Pittsburgh Press, 1974. p 262.

8   The Allegheny River valley town of Oakmont.

9   Western University of Pennsylvania is now the University of Pittsburgh.

10   *The Courant*

11   Public Broadcasting System. Biographies: Robert Lee Vann. http://www.pbs.org/blackpress/news_bios/ (accessed October 5, 2013). At Cleveland's St. James Literary Forum in 1932.

12   Roosevelt to be president. Black, Samuel. "America's Best Weekly: 100 Years of *The Pittsburgh Courier*." Western Pennsylvania History, 2010, Spring ed.: 22-29.

[13] Buni, 1974. p 142. Economists might debate the wisdom of Vann's advice in 1927, three years before the Great Depression: "Don't borrow money to spend; it is a sin. Borrow money to invest; it is good sense."

[14] Public Broadcasting System.

[15] Buni, 1974. p 145. In 1919.

[16] At 2628 Centre Avenue.

[17] Black, 2010. Black's article and exhibit included an image of the newsroom captured by *Courier* photographer Charles "Teenie" Harris called "Group in Office."

[18] Buni, 1974. p 257. Estimates of the *Courier*'s actual circulation vary widely. Buni refers to ABC audit numbers to show circulation peaking at 250,000. But he also cites the N.W. Ayer and Sons' *Directory of Newspapers and Periodicals*, which listed the 1938 circulation at 145,022 and in 1940 at 126,962. The newspaper reached its all-time peak circulation in May 1947 at 357,212 copies, Buni says, citing a research thesis by Henry LaBrie, "Robert Lee Vann and the Editorial Page of the *Pittsburgh Courier*," West Virginia University, 1970. Throughout its history, the newspaper had about 20,000 local subscribers, Buni writes, based on a 1973 interview with P.L. Prattis, the *Courier*'s executive editor, who worked at the paper in various positions from 1936 until 1965.

[19] Whitaker, John T. "Hitler Can't Win, High-Ranking Nazis Admit in Private." *The Pittsburgh Press*, June 18, 1941: 1.

[20] Field, Bryan. *This Day in Sports.* June 7, 2004. http://www.nytimes.com/packages/html/sports/year_in_sports/06.07.html (accessed October 15, 2013).

[21] "Ted Williams hits .406 in 1941". http://www.baseball-almanac.com/players/p_wilt5.shtml (accessed October 15, 2013).

[22] Scheffels, Paul. "Joe Runs Hitting Streak to 29 Straight." United Press, *The Pittsburgh Press*, June 17, 1941: 24.

[23] Smith, Chester L. "Great! Ray Praises High Fighter; Billy Promises To Win Next Time." *The Pittsburgh Press*, June 19, 1941: 22.

[24] Washington, Chester L. "Sez Ches: What Happened to the Wise Guys Who Said It Was 'Fixed?'." *The Pittsburgh Courier*, June 1941.

[25] Cuddy, Jack. "Louis 13-5 To Win, 3-2 To Kayo Conn; Big Gate Expected." *The Pittsburgh Press*, June 15, 1941: 24.

[26] United Press. "Irate Father Says He'll Punch Conn If Billy Tried to Marry Daughter." *St. Petersburg Times*, June 18, 1941: 11.

[27] "Irate Father of Girl, 18." *The Pittsburgh Press*. June 18, 1941: 1.

[28] Buni, 1974. pp 252-252. "Vann went to nearly every Louis fight along with members of his staff. Vann… usually went by train, because Vann disliked air travel; the others went by plane."

[29] Buni, 1974. p 145.

[30] O'Toole, Andrew. *Sweet William: The Life of Billy Conn*. Urbana, Illinois: University of Illinois Press, 2008. p. 201.

[31] Ross, Charles K. *Outside the Lines: African Americans and the Integration of the National Football League*. New York: New York University Press, 1999. p. 119. Born in Virginia, Lewis enrolled in the state's first college for blacks, the Virginia Normal and Collegiate Institute (now Virginia State University) but transferred to Amherst College in Massachusetts. He played five seasons of football: three at Amherst, including two as captain, and two at Harvard University while attending law school. He played center: "Although he weighed only 175 pounds, considered light for a lineman, his intelligence, quickness, and maturity gave him a substantial advantage; many considered him the best to have played the position up to that time." He was selected as an All-American in 1892 and 1893. After finishing law school, Lewis coached defense and the front line at Harvard for 12 seasons, when it posted a record of 114 wins, 15 losses and five ties. He wrote one of the first books on the game, *A Primer of College Football* (1896) and in 1904 he wrote a chapter on defense for Walter Camp's annual primer, *Spalding's How to Play Football*. President Theodore Roosevelt appointed Lewis U.S. attorney for Boston in 1903, a first for blacks. In 1910, President Taft appointed Lewis assistant attorney general, the highest executive branch office ever held by a black at that time.

[32] Ross, 1999, p. 6; Albright, Evan J. "A Slice of History." Amherst Magazine, Winter 2007.; Columbus Daily Enquirer-Sun (Columbus, Ga.). "Negro Gets High Office. One to be Named as Assistant Attorney General of United States." October 27, 1910: 1.; "Selected Profiles of Massachusetts Judges and Lawyers: William H. Lewis." http://www.masshist.org/longroad/03participation/profiles/lewis.htm (accessed October 18, 2013)

[33] Ross, 1999, pp. 10-18.; Charles Thomas, 2009. Four blacks played as professionals before the formation of the American Professional Football Association, the precursor to the NFL, in 1920: Follis, Baker, McDonald and Smith. Charles W. Follis, known as "The Black Cyclone," is credited with being the first black professional football player, signing a contract on September 15, 1904 to play for the Shelby Athletic Club's Shelby Blues of the Ohio League. Shelby is about an hour

southwest of Cleveland. Follis played two years before he was paid, and he continued playing until 1906. Follis had started playing football at Wooster High School in Ohio, where he helped start the varsity program. He was the high school team's first captain and right halfback, once helping the team score 122 points to its opponents' zero. Follis entered the College of Wooster in 1901. Through baseball, Follis met Branch Rickey, who integrated major league baseball as general manager of the Brooklyn Dodgers when he signed Jackie Robinson, who debuted in 1947. Rickey played baseball against Follis at Ohio Wesleyan University and the two played football together for the Shelby Blues. "Follis was a man of great pride," Ross writes. "Although he was the frequent target of verbal and physical abuse from white fans and opponents, even on the most trying occasions he never resorted to belligerent behavior or open hostility. Follis' attitude appears to have left a lasting impression on Rickey." Follis encountered frequent racial abuse. *The Toledo Evening News Bee* reported on November 29, 1905: "Follis, the Shelby halfback, is a Negro and the crowd got after him, advising the local players to put him out of the game. Toledo captain Jack Tattersoll stopped the game and yelled to the crowd: 'Don't call Follis a nigger. He is a gentleman and a clean player and please don't call him that.' He was applauded for his sentiment and the colored player was not molested during the remainder of the game." Another time, the Blues went to a Shelby tavern after practice, with white players inviting Follis to tag along. The tavern owner refused to serve Follis, who left on his own. Charles "Doc" Baker, halfback for the Akron Indians, was the second black pro (1906-08, 11). Henry "the Motorcycle" McDonald, a Haitian immigrant who played running back, was the third black pro. He played from 1911 to 1920 for teams including the Oxford, N.Y., Pros in 1911 and the Rochester Jeffersons in 1912. Late in his life, McDonald recalled a racial incident in which Jim Thorpe interceded on his behalf. A player on the opposing Canton Bulldogs jumped up after a play, cocked his fist and shouted, "Black is black and white is white, and where I come from they don't mix." Jim Thorpe jumped between the two players and said, "We're here to play football." McDonald recalled how "Thorpe's word was law on the field," and that the black player did not face any more problems in that game. Gideon E. Smith, who played tackle for the Canton Bulldogs in 1915, was the fourth black pro. He played only once that season. He also attended Michigan Agricultural College, which is now Michigan State University, graduating in 1916.

[34] Ross, 1999, p. 19. Thorpe had been forced to attend the Carlisle Indian School in Carlisle, Pa. as a child. While he served as league commissioner and president, from 1920 to 1921, he also played for the Canton Bulldogs.

[35] Ross, 1999, pp. 21, 25-26, 31. Note: Ross cites the interview back to *Illustrated History of the Black Athlete*. Rust, Edna and Rust, Art Jr. New York. Doubleday. 1985. 231-32. Pollard attended Brown University and led the school to the Rose Bowl on Jan. 1, 1916. He had tried to attend college and play football at several schools and either did not like them or was turned away. But when he played a high school game in New York for Lane Tech, he was spotted by John D. Rockefeller, a Brown University benefactor, who convinced him to enroll there. Pollard was the first black man to live on campus, and the Rockefellers paid his tuition. "Playing football for Brown was rough," Pollard said. "They'd call me 'nigger' from the stands. … 'Kill the nigger! Don't let him do that!' was all I heard. That was the first year and then things started working out." At the Rose Bowl, officials didn't want Pollard to play but his team and manager refused to play unless he was included. So he was allowed. At the end of the next season in 1916, Pollard was named to Walter Camp's All-America team. In the pros, Pollard co-coached the Akron Pros from 1919-21, making him the first black head coach in the APFA/NFL.

[36] Hall of Famers: Fritz Pollard. http://www.profootballhof.com/hof/member.aspx?player_id=242 (accessed November 19, 2013). In 1922, the first year of the renamed NFL, the league had five blacks: Pollard, who played for and coached the Milwaukee Badgers; Paul Leroy Robeson, also with the Badgers; Fred "Duke" Slater, a tackle for Milwaukee and Rock Island; Jay "Inky" Williams, a Hammond left end; and John Shelbourne, a Hammond fullback. That level of diversity, meek as it was, lasted through 1926 when the league had five blacks. On Nov. 5, 1926, New York Giants players refused to take the field at the Polo Grounds to play against Canton because of its black player, Sol Butler. Butler withdrew from the game and did not play. In 1927, the league had just one black: Duke Slater of the Chicago Cardinals. In 1928, it had two, Slater and Harold Bradley, a guard on the Cardinals. In 1929, Slater was alone again. In 1930, Slater played along with David Myers, a left guard for the Staten Island Stapletons. In 1931, Slater's last year, he was alone. In 1932, Joe "the Midnight Express" Lillard played for the Chicago Cardinals as a right halfback. The following year, in 1933, the startup Pittsburgh Pirates played Ray Kemp, a black standout from Pittsburgh's Duquesne University. Kemp and Lillard played against each other in the first game that season: Lillard passed for a 60-yard touchdown but the Pirates won 14-13. Kemp was either cut from the team or stopped playing after three games; he came back for the final game against the New York Giants at the Polo Grounds. After the season, Lillard and Kemp were both released. Cardinals Coach Paul Schlissler said in 1935 that he had no choice but to cut Lillard: "He was a marked man, and I don't mean that just the Southern boys took it out on him either; after a

while whole teams, Northern and Southern alike, would give Joe the works, and I'd have to take him out." The whole team was "marked," he added: "We had to let him go, for our own sake, and for his, too!"

[37] Ross, 1999, pp. 21-45. Note: Ross cites Smith, Thomas G. "Outside the Pale: The Exclusion of Blacks from the National Football League, 1934-46." *Journal of Sport History* 15, no. 3 (winter) 1988), 256. Thirteen blacks played as pros for the APFA/NFL before segregation in 1933. Pollard and Robert Wells "Bobby" Marshall, of the Rock Island Independents, were the first black players in the APFA, in 1920. Marshall, at the University of Minnesota, was the first black to play in the Big Nine (which became the Big Ten Conference). Then he played for the NFL's Minneapolis Marines in 1920, as well as other teams.

[38] Buni, 1974. p 144, citing the *Courier*, December 21, 1929. Washington graduated from Virginia Union University, where Vann had attended as an undergraduate. Writing from the cold, gray, factory-soot-polluted Pittsburgh in December 1929, he spared few adjectives in revealing his black college All-America picks: "Challenging the brilliancy of even the sun itself, five sparkling stars of Gridironia have upheld the athletic glory of the sunshine-polluted far South by winning for Dixie five places" on the *Courier*'s All-America team.

[39] "*Courier* All-Americans 90 Per Cent Pro Prospects." September 26, 1964: 22.; Roberts, Ric. "Five *Courier* Chosen Aces Among 'Greats'." *Pittsburgh Courier*, September 26, 1964: 22.; Black College Nines. "Harry 'Wu Fang' Ward (Wilberforce) — All Around Athlete." January 6, 2010. http://blackcollegenines.com/?p=680 (accessed January 22, 2013). The *Pittsburgh Courier* published its first All-America team of black college players in the December 19, 1925, edition: Ends – Duncan, of Tuskegee Institute in Alabama, and Gaiters, of West Virginia State University; tackles – Lee, of Hampton Normal and Agricultural Institute in Virginia, and Kinman, of Wiley College in Marshall, Texas; guards – Calloway, of Lincoln University in Philadelphia, and Alexander, of Hampton; center – Tadlock, of Tuskegee; backs – "Pops" Turner, of West Virginia State, "Big Ben" Stevenson, of Tuskegee, "Tick" Smith, of Howard, and Harry "Wu Fang" Ward, of Wilberforce University in Ohio. "They were born 22 years too soon," Ric Roberts wrote in the *Courier* in 1964. "The door to financial independence, the absolute 'must' for any nation, any people, any person – in our secular society – opened in 1947. Tank Younger lighted that first torch, in a quest for human dignity … and gold." Ward played as Wilberforce's fullback and kicker: "Whether it be, as reported, that he had a Chinese relative or because it was the name of one of the popular film and comic book characters of the first quarter of the twentieth century, Ward's nickname brought attention to the lore and legend he was in

the late 1920s." After college, he played baseball with the black semi-pro Cincinnati Tigers, and spent one year with the team when it joined the Negro American League before disbanding. Later, Ward worked as an umpire in the Cincinnati area, and he worked the 1945 Negro leagues East-West All-Star game, featuring Jackie Robinson and Roy Campanella.

40 Buni, 1974. pp 258-259, citing the Courier, August 8, 1936.

41 Jack Johnson. http://www.britannica.com/EBchecked/topic/305329/Jack-Johnson (accessed October 10, 2013).

42 Buni, 1974. pp 251-253.

43 Buni, 1974. pp 253-254. Citing the Courier, June 20, 1935.

44 Sitting at home in Homewood on the night of the Conn fight, Bill Jr. instinctively felt a surge of pride thinking about Louis getting ready in New York: "When Joe came along and blacks began almost dominating the fight game, naturally in every weight division, you were rooting for black guys," he later recalled.

45 Buni, 1974. p 254. Citing an interview with Bill Nunn Sr. from March 13, 1969.

46 Buni, 1974. p 256. Citing the Courier from June 25, 1938.

47 Rooney, Dan, Andrew E. Masich, and David F. Halaas. Dan Rooney: My 75 years with the Pittsburgh Steelers and the NFL". Cambridge, Massachusetts: Da Capo Press, 2007. P 20-21.

48 Beachler, Eddie. "Billy's Mother 'Awfully Proud' of Son's Fight." *The Pittsburgh Press*, June 19, 1941: 2.

49 "'Conn Clan' Shows Anguish at Knockout Blow." *The Pittsburgh Press*, June 19, 1941: 2. *The Pittsburgh Press* ran a photograph that shows the women reacting at the moment of the broadcast when Conn is knocked out. *The Pittsburgh Post-Gazette* re-ran the photo online as part of its "The Digs" column on January 23, 2013, by Steve Mellon.

50 Welsh, Regis M. "Conn Razor Sharp, Confidence May Be Biggest Menace." *The Pittsburgh Press*, June 17, 1941: 23.

51 *The Pittsburgh Press*. "54,487 Fans Make Gate of $451,776." *The Pittsburgh Press*, June 19, 1941: 22. Estimates of the boxers' take from the fight vary but *The Press* cites very specific numbers on the day after the fight, giving a total gate of $451,743 and a net take of $385,012, with Louis receiving 42½ percent and Conn, 16½ percent. Even then, the gate estimates in the headline and story differ by $33.

52 *The Pittsburgh Press* . "Pittsburgh Sportsmen's Special to New York" — advertisement. June 15, 1941: 8.

53 *The Pittsburgh Press.* Hotel Paris — advertisement. June 17, 1941: 23.

54 Welsh, Regis M. "Conn-Louis Bout Recalls Other Heavyweight Thrills." *The Pittsburgh Press*, June 15, 1941: 24.

55 O'Toole, 2008. p 201.

56 Welsh, Regis M. "Conn Razor Sharp, Confidence May Be Biggest Menace." *The Pittsburgh Press*, June 17, 1941: 23.

57 Williams, Joe. "Conn Loves to Fight But He'll Be Fighting for Love Tomorrow." *The Pittsburgh Press*, June 17, 1941: 23.

58 Kennedy, Paul F. *Billy Conn: The Pittsburgh Kid.* Bloomington, IN: AuthorHouse, 2007. p 151.

59 "The Village Smithy: Notes Copied From A Reporter's Cuff." *The Pittsburgh Press*, June 19, 1941: 22.

60 Holloway, Bessie. "From Every Hamlet They Came To See Joe Louis Win." *The Pittsburgh Courier*, June 1941.

61 Crouch, Stanley. *One Shot Harris: The Photographs of Charles 'Teenie' Harris.* New York: Harry N. Abrams, 2002.

62 Nunn Jr., Bill, interview by Andrew Conte. (July 11, 2013).

63 Buni, 1974. p 249.

64 Along Frankstown Road.

65 *The Pittsburgh Press.* "Fight Makes Forbes Field Crowd Forget Ball Game." June 19, 1941: 24.

66 Patterson, Harry. "The Main Event: When the Forbes Field crowd heard the Louis-Conn fight." *Pittsburgh Post-Gazette*, June 16, 2001: 7.

67 *Pittsburgh Sun-Telegraph.* June 19, 1941.

68 *Pittsburgh Sun Telegraph.* June 18, 1941.

69 "Hall of Famers." http://baseballhall.org/hall-famers/members/bios (accessed October 21, 2013).

70 *Pittsburgh Courier.* "Harriett Tubman Guild Chapter Plans to Hear Fight at Their Party." June 1941.

71 Pesca, Mike, and Rachel Martin. "Racial History of American Swimming Pools." National Public Radio. May 6, 2008.

72 Wolcott, Victoria W. *Race, Riots, and Roller Coasters: The Struggle Over Segregated Recreation in America*. Philadelphia: University of Pennsylvania Press, 2012. p 105.

73 Nunn Jr., Bill, interview by Andrew Conte. (November 30, 2012). "When you start talking about the South, you got to talk about the North. ...So many people have no idea about the way things were."

74 Nunn Jr., Bill, interview by Andrew Conte. (November 30, 2012). "It was frustrating for me in junior high school when I couldn't make my junior high school team for some jive white guys that couldn't play on the playground with us. … I was dominant but I couldn't play because supposedly I had an attitude." As a senior captain at Westinghouse High School, Nunn Jr. led the players in insisting that the coach play the best players – even though that meant putting three blacks in the starting lineup. After a meeting with the school principal, the coach agreed and the team won the city title with two black players leading the entire city in scoring.

75 Mullins. "Powder Puff and Powder Keg." *The Pittsburgh Press*, June 14, 1941: 6.

76 "Majority of Pittsburghers Select Conn to Win Title." *The Pittsburgh Press*, June 15, 1941.

77 Nunn Sr., William G. "Conn to Beat Joe? With What! ... Asks *Courier's* Bill Nunn." *The Pittsburgh Courier*, June 1941.

78 O'Toole, 2008. pp 187-8.

79 *The Pittsburgh Press*. "Fight Makes Forbes Field Crowd Forget Ball Game." June 19, 1941: 24.

80 Patterson, Harry. "The Main Event: When the Forbes Field crowd heard the Louis-Conn fight." *Pittsburgh Post-Gazette*, June 16, 2001: 7.

81 Various videos of the fight exist on the Internet.

82 "Couldn't Stand Prosperity — Conn Only Boxer to Win, Lose Title the Same Night." *The Pittsburgh Press*, June 19, 1941: 22.

83 "Sez Ches: What Happened to the Wise Guys Who Said It Was "Fixed?" *The Pittsburgh Courier*, June 1941.

84 Ferguson, Harry. "'Joe, I Got You,' Conn Tells Baffled Louis in Ninth — Then He Made Mistake." *United Press*, The Pittsburgh Press, June 19, 1941: 22.

85 Smith, Wendell. "Billy Conn is Game and Tough — Champion Joe Louis." *The Pittsburgh Courier*, June 19, 1941.

86   Associated Press. "Billy Conn's Mother 'Battles' Illness." *Gettysburg Times*, June 18, 1941: 3.

87   Beachler, Eddie. "Billy's Mother 'Awfully Proud' of Son's Fight." *The Pittsburgh Press*, June 19, 1941: 2.

88   Smith, Wendell. "Billy Conn is Game and Tough — Champion Joe Louis." *The Pittsburgh Courier*, June 19, 1941.

89   Ferguson, Harry. "'Joe, I Got You,' Conn Tells Baffled Louis in Ninth — Then He Made Mistake." United Press, *The Pittsburgh Press*, June 19, 1941: 22.

90   Smith, Wendell. "Billy Conn is Game and Tough — Champion Joe Louis." *The Pittsburgh Courier*, June 19, 1941.

91   Beachler, Eddie. "Billy's Mother 'Awfully Proud' of Son's Fight." *The Pittsburgh Press*, June 19, 1941: 2.

92   Rooney, Masich, & Halaas, 2007. "That was a real eye-opener for me," Rooney recalled in his autobiography. "Joe Louis was their hero because he was black and they identified with him. Joey and Clarence remained friends, but in this case raced trumped neighborhood loyalty."

93   Welsh, Regis M. "Conn's Cocksureness Costs Him Boxing's Greatest Prize." *The Pittsburgh Press*, June 19, 1941: 22.

94   United Press. "'Maybe I Had Too Much Guts,' Says Conn." *The Pittsburgh Press*, June 19, 1941: 22.

95   Beachler, Eddie. "Billy's Mother 'Awfully Proud' of Son's Fight." *The Pittsburgh Press*, June 19, 1941: 2.

96   Smith, Chester L. "Great! Ray Praises High Fighter; Billy Promises To Win Next Time." The Pittsburgh Press, June 19, 1941: 22.

97   Ferguson, Harry. "'Joe, I Got You,' Conn Tells Baffled Louis in Ninth — Then He Made Mistake." United Press, *The Pittsburgh Press*, June 19, 1941: 22.

98   Beachler, Eddie. "Billy's Mother 'Awfully Proud' of Son's Fight." *The Pittsburgh Press*, June 19, 1941: 2.

99   *Pittsburgh Post-Gazette.* "Margaret McFarland Conn dies at home." June 28, 1941.

100 *Pittsburgh Sun-Telegraph.* June 19, 1941.

101 *Pittsburgh Press.* "Billy Conn Fan Dies During Broadcast." June 19, 1941.

[102] *The Pittsburgh Press*. "Fight Makes Forbes Field Crowd Forget Ball Game." June 19, 1941: 24.

[103] Patterson, Harry. "The Main Event: When the Forbes Field crowd heard the Louis-Conn fight." *Pittsburgh Post-Gazette*, June 16, 2001: 7.

[104] *The Pittsburgh Press*. June 19, 1941: 1.

[105] O'Toole, 2008. p 214. He cited *Pittsburgh Courier*, June 21, 1941.

[106] Holloway, Bessie. "From Every Hamlet They Came To See Joe Louis Win." *The Pittsburgh Courier*, June 1941.

CHAPTER 2

[107] WWII Multimedia Timeline: December 7-8, 1941: Pearl Harbor. July 15, 2012. http://www.authentichistory.com/1939-1945/1-war/2-PH/19411207_1600c_WCAE_Pittsburgh_News_Summary.html (accessed October 30, 2013); "Day of Infamy" - December 7th, 1941. June 14, 2004. http://library.umkc.edu/spec-col/ww2/pearlharbor/ph-txt.htm#radio (accessed October 30, 2013). WCAE Pittsburgh, December 7, 1941, c. 4:00 pm EST: "Japan's game became crystal clear today. Her desire was war – war with The United States. The peace talks now appear to have been just a subterfuge, an attempt to gain time for her fleet to sail within battle range of the American bases in the Philippines. The blow struck the American public with lightning-like suddenness. Entirely unsuspecting and apathetic to the brewing war clouds, the public entered another calm weekend, stirred only to mild interest when the President last night, in a dramatic attempt to appeal to the Emperor of Japan, to keep alight the lamp of civilization. But suddenly this afternoon a grave-faced Secretary Steve Early appeared and announced that Japan has attacked Hawaii, with airplanes. … The Japanese have drawn first blood. The attack was a complete surprise. At Pearl Harbor, only minimum forces of the army and navy were on Sunday morning duty. A pall of heavy black smoke hung over Pearl Harbor. …"

[108] Randolph, A. Phillip. "Negro Blood Donors Get Navy's O.K. ... But Red Cross Says "No!" *Pittsburgh Courier*, January 24, 1942: 3.

[109] Scott, Emmett J. "Negroes To Play Creditable Part In Present War With Enemies — Scott." *Pittsburgh Courier*, December 20, 1941: 13.

[110] *Pittsburgh Courier*. "Houston Raps Navy's So-Called 'Efficiency'." December 27, 1941: 18.

[111] Rogers, J.A. "Only One Course For Race In War, "Back Our Boys." *Pittsburgh Courier*, December 27, 1941: 7.

[112] Jones, Jule B. "It's a Family Affair!" *Pittsburgh Courier*, December 13, 1941: 9.

[113] Bibb, Joseph D. "To Tokio — Berlin: It Is Our War And We Are In It To Win." *Pittsburgh Courier*, December 20, 1941: 13.

[114] *Pittsburgh Courier*. "We Are Americans, Too!" December 13, 1941: 1.

[115] Nunn Jr., Bill, interview by Andrew Conte. (November 30, 2012).

[116] "Steagles: When the Steelers and Eagles were One in the Same." September 17, 2008. http://www.behindthesteelcurtain.com/2008/9/17/616457/steagles-when-the-steelers (accessed December 12, 2013).

[117] Football and America: World War II. http://www.profootballhof.com/history/general/war/worldwar2/page2.aspx (accessed November 8, 2013); Eagles Team History. http://www.profootballhof.com/history/team.aspx?FRANCHISE_ID=24 (accessed November 8, 2013).

[118] Thompson, James G. "Should I Sacrifice To Live 'Half-American?'" *Pittsburgh Courier*, January 31, 1942: 3.

[119] *Pittsburgh Courier*. "'Double V' Originator At Camp Davis, N.C." March 13, 1943: 4.

[120] Ross, 1999. p. 63.

[121] Ross, 1999. p. 66.

[122] Ross, 1999, pp. 66-7. The Pacific Coast League was formed by Paul Schlissler, the Chicago Bears coach who had cut Joe Lillard, one of the two last blacks in the NFL in 1933. The league included teams in San Diego, Fresno, Salinas, Hollywood and Los Angeles. Strode received $100 a game, plus a percentage of the gate; Washington received $200, plus a percentage. For context, Don Hutson, an end with the NFL's Green Bay Packers made $175 a week. Tickets were printed: "The Hollywood Bears with Kenny Washington vs. …"

[123] Hill, H. (1942, January 3). "Kenny Sparks Bears To Pro Coast Title." *Pittsburgh Courier*, p. 16.

[124] Washington, K., & Hill, H. (1943, May 15). "Kenny Washington Had Many Thrills." *Pittsburgh Courier*, p. 19.

[125] *Pittsburgh Courier*. "Grid Mates Part." April 18, 1942: 16.; *Pittsburgh Courier*. "Kenny Washington in 1-A." May 6, 1944: 12.; Hill, Herman. "No Football For Kenny Washington." *Pittsburgh Courier*, September 5, 1942: 17.

[126] History of Cheyney University. http://www.cheyney.edu/about-cheyney-university/cheyney-history.cfm (accessed November 12,

2013). Cheyney University was established on February 25, 1837, through the bequest of Richard Humphreys, making it the first institution of higher learning for African-Americans. At its founding in 1837, the university was named the African Institute. The name was changed several weeks later to the Institute for Colored Youth. It was renamed Cheyney Training School for Teachers in 1914, Cheyney State Teacher's College in 1951, Cheyney State College in 1959, and Cheyney University of Pennsylvania in 1983.

[127] U.S. Department of Education. HBCUs and 2020 Goal. 2011. http://www.ed.gov/edblogs/whhbcu/ (accessed January 17, 2012).

[128] Roth, Mark. Homestead Works: Steel lives in its stories. July 30, 2006. http://www.post-gazette.com/businessnews/2006/07/30/Homestead-Works-Steel-lives-in-its-stories/stories/200607300258 (accessed November 12, 2013).

[129] Trotter, Joe William, and Jared N. Day. Race and Renaissance: African Americans in Pittsburgh Since World War II. Pittsburgh: University of Pittsburgh Press, 2010. pp 38-39.

[130] *Pittsburgh Courier*. "'Messman Hero' Identified." March 14, 1942: 1.

[131] "Cook Third Class Doris Miller, USN." http://www.history.navy.mil/faqs/faq57-4.htm (accessed December 6, 2013).

[132] Scott, Emmett J. "Gallant Exploit of Negro Sailor At Pearl Harbor Deserves Fair Policy." *Pittsburgh Courier*, January 10, 1942: 13.

[133] "NAACP Urges Navy to Lift Ban n Negroes As Tribute To Miller." *Pittsburgh Courier*, March 21, 1942: 1.

[134] Rouzeau, Edgar R. "Pressure On Navy Grows." *Pittsburgh Courier*, March 28, 1942: 1.

[135] "This Is An Example Of How The Jim-Crow Policy And The Jim-Crow Attitude Work." *Pittsburgh Courier*, July 25, 1942: 12.

[136] Pittsburgh Courier. "Freedom's Contrast." *Pittsburgh Courier*, January 1, 1944.

[137] United Press. "Cadets Maul Owls, 34-0." *Reading Eagle*, October 24, 1942: 9.

[138] Nunn, William G. "Top Command Is Responsible For Policy Which Segregates Men In Naval Services." *Pittsburgh Courier*, February 5, 1944: 5.

[139] Smith, Wendell. "Illinois Counts on 'Bronze Bullets'." *Pittsburgh Courier*, October 7, 1944: 12.

[140] *Pittsburgh Courier.* "Great Lakes Tied, 26-26, In Thriller." October 7, 1944: 12.

[141] Rhoden, William C. "When Paul Brown Smashed the Color Barrier." *The New York Times,* September 25, 1997. Mike Brown said his father had roots with black players that went beyond expedience. "When he coached at Massillon High School, he had many black players on his teams," Brown recalled. "When he coached at Ohio State, he had many black players on his team. When he coached in the service, the same thing was true."

[142] Ross, 1999. p. 73.

[143] "I never considered football players black or white, nor did I keep or cut a player just because of his color. … I didn't care about a man's color or his ancestry; I just wanted to win football games with the best possible people." Ross, 1999, p. 86. Citing Paul Brown, with Jack Clary, *PB: The Paul Brown Story,* 129.

[144] Ross, 1999. pp. 73-4.

[145] Smith, Wendell. "Time Marches On!" *Pittsburgh Courier,* January 3, 1942: 17.

[146] Minniear, Steve. *Fleet City and World War II: Camp Parks, Camp Shoemaker and Naval Hospital Shoemaker.* April 30, 2012. http://www.militarymuseum.org/FleetCity.html (accessed November 16, 2013).

[147] *Pittsburgh Courier.* "Buddy Young Playing With 'Bluejackets'." October 6, 1945; *Pittsburgh Courier.* "Buddy Young and Company Win Another." October 20, 1945: 17.

[148] *Pittsburgh Courier.* "Buddy Young Thrills 60,000 Fans." November 17, 1945: 16.

[149] "Nation Lauds Courier's 'Double V' Campaign." *Pittsburgh Courier,* March 7, 1942: 12.

[150] *Pittsburgh Courier.* ""Double V' Club News." July 4, 1942: 15.

[151] *Pittsburgh Courier.* "'Double V' Club News." July 11, 1942: 15.

[152] *Pittsburgh Courier.* "Nation-wide Support Grows For 'Double V'." March 14, 1942: 12.

[153] *Pittsburgh Courier.* "NAACP Joins Courier's 'Double Victory' Drive." May 23, 1942: 4.

[154] *Pittsburgh Courier.* "Milwaukee's Mayor Prases 'Double V'." March 21, 1942: 12.

[155] *Pittsburgh Courier.* "Unity At Home — Victory Abroad." September 11, 1943: 8. Clifton Fadiman: "I am for racial tolerance simply because I love my country and because I fear for its future if the German theory of race hatred and race superiority makes any real headway here. If that German theory does make headway, we will in effect have become Germans. We will have lost the war, no matter how decisively we beat the Germans and the Japanese. We will have lost this war and planted the seeds of another and more terrible one."

[156] *Pittsburgh Courier.* "DiMaggio, Kenny Star in Coast Game." June 16, 1943.

[157] Williams, Christopher M. "Making a Difference: Profiles in Black History — Will Robinson." http://www.wnba.com/shock/news/wrobinson_070215.html (accessed November 18, 2013).

[158] Vernon, John. "Jim Crow, Meet Lieutenant Robinson: A 1944 Court-Martial." *Prologue Magazine*, Spring 2008. Vernon's article describes Robinson's experience in great detail and includes links to original source documents such as his hand-written letters.

[159] Dixon, Randy. "Uncle Sam Ignores Negro Footballers." *Pittsburgh Courier*, September 5, 1942: 16.

[160] Football and America: World War II. http://www.profootballhof.com/history/general/war/worldwar2/page2.aspx (accessed November 8, 2013).

[161] Smith, Wendell. "Pro Football Follows Big League Pattern." *Pittsburgh Courier*, January 22, 1944: 14.

[162] Stuart, M.S. "Local Race Leaders Should Organize Now to Forestall Trouble When Negro Soldiers Return." *Pittsburgh Courier*, August 25, 1945: 6.

[163] "Unemployment is here." *Pittsburgh Courier*, August 25, 1945: 6.

[164] Coleman, Ted. "Chicago Men In Spotlight." *Pittsburgh Courier*, August 18, 1945: 17.

[165] Dr. J. Ernest Wilkins Jr. Obituary. May 4, 2011. http://www.legacy.com/obituaries/chicagotribune/obituary.aspx?n=j-ernest-wilkins&pid=150779097 (accessed November 21, 2013).

[166] Absher, A. Taylor, Moddie Daniel (1912-1976). http://www.blackpast.org/aah/taylor-moddie-d-1912-1976 (accessed November 21, 2013).

[167] Patterson, Robert P. "To The Men And Women Of Manhattan District Project." *Pittsburgh Courier*, August 18, 1945: 17.

168 Associated Press. "Klan Disbands As National Body; Claimed 5,000,000 Roll In 1920s." *The New York Times*, June 4, 1944.

169 The Legacy of Harry T. Moore. 2000. http://www.pbs.org/harrymoore/terror/k.html (accessed November 21, 2013).

170 "The Klan's Post-War Plans." *Pittsburgh Courier*, November 25, 1944: 6.

171 "The Klan's Post-War Plans." *Pittsburgh Courier*, November 25, 1944: 6.

172 Lloyd, Earl, interview by Andrew Conte. (November 25, 2013).

173 Wilson, Bob, interview by Andrew Conte. (November 25, 2013).

174 Whiteford, Mike. "Blazing a Trail to the NBA, Lloyd Grateful for Opportunities Afforded Him at State." *The Charleston Gazette*, June 21, 2003.

175 Angst, Frank. "W.Va. State Basketball Dominated in Late 1940s." *The Charleston Gazette*, July 20, 1999.

176 WVSU Athletic Court to be Named for Mark Cardwell.

177 (Whiteford, 2003)

178 Time Trail, West Virginia. March 1998. http://www.wvculture.org/history/timetrl/ttmar.html (accessed December 5, 2013).

179 Wilson, Bob, interview by Andrew Conte. (November 25, 2013). "You looked at it and you said, 'If I got a shot, we could take care of some of them,'" Wilson said. "Maybe not all of them, but we could have established a pretty good record."

CHAPTER 3

180 Cohen, Haskell. "Flickers of Sunshine: 92nd Division Has Own Laugh-Making Service." *Pittsburgh Courier*, December 23, 1944: 18.

181 Cohen, Haskell. "Atlanta GI Made the Grade: Delivering Babies Wasn't Exactly In His Line, But...." *Pittsburgh Courier*, December 9, 1944: 9.

182 Cohen, Haskell. "Joe Louis Bowed to Them: 92nd Division MPs Rank High in Intelligence and Strength." *Pittsburgh Courier*, December 16, 1944: 18.

183 Cohen, Haskell. "Nazis Try To Create Discord On Battlefield." *Pittsburgh Courier*, January 6, 1945: 4.

184 Cohen, Haskell. "Men of 92nd Win Hearts Of Italians With Kindness." *Pittsburgh Courier*, December 30, 1944: 9.

[185] Cohen, Haskell. "Joe Tells Conn To Be Careful In War Zone." *Pittsburgh Courier*, December 23, 1944: 12.

[186] Cohen, Haskell. "Spaghetti Bowl Hero: John Moody Big Star In Army Bowl Game." *Pittsburgh Courier*, January 6, 1945: 14.

[187] *Pittsburgh Courier*. "Magazine Features Story on 'Trotters'." March 10, 1945: 16.

[188] Nunn Jr., Bill, interview by Andrew Conte. (July 11, 2013). Cohen went on to work as public relations director for the National Basketball Association in 1950 after the league changed its name. He created the first NBA all-star game and structured the first league draft. Also as a contributing editor to the Parade newspaper magazine, he started its High School All-America teams for football, basketball and soccer. Goldstein, Richard. "Haskell Cohen, 86, Publicist; Created N.B.A. All-Star Game." *The New York Times*, July 3, 2000. The Pillar of Achievement: Haskell Cohen. June 28, 2000. http://www.jewishsports.net/PillarAchievementBios/HaskellCohen.htm (accessed January 11, 2014).

[189] Ross, 1999. p. 44.

[190] Ross, 1999. p. 45.

[191] Ross, 1999. p. 44.

[192] Ross, 1999. p. 45.

[193] "Hall of Famers: Bob Waterfield." http://www.profootballhof.com/hof/member.aspx?PLAYER_ID=226 (accessed January 16, 2014).

[194] *Pittsburgh Courier*. "Coast Athlete, Beauty Marry." November 7, 1942: 10.

[195] "Halley Harding." February 12, 2013. http://agatetype.typepad.com/agate_type/2013/02/halley-harding.html (accessed January 16, 2014).

[196] *Los Angeles Times*. "Herman Hill; USC's First Black Basketball Player Was Activist." October 1, 1991.

[197] *Pittsburgh Courier*. "Form 'Fair Practices' Baseball Committee." May 8, 1943: 19.

[198] Hill, Herman."Pickets Protest Ban on Negro Ball Players." *Pittsburgh Courier*, May 29, 1943: 19.

[199] *Pittsburgh Courier*. "Pro Grid Bias May Be Problem For Rams." January 19, 1946: 15.

[200] Ross, 1999. p. 78.

201 Strode, Woodrow Jr., and Pamela Strode. "Strode Road: The Extraordinary Life of Woody Strode." May 12, 2009.

202 *Pittsburgh Courier*. ""Pro Grid Champs Say They Want Buddy Young"." January 26, 1946: 14. This article calls Harding's speech "dramatic and unsuspected" but others have suggested that the moment might have been scripted.

203 "Nightlife and Restaurants in West Adams and Nearby Communities." http://www.westadams-normandie.com/lapl/Nightlife-restaurants.php (accessed January 17, 2014).

204 "Four people sitting together at a table in the Last Word Club, 1950." University of Southern California Libraries. http://digitallibrary.usc.edu/cdm/ref/collection/p15799coll83/id/40 (accessed January 17, 2014).

205 Fentress, J. Cullen. "Los Angeles '11' Interested in Young and Kenny." *Pittsburgh Courier*, February 2, 1946: 26. The meeting included Lowrence F. LaMar, Negro Press Bureau; David K. Carlisle and Halley Harding, *Los Angeles Tribune*; Leon Hardwick and Eddie Burbridge, *California Eagle*; Donald Joseph, Neighborhood News; Joe Harris, Criterion; Don Durham and Dave Washington, *Spotlight*; Herman Hill and J. Cullen Fentress, *The Pittsburgh Courier*; along with Walsh's brother-in-law, M.E. Brown, and Maxwell Stiles, the Rams' director of publicity.

206 Smith, Jay T. "Chicago's Harlem Globetrotters." http://www.wttw.com/main.taf?p=1,7,1,1,18 (accessed January 20, 2014).

207 "Our Story." http://www.harlemglobetrotters.com/our-story (accessed January 20, 2014).

208 Thornley, Stew. "Minneapolis Lakers vs. Harlem Globetrotters." 1989. http://stewthornley.net/mplslakers_trotters.html (accessed January 20, 2014).

209 O'Toole, 2008. pp. 89-91.

210 O'Toole, 2008. pp. 94-97.

211 O'Toole, 2008. pp. 98-99.

212 "NFL Franchise Nicknames." 2004-2009. http://www.nflteamhistory.com/nfl_franchise_nicknames.html (accessed January 21, 2014).

213 O'Toole, 2008. p. 120.

214 O'Toole, 2008. p. 120.

215 Historical references are unclear about whether Nunn also captained the West Virginia State football team.

216 Fentress, J. Cullen. "Rams Sign Kenny Washington." *Pittsburgh Courier*, March 30, 1946: 26.

217 Ross, 1999. p. 84. Citing Strode and Young, *Goal Dust*, 142. In his autobiography, Strode wrote: "When Kenny signed, they had to get him a roommate. He could have gotten along with the white boys on the team … But the thinking then was that he had to have a running mate, another black person to live with on the road. They asked him to select somebody. Kenny told them he wanted me."

218 Strode, Woody, and Sam Young. *Goal Dust: The warm and candid memoirs of a pioneer black athlete and actor*. Lanham, Massachusetts: Madison Books, 1990. p 142.

219 *Pittsburgh Courier*. "Tim Mara Says: Ken, Strode To Help New Grid League." June 1, 1946: 27.

220 *Pittsburgh Courier*. "Negro Stars Play In 'Dream' Game." August 31, 1946: 25.

221 *Pittsburgh Courier*. "Strode Among 53 Vets on Rams' Squad." July 13, 1946: 26.

222 *Pittsburgh Courier*. "Rams-'Skins Game May Set Record." July 5, 1947: 15.

223 *Pittsburgh Courier*. "Say Archie Harris Was Barred." August 24, 1946: 25.

224 *Pittsburgh Courier*. "N. Y. Yank Grid Team Signs Archie Harris to Join Buddy." June 14, 1947: 15.

225 Francis, Charles E. *The Tuskegee Airmen: The Men who Changed a Nation*. 4th. Boston: Branden Publishing Company, 1997. p 448.

226 Smith, Wendell. "Pro Football Stays Lily-White." *Pittsburgh Courier*, January 12, 1946: 16.

227 Ross, 1999. p. 77.

228 O'Toole, 2008. pp. 104-5.

229 O'Toole, 2008. pp. 120-122. O'Toole recreated the conversations in this section by citing a *Cleveland Plain Dealer* article and a 1970 book by Myron Cope called *The Game That Was: The Early Days of Pro Football*, published by World Publishing in Cleveland. Cope gained fame as a football announcer for the Pittsburgh Steelers with the catch phrases "Yoi" and "Double Yoi." He also inspired the creation of the Steelers' Terrible Towel.

[230] Ross, 1999. p. 86.

[231] O'Toole, 2008. p. 122.

[232] *Pittsburgh Courier*. "*Courier* All-Americans 90 Per Cent Pro Prospects." September 26, 1964: 22.

[233] Stein, Jaime. "Celebrating Black History Month". February 9, 2007. http://www.cfl.ca/article/celebrating_black_history_month (accessed January 22, 2013).

[234] Canadian Football Hall of Fame. "Herb Trawick." http://www.cfhof.ca/page/trawickherb (accessed January 22, 2013). Trawick played 12 seasons for the Alouettes, from 1946-57, including seven all-star selections. He played in four Grey Cups, winning the championship in 1949. He was inducted to the CFL Hall of Fame in 1975: "Herb Trawick was amazingly quick for a big man, and although offensive linemen usually remain fairly anonymous, he was well-known for his great speed." Montreal named a park for him: Parc Herb-Trawick. http://bit.ly/10n0wW8

[235] Strode & Young, 1990. pp. 151-152.

[236] Strode & Young, 1990. pp. 155-156. Strode went on to pursue a successful career, acting in dozens of Hollywood movies through 1985. He died in 1994.

[237] Nunn Jr., Bill, interview by Andrew Conte. (June 9, 2012).

[238] Pluto, Terry. *Tall Tales: The Glory Years of the NBA*. New York: Simon & Schuster, 1992. p 18.

[239] Smith, Wendell. "Riding The Rails With The 'Bums.'" *Pittsburgh Courier*, June 21, 1947: 14.

[240] Smith, Wendell. "'Stop Race Baiting' — Chandler." *Pittsburgh Courier*, May 10, 1947: 1.

[241] Smith, Wendell. "Fans Plead for Jackie's Autograph...." *Pittsburgh Courier*, April 19, 1947: 18. "When he finally reached the street, he was mobbed again. There seemed to be a thousand people standing directly outside that door. When he stepped out, they gave a deafening roar and surged upon him. Despite the efforts of another squadron of police, he was absorbed in a sea of slapping hands and was literally carried away. Flash bulbs were exploded with machinegun-like rapidity and the whole world seemed to be screaming in unison: 'Jackie Robinson!' He finally made his way to the car which was to take him to his hotel. But it was a hard struggle. They almost pulled his clothes off him. They pushed him all direction at the same time, trying desperately to get his autograph. They screamed and hollered

like people who had escaped a concentration camp. They stepped on his feet and some begged him to merely cast a look in their direction."

[242] Smith, Wendell. "Robinson's No Longer A 'Sideshow'." *Pittsburgh Courier*, June 28, 1947: 14.

[243] Thornley, Stew. "Minneapolis Lakers vs. Harlem Globetrotters." 1989. http://stewthornley.net/mplslakers_trotters.html (accessed January 20, 2014)

[244] Green, Ben. *Spinning the Globe*. New York: HarperCollins Publishers, 2005. p. 4.

[245] Nunn Sr., William G. ""Pride of Morris Brown College: Dedicate $250,000 Stadium in Atlanta, Ga." *Pittsburgh Courier*, October 2, 1948: 2.

Chapter 4

[246] Nunn Jr., Bill. "The First Step Is Taken." *Pittsburgh Courier*, May 6, 1950: 24.

[247] O'Connel, Jack. "Robinson's many peers follow his lead". April 13, 2007. http://mlb.mlb.com/news/article.jsp?ymd=20070412&content_id=1895202&vkey=news_mlb&fext=.jsp&c_id=mlb (accessed April 23, 2014). Three teams signed black players in 1947 – the Dodgers in the National League and the American League's Cleveland Indians, with Larry Doby, and St. Louis Browns, with Hank Thompson. No teams added a black player in 1948.

[248] Nunn Jr., Bill. "West Wins 6th Straight Over East, 3-0." *Pittsburgh Courier*, August 28, 1948: 10.

[249] Nunn Jr., Bill. "Robinson Ejected From First Major League Game." *Pittsburgh Courier*, September 4, 1948: 12.

[250] Nunn Jr., Bill. "Jackie Is Running Again for the Bums." *Pittsburgh Courier*, July 31, 1948: 8.

[251] Nunn Jr., Bill. "Campanella's Bat Explodes for Brooklyn Bums." *Pittsburgh Courier*, July 10, 1948: 10.

[252] Nunn Jr., Bill. "Robinson Ejected From First Major League Game." *Pittsburgh Courier*, September 4, 1948: 12.

[253] *Pittsburgh Courier*. "Tell What Rams' Kenny, Strode Did Last Year." February 1, 1947: 17.

[254] Strode & Young, 1990, pp. 148-149.

[255] *Pittsburgh Courier*. "Tell What Rams' Kenny, Strode Did Last Year." February 1, 1947: 17.

256 Strode & Young, 1990. p. 154.

257 Strode & Young, 1990. p. 154.

258 Strode & Young, 1990. p. 155.

259 Ross, 1999, p. 100.

260 The building originally existed as Elks Temple, Lodge No. 99.

261 *Pittsburgh Courier*. "Movie Stars To Perform At Sports Banquet." February 2, 1946: 27.

262 Smith, Wendell. "Why Is Buddy Returning to Illinois?" *Pittsburgh Courier*, July 13, 1946: 26.

263 Smith, Wendell. "Bias at the University of Illinois...." *Pittsburgh Courier*, July 20, 1946: 26.

264 Dunmore, Al. "Young on Draft List Of Dons." *Pittsburgh Courier*, January 4, 1947: 12.

265 Hill, Herman. "Rose Bowl Rose." *Pittsburgh Courier*, January 11, 1947: 14.

266 Griffin, Earl. "Photo Standalone 20." *Pittsburgh Courier*, January 11, 1947: 14.

267 Smith, Wendell. "Missouri Could Have Used Them, Too!." *Pittsburgh Courier*, June 11, 1947: 18.

268 *Pittsburgh Courier*. "Grid Game Called Off on Coast; Young May Play With L.A. Dons." February 1, 1947: 17.

269 *Pittsburgh Courier*. "Hint Buddy Young Offered $125,000." January 25, 1947: 1.

270 *Pittsburgh Courier*. "Grid Game Called Off on Coast; Young May Play With L.A. Dons." February 1, 1947: 17.

271 *Pittsburgh Courier*. "Buddy's Pay Irked Pros." February 8, 1947: 17.

272 Smith, Wendell. "Should Buddy Wait Two More Years?" *Pittsburgh Courier*, January 25, 1947: 16.

273 Cole, Haskell. "Motley, Willis, Gillom Help Cleveland Win AAC Grid Title." *Pittsburgh Courier*, December 20, 1947: 14.

274 Ross, 1999. p. 100.

275 Nunn Jr., Bill, interview by Andrew Conte. (July 11, 2013). "My father hardly ever sat down and ate dinner. I ate with my mother. My father worked at the paper every day – seven days. Even when there were days when he would play golf, he would end up back at the paper. He was not what you would call an early guy but he'd be at the paper at

10-11 o'clock at night when other people might be gone. But now he might not go to work until 10 or 10:30. So his style was a little bit different." 29:25

[276] "Linotype, The Film." http://www.linotypefilm.com/ (accessed February 18, 2014).

[277] Dan Bankhead. http://coe.k-state.edu/annex/nlbemuseum/history/players/bankheadd.html (accessed February 18, 2014).

[278] "Crossing the Color Barrier: Jackie Robinson and the Men Who Integrated Major League Baseball." http://www.la84.org/crossing-the-color-barrier-jackie-robinson-and-the-men-who-integrated-major-league-baseball/ (accessed February 18, 2014).

[279] Satchel Paige Biography. http://www.satchelpaige.com/bio2.html (accessed February 18, 2014).

[280] Smith, Wendell. "Hard to Find Negro Baseball Talent." *Pittsburgh Courier*, October 2, 1948: 10.

[281] Friday, August 13, 1948, Comiskey Park I. http://www.baseball-reference.com/boxes/CLE/CLE194808200.shtml (accessed February 18, 2014).

[282] Bibb, Joseph D. "Color Pays Off: Promoters Reap Harvest By Presenting Stellar Athletes of Color." *Pittsburgh Courier*, September 4, 1948: 19.

[283] O'Toole, 2008. p. 137. O'Toole cites *Sport* magazine, November 1948.

[284] Cole, Haskell. "Motley, Willis, Gillom Help Cleveland Win AAC Grid Title." *Pittsburgh Courier*, December 20, 1947: 14.

[285] O'Toole, 2008. O'Toole cites *Cleveland Press*, December 15, 1947.

[286] Shribman, David. "The Birth of American Football." The Princeton-Dartmouth football program, October 14, 1972: 40. Historians dispute when the first game was played. Shribman points out that where "the 'experts' disagree is in the definition of modern American football." He cites Ivy League football historian Harold Kennard who argues that the first American football game took place June 4, 1875, with Tufts University defeating Harvard University. Harvard and Yale University met for the first in the series of "The Game" that fall.

[287] Renamed Johnson C. Smith University in the early 1920s after Jane Berry Smith of Pittsburgh left an endowment for the school in honor of her husband. "Our History." http://www.jcsu.edu/about/our_university/history (accessed March 8, 2014).

[288] Rivera Jr., A.M. "That First Game Was a Thriller." *Pittsburgh Courier*, November 13, 1948: 10.

[289] "…Rah, rah, ris; Universitatis; Ha, ha, ha; Here we are; Atlas, Atlas, Atlas."

[290] Dressman, Denny. Eddie Robinson: "...he was the Martin Luther King of football." Greenwood Village, CO: ComServ Books, 2010. p. 74.

[291] Dressman, Eddie Robinson: "...he was the Martin Luther King of football", 2010. p. 75.

[292] Nicholson, Collie J. "Coach Eddie Robinson Seeks Power at Grambling." *Pittsburgh Courier*, September 18, 1948: 12.

[293] Nunn Jr., Bill, interview by Andrew Conte. (June 9, 2012).

[294] Nunn Sr., William G. "Pride of Morris Brown College: Dedicate $250,000 Stadium in Atlanta, Ga." *Pittsburgh Courier*, October 2, 1948: 2.

[295] Nunn Jr., Bill. "They're Off! College Grid Teams in First Battles of '48." *Pittsburgh Courier*, September 25, 1948: 10.

[296] Nunn Jr., Bill. "Sepia Colleges Eye Coming Gridiron Season." *Pittsburgh Courier*, September 11, 1948: 12.

[297] Nunn Jr., Bill. "Union Tops W.Va. on Field Goal." *Pittsburgh Courier*, October 2, 1948: 10.

[298] Nunn Jr., Bill. "Wilberforce Power Humbles Tennessee State 26-7." *Pittsburgh Courier*, October 30, 1948: 10.

[299] Nunn Jr., Bill. "W.Va. Spoils Va. State's Perfect Season, 18 to 2." *Pittsburgh Courier*, November 13, 1948: 11.

[300] Nunn Jr., Bill . "Thorobreds Spearheaded By Spruling." *Pittsburgh Courier*, November 27, 1948: 11.

[301] Pittsburgh Courier. "Courier All-Americans 90 Per Cent Pro Prospects." September 26, 1964: 22.

[302] Sprigle, Ray. "I Was A Negro." *Pittsburgh Post-Gazette*, August 9, 1948: 1.

[303] *Pittsburgh Courier*. "Sellout Improbable, Race Fans Admitted." October 9, 1948: 24.

[304] *Pittsburgh Courier*. "Refused to Eat: Grid Squad Licks Dining Car Jim Crow." October 23, 1948: 1.

[305] Nunn Jr., Bill, interview by Andrew Conte. (November 30, 2012).

306 *Pittsburgh Courier*. " Mother, Two Sons Sentenced to Die." February 7, 1948: 1.

307 Jones, J. Richardson. "'My Children Need Me,' Doomed Mother Cries." *Pittsburgh Courier*, February 21, 1948: 1.

308 *Pittsburgh Courier*. "New Survey Supports Courier Expose: 'U.S. Capital Seat of Bias'." December 18, 1948: 1.

309 *Pittsburgh Courier*. "The Disgrace of the District of Columbia." December 25, 1948: 16.

310 *Pittsburgh Courier*. "White House Must Act To End U.S. Army Bias." September 18, 1948: 1.

311 Schuyler, George S. "What's Good About the South?" *Pittsburgh Courier*, December 4, 1948: 14.

312 Schuyler, George S. "Neil Scott and His Plan to End Constitution Hall Bias." *Pittsburgh Courier*, December 18, 1948: 17.

313 Hill, Herman. "Kenny Washington Rings Down Glorious Grid Career on Coast." *Pittsburgh Courier*, December 18, 1948: 10.

314 Smith, Wendell. "Southern National Champions...." *Pittsburgh Courier*, November 27, 1948: 10.

315 *Pittsburgh Courier*. "The Courier Salutes." December 25, 1948: 13.

316 Smith, Wendell. "Here's Football's Dream Team — The Courier All-America!" *Pittsburgh Courier*, December 25, 1948: 11.

317 Dawson, James P. "Louis Stops Conn in Eighth Round and Retains Title." *The New York Times*, June 20, 1946: 1.

318 *The New York Times*. "Billy Conn, 75, an Ex-Champion Famed for His Fights With Louis." May 30, 1993.

319 Guggenheim, Ken. "Billy Conn takes on young store robber." *The Pittsburgh Press*, January 11, 1990: B1. Conn was not done fighting entirely. He and his wife, Mary Louise, stopped for coffee at a Uni-Mart on their way home from church in 1990. As they waited in line, a robber grabbed $80 from the cashier. Conn, at age 72, took a swing at the robber, and they ended up scuffling on the floor. "My instinct was to get help," Mrs. Conn said. "Billy's instinct was to fight."

320 *Pittsburgh Courier*. "Team Members Not Consulted On Race Issue." December 4, 1948: 10.

321 Robinson, Will. "Negro Stars Snubbed at Dinner for Sports Champs." *Pittsburgh Courier*, December 25, 1948: 10.

322 Ross, 1999. pp. 100, 120.

[323] Dressman, Eddie Robinson: "...he was the Martin Luther King of football", 2010. pp. 66-69. I relied heavily on Dressman's account for this section and also to learn about the impacts of Coach Eddie Robinson and Grambling football.

[324] Nunn Jr., Bill. "Here's The Courier's 19th Annual All-American Team." *Pittsburgh Courier*, December 24, 1949: 23.

[325] Schall, Andrew. "The Next Page / Wendell Smith: The Pittsburgh journalist who made Jackie Robinson mainstream." *Pittsburgh Post-Gazette*, June 5, 2011.

[326] Smith, Wendell. "The Baseball Writers Aren't Right...." *Pittsburgh Courier*, September 24, 1949: 22.

[327] *Pittsburgh Courier*. "Show-Down Due in Ban on Baseball Reporter." October 8, 1949: 24.

[328] Nunn Jr., Bill. "The First Step Is Taken." *Pittsburgh Courier*, May 6, 1950: 24.

CHAPTER 5

[329] Hanson, Dave. "Bright not bitter: Blow helped clean up sports." *Des Moines Tribune*, November 13, 1980.

[330] Ultang, Don, and John Robinson. "Iowa Fails, 21-0; Iowa State Wins — Bright's Jaw Broken, Drake Streak Ends, 27-14." *Des Moines Register*, October 21, 1951: Sports front page.

[331] Ultang, Don, and John Robinson. "Iowa Fails, 21-0; Iowa State Wins — Bright's Jaw Broken, Drake Streak Ends, 27-14." *Des Moines Register*, October 21, 1951: Sports front page.

[332] White, Maury, Don Ultang, and John Robinson. "Mugging of Bright made history." *Des Moines Register*, June 11, 1990.

[333] Ultang, Don, and John Robinson. "Iowa Fails, 21-0; Iowa State Wins — Bright's Jaw Broken, Drake Streak Ends, 27-14." *Des Moines Register*, October 21, 1951: Sports front page.

[334] White, Maury, and Don Ultang. "Aggies Outlast Drake 27-14." *Des Moines Register*, October 21, 1951.

[335] Drake University News Bureau. Drake University, Cowles Library, special collections.

[336] Becker, Philip. "Letter to Frank N. Gardner, president of Drake University's Athletic Council." Drake University, Cowles Library, special collections, December 4, 1951.

337 Hanson, Dave. "Bright not bitter: Blow helped clean up sports." *Des Moines Tribune*, November 13, 1980.

338 *Pittsburgh Courier*. "Pittsburgh's Maids and Matrons Post for Easter." April 23, 1949.

339 Harris, Charles "Teenie". "Still Counting 'Em." *Pittsburgh Courier*, March 12, 1949.

340 Harris, Charles "Teenie". "Women staff in Pittsburgh Courier office, including Ida Mae Mauney, Frances Bell Nunn, Myrtle Lewis, Revella Tunie (Hopson), Bea Williams, Ms. Robinson, Elizabeth Barrow, and Betty Stokes with Johnny Roventini, the Philip Morris bellhop." Carnegie Museum of Art. Teenie Harris Archive. Pittsburgh, PA.

341 *Pittsburgh Courier*. August 19, 1950.

342 Harris, Charles "Teenie". "Various photos." Carnegie Museum of Art. Teenie Harris Archive. Pittsburgh, PA.

343 *Pittsburgh Post-Gazette*. "Charles Takes Exception to Walcott Crack." July 12, 1951.

344 Pro Football Hall of Fame. *History: African-Americans in Pro Football*. http://www.profootballhof.com/history/general/african-americans.aspx (accessed January 31, 2013).

345 Pro Football Hall of Fame. *History: African-Americans in Pro Football*. http://www.profootballhof.com/history/general/african-americans.aspx (accessed January 31, 2013).

346 "History of USTA." May 25, 2008. http://www.usta.com/Archive/News/Community-Tennis/Volunteers/95424_USTA_History/ (accessed April 14, 2014). USLTA was a precursor to the USTA, before the name was shortened in 1975.

347 Ross, 1999. p. 119. Ross helpfully provides this list of firsts.

348 Nunn Jr., Bill. "The Path That Fate Takes." *Pittsburgh Courier*, January 14, 1950: 22.

349 "About the Foundation." http://chuckcooperfoundation.org/about/ (accessed April 14, 2014).

350 Sullivan, George. "The Celtics, Chuck Cooper and the Struggling N.B.A." *The New York Times*, April 27, 1980: S2. This quoted exchange has been often cited but Sullivan appears to be the first to have written it down in a news article.

351 Howell, Dave. "Six Who Paved the Way: Pistons Celebrate Black History Month."http://www.nba.com/pistons/news/bhm_sixwhopavedtheway.html (accessed April 14, 2014). Many people believe

that Nat "Sweetwater" Clifton was the first to sign an NBA contract, but he was second. Harold Hunter signed first, but never made it out of training camp. Howell provides a nice list of NBA black firsts: April 25, 1950 – Chuck Cooper drafted by Boston Celtics in second round; Earl Lloyd drafted by Washington Capitols in ninth round; Harold Hunter drafted by Washington Capitols in tenth round. April 26, 1950 – Hunter signs training camp contract. May 1950 – Nat Clifton signs with New York Knicks. October 31, 1950 – Lloyd debuts with Washington Capitols. November 1, 1950 – Cooper debuts with Boston Celtics. November 4, 1950 – Clifton debuts with New York Knicks. December 3, 1950 – Hank DeZonie signs with Tri-Cities Hawks.

[352] *Pittsburgh Courier.* "Caps Draft Two Sepia Cage Stars Into NBA." April 29, 1950: 23.

[353] Lloyd, Earl, interview by Andrew Conte. (November 25, 2013).

[354] Howell, Dave. "Six Who Paved the Way: Pistons Celebrate Black History Month." http://www.nba.com/pistons/news/bhm_sixwho pavedtheway.html (accessed April 14, 2014).

[355] Lloyd, Earl, interview by Andrew Conte. (November 25, 2013).

[356] Branton, B.B. "USF Dons - Perfect Football Season: '51 Grid Team Had 3 Hall of Famers." *The Chattanoogan*, August 25, 2011.

[357] "Uninvited: The 1951 USF Football Team." College Sports Television (CSTV), CBS. February 14, 2007.

[358] "Uninvited: The 1951 USF Football Team." College Sports Television (CSTV), CBS. February 14, 2007.

[359] Dressman, 2010. pp. 85-6.

[360] Beisler, Frank M., and C. Dennis Norred. "Preliminary Statement." Florida Attorney General, 2006. Florida Attorney General Charlie Christ in 2004 reopened the investigation of the murders of Harry and Harriette Moore. The investigators completed their work and issued this report in mid-2006. It provides rich details about the Moores' lives, their home on the night of the bombing and the investigations that followed. Investigators determined there was a "strong circumstantial basis" that four men they identified by name might have been part of an ongoing conspiracy and a Ku Klux Klan operation to bomb the Moore's home. The investigators said they strongly believed others were involved in the bombing but information could not be uncovered "primarily due to the passage of time, lost, misplaced or hidden information and people being afraid to come forward, including current members of the KKK."

361 Rich, Dave, ed. "Harry T. Moore Homesite." http://www.nbbd.com/godo/moore/ (accessed April 18, 2014).

362 Diaz, John A. "'I Know Who Did It!' Stricken Wife Tells Courier Moore Murder Planned; 'Do Something,' Shocked Nation Urges Pres. Truman." *Pittsburgh Courier*, January 5, 1952: 1.

363 Diaz, John A. "Florida Buries Her Native Son, Martyr Harry Moore: Slain State Leader Given Last Tribute At Impressive Rites." *Pittsburgh Courier*, January 12, 1952: 5.

364 Now Bethune-Cookman University.

365 Diaz, John A. "Lips Sealed?" *Pittsburgh Courier*, January 12, 1952: 1.

366 Ratcliffe, Robert M. "A Seat Is But a Seat!" *Pittsburgh Courier*, December 3, 1955: 22.

367 *Pittsburgh Courier*. "Georgia Pardon Board To Hear Ingram Appeal on Merit." January 12, 1952: 5.

368 "Permanent reintegration of pro football." http://www.profootballhof.com/story/2010/2/19/permanent-reintegration-of-pro-football/ (accessed April 23, 2014).

369 O'Connel, Jack. "Robinson's many peers follow his lead." April 13, 2007. http://mlb.mlb.com/news/article.jsp?ymd=20070412&content_id=1895202&vkey= news_mlb&fext=.jsp&c_id=mlb (accessed April 23, 2014). By 1952, integrated baseball teams included the National League's Dodgers, Giants and Braves and the American League's Indians, Browns and White Sox.

370 Nunn Jr., Bill. "Says They'll Take Over Our Jobs." *Pittsburgh Courier*, September 17, 1949: 22.

371 "1952 NFL Player Draft." http://www.databasefootball.com/draft/draftyear.htm?lg=NFL&yr=1952 (accessed April 18, 2014).

372 "Medalist Search Results: Ollie Matson (USA)." http://www.olympic.org/content/results-and-medalists/searchresultpercountry/?athletename=matson&country=&sport2=&games2=1952%2F1&event2=&mengender=true&womengender=true&mixedgender=true&goldmedal=true&silvermedal=true&bronzemedal=true&worldrecord=false&ol (accessed April 23, 2014).

373 "Hall of Famers: Ollie Matson." http://www.profootballhof.com/hof/member.aspx?PLAYER_ID=143 (accessed April 23, 2014).

[374] "Johnny Bright." Canadian Football Hall of Fame. http://www.cfhof.ca/hall-of-fame-members/players/johnny-bright/?pageId=203&tracking_page=Players (accessed March 31, 2014).

[375] Willie Thrower, who grew up in the Pittsburgh suburb of New Kensington, became the first black quarterback after reintegration when he played for the Chicago Bears behind George Blanda. Thrower often said he "felt like the Jackie Robinson of football." He was a pioneer at the quarterback position from high school, through Michigan State University, where he was the first Big Ten black quarterback, and into the NFL. Van Atta, Robert B. *Willie Thrower: The First Black QB in the NFL*. 1986.

[376] The author gratefully relied on the insights of Pittsburgh architect Mark O'Matz.

[377] Nunn Jr., Bill. "Keep a Grid Eye on Southern, Tenn., Fla., N.C.: All Expected to Field Powerhouses." *Pittsburgh Courier*, September 10, 1955: 23.

[378] Dressman, 2010. p. 83.

[379] Dressman, 2010. p. 85.

[380] "That Baton Rouge Bus Boycott of 1953 ... a recaptured past." LSU Libraries. http://www.lib.lsu.edu/special/exhibits/e-exhibits/boycott/ (accessed September 8, 2014).

[381] Dressman, 2010. p. 84.

[382] Nunn Jr., Bill. "Keep a Grid Eye on Southern, Tenn., Fla., N.C.: All Expected to Field Powerhouses." *Pittsburgh Courier*, September 10, 1955: 23.

[383] Ratcliffe, Robert M. "A Seat Is But a Seat!" *Pittsburgh Courier*, December 3, 1955: 22.

[384] Boyack, James E. "State Calls Killing Brutal." *Pittsburgh Courier*, October 1, 1955: 17.

[385] Samels, Mark. "The Murder of Emmett Till: The brutal killing that mobilized the civil rights movement." http://www.pbs.org/wgbh/amex/till/ (accessed September 11, 2014).

[386] Coleman, Theodore. "Bitter, Anguished Mourners Weep at Bier of Lynched Boy." *Pittsburgh Courier*, September 10, 1955: 1.

[387] Nunn Jr., Bill. "Change of Pace." *Pittsburgh Courier*, April 9, 1955: 23.

[388] Nunn Jr., Bill. "Tenn-U., Alcorn, B.-C., Prairie View Battered." *Pittsburgh Courier*, October 15, 1955: 23.

389 Rogers, J.A. "History Shows...." *Pittsburgh Courier*, December 3, 1955: 11.

390 *Pittsburgh Courier*. "Local Officials Ignore Race Issue in Bowl Game." December 10, 1955: A29.

391 Curry, Butch. "Grier Ready for Sugar Bowl Game." *Pittsburgh Courier*, December 31, 1955: 24. In 1941, the Sugar Bowl invited Boston College, which had a black player, but he was not allowed to play in the game because of bowl officials' segregation policy.

392 Bird, David. "Marvin Griffin, 74, Former Governor." *New York Times*, June 14, 1982.

393 Mays, Benjamin E. "My View: Bobby Grier." *Pittsburgh Courier*, December 31, 1955: A8.

394 Smith III, Charles J. "Expect 50,000 Fans to Pack Classic for FAMU-Grambling." *Pittsburgh Courier*, December 3, 1955: A26.

395 *Pittsburgh Courier*. "Orange Blossom Gets Grambling." November 26, 1955: A21.

396 Freedman, Samuel G. "Black Gridiron: Orange Blossom Classic — The first black Rose Bowl." *Miami Herald*, September 15, 2013.

397 Nunn Jr., Bill. "Orange Blossom Top Classic of Them All." *Pittsburgh Courier*, December 3, 1955: A26.

398 *Pittsburgh Courier*. "Classic Receipts Set Mark." December 24, 1955: 27.

399 Nunn Jr., Bill. "Grambling Beats Rattlers 28-21." *Pittsburgh Courier*, December 10, 1955: 28.

400 While Coach Eddie Robinson received the attention, many – including Bill Nunn Jr. – point to Grambling's first sports information director, Collie J. Nicholson, as the reason. Nicholson used his often colorful words and creative marketing strategies to bring national prominence to Grambling's football program. Doug Williams, former Grambling quarterback and coach: "When people think of Grambling, they think of (legendary former football coach) Eddie Robinson, and rightfully so. But the one who taught people about him was Collie J. He's the reason all of America knows about all that we did." "Collie J. Nicholson." Grambling Legends. http://www.gramblinglegends.net/#!legends/cnmx (accessed September 11, 2014).

401 Nunn in later life felt frustrated that so many other black college coaches, many with better records, were overlooked. Ace Mumford at Southern University in Baton Rouge won five black college champi-

onships and his teams tormented Grambling football, but he did not have Robinson's public relations team.

402 Robinson was not all flash either. W.C. Gorden, a member of the College Football Hall of Fame who won a black college national championship at Mississippi's Jackson State University, summed up Robinson's legacy in 10 words to author Denny Dressman: "To me, he was the Martin Luther King of football." (Dressman, 2010, p. 2)

403 Nunn Jr., Bill. "25th Annual Courier All-American Is Tops." *Pittsburgh Courier*, December 17, 1955: 29.

404 *Pittsburgh Courier*. "Four Courier All-Americans Picked in NFL Annual Draft." January 28, 1956: 29.

405 Curry, Butch. "Orleans to Welcome Grier." *Pittsburgh Courier*, December 10, 1955: A27.

406 *Pittsburgh Courier*. "Some Fans Are Asking: Why Wasn't Bobby Grier Given Chance Monday to Carry Ball More Often?" January 7, 1956: 1.

407 Dressman, 2010. pp. 104-5. The Rose Bowl in 1956 featured UCLA, with six black players, and Michigan State, with seven.

408 Nunn Jr., Bill. "Sports Thrills Galore During '55." *Pittsburgh Courier*, December 31, 1955: 27.

409 Ratcliffe, Robert M. "Behind the Headlines." *Pittsburgh Courier*, January 14, 1956: 14.

410 Nunn Jr., Bill. "No 'Incident' With Pitt's Grier ... But." *Pittsburgh Courier*, January 14, 1956: 29.

411 The school changed its name to Mississippi Valley State College in 1964, and later to Mississippi Valley State University.

412 Nunn Jr., Bill. "MVC and Jackson in 6-6 Stalemate." *Pittsburgh Courier*, October 6, 1956: 21.

413 Segall, Grant. "Earl Cochran helped develop Cleveland housing programs." *The Plain Dealer*, June 21, 2010.

414 Nunn Jr., Bill, interview by Andrew Conte. (November 30, 2012). Nunn related this entire story to me, with facts corroborated by Earl Cochran's obituary in *The Plain Dealer* and Nunn's own article in the *Pittsburgh Courier* about the football game.

415 Phases of the Moon: 1901 TO 2000. http://eclipse.gsfc.nasa.gov/phase/phases1901.html (accessed September 30, 2014).

[416] Roberts, Ric. "Five Tan Players Ready for Series." *Pittsburgh Courier*, October 1, 1960: 16.

[417] Nunn Jr., Bill. "Change of Pace." *Pittsburgh Courier*, October 22, 1960: 18.

[418] http://www.youtube.com/watch?v=FE1nYMg-jU4

[419] Maranis, David. *Clemente: The Passion and Grace of Baseball's Last Hero*. New York: Simon & Schuster, 2006.

[420] Clemente Jr., Roberto, interview by Andrew Conte. (May 2014). Roberto Clemente Jr.: "When he got to the states, it was happening. Segregation and racism was a big issue at that time. He had to overcome the treatment as a human being for being the color that he was and also with the language, the culture shock also. … He was actually dealing not only with the fact that the issues of racism were right in his face and affected him not being able to eat or to stay in certain places, but the fact that he needed to come up to par very quickly with the language and the culture… including having to play, compete and play baseball."

[421] Nunn Jr., Bill. "Young Outfielder Displays Class: Clemente May Bring 'Rookie of the Year' Laurels to Pirates." *Pittsburgh Courier*, June 18, 1955: 33.

[422] Maranis, 2006. Maranis cites a *Pittsburgh Courier* story that appeared on June 25, 1960.

[423] Nunn Jr., Bill. "Change of Pace." *Pittsburgh Courier*, October 22, 1960: 18.

[424] Nunn Jr., Bill. "Clemente" 'Forgotten Man of the Pirates'." *Pittsburgh Courier*, February 25, 1961: A28.

[425] Curry, Jack. "BASEBALL; Never Too Late To Make Debut In the Majors." *The New York Times*, May 13, 2000.

[426] Nunn Jr., Bill. "World Champion Pirates Live in Two Worlds at Ft. Myers Spring Camp." *Pittsburgh Courier*, March 25, 1961: A27.

[427] Nunn Jr., Bill. "Bucs End Training Camp Bias." *Pittsburgh Courier*, January 19, 1963: 1.

[428] Nunn Jr., Bill. "World Champion Pirates Live in Two Worlds at Ft. Myers Spring Camp." *Pittsburgh Courier*, March 25, 1961: A27.

[429] White, Bill. "When baseball defied segregation off the field." May 14, 2011. http://www.cnn.com/2011/OPINION/05/14/white.baseball.desegregation/ (accessed November 14, 2014).

[430] Nunn Jr., Bill, interview by Andrew Conte. (November 30, 2012).

[431] Nunn Jr., Bill. "Baker, Clemente Deny Liking Ft. Myers' Bias in Housing." *Pittsburgh Courier*, February 25, 1961: 1.

[432] Fountain, Charles. *Under the March Sun: The story of spring training.* New York: Oxford University Press, 2009. p 119.

[433] Nunn Jr., Bill. "World Champion Pirates Live in Two Worlds at Ft. Myers Spring Camp." *Pittsburgh Courier*, March 25, 1961: A27.

[434] Major League Baseball played two All-Star Games each year from 1959 to 1962.

[435] Nunn Jr., Bill. "Diamond Stars Meet Over Florida Prejudice." *Pittsburgh Courier*, August 5, 1961: A27.

[436] Smith, Wendell. "Housing Bias On Way Out in Florida." *Pittsburgh Courier*, March 3, 1962: A30.

[437] White, Bill. "When baseball defied segregation off the field." May 14, 2011. http://www.cnn.com/2011/OPINION/05/14/white.baseball.desegregation/ (accessed November 14, 2014).

[438] Nunn Jr., Bill. "Bucs End Training Camp Bias." *Pittsburgh Courier*, January 19, 1963: 1.

[439] MacCambridge, Michael. *America's Game: The epic story of how pro football captured a nation.* New York: Anchor Books, 2004. pp 118-121.

[440] MacCambridge, Michael. *America's Game: The epic story of how pro football captured a nation.* New York: Anchor Books, 2004. p. 124.

[441] *Pittsburgh Courier.* "Haynes Lured by New Loop ." December 12, 1959: 22.

[442] *Pittsburgh Courier.* "Fifty Pro Gridders Up From Tan Colleges." August 5, 1961: A32.

[443] Nunn Jr., Bill. "Annual Courier All-America Loaded With Talent." *Pittsburgh Courier*, December 22, 1962: 27.

[444] Roberts, Ric. "Marshall Felt, Still Convinced, Racism is Right." *Pittsburgh Courier*, August 26, 1961: A29.

[445] Roberts, Ric. "Marshall Felt, Still Convinced, Racism is Right." *Pittsburgh Courier*, August 26, 1961: A29.

[446] Nunn Jr. Bill. "Change of Pace." *Pittsburgh Courier*, December 31, 1960: 21.

[447] *Pittsburgh Courier.* "Povich and Cobbledick Rip Redskins' Bias!" January 7, 1961: 14.

448 *Pittsburgh Courier*. "Povich and Cobbledick Rip Redskins' Bias!" January 7, 1961: 14.

449 Ross, 1999. pp. 148-157. This section on the Redskins' racial integration draws on Ross' detailed research.

450 Pittsburgh Courier. "Govt. Does What NFL Wouldn't." April 1, 1961: A31.

451 Ross, 1999.

452 Nunn Jr. Bill. "Jackson Roars Past Tex. Southern, 12-7, To Lead Southwest." *Pittsburgh Courier*, November 18, 1961: A28.

453 Schwartz, Seth. "Black History Month: The Roy Curry Story by Seth Schwartz." 2011. http://www.takingit2thehouse.com/2012/02/black-history-month-the-roy-curry-story-by-seth-schwartz/ (accessed November 20, 2014).

454 *Pittsburgh Courier*. "Steelers Sign Jackson QB, Say He'll Get Chance." January 26, 1963: 28.

455 *Pittsburgh Courier*. "Steelers Sign Jackson QB, Say He'll Get Chance." January 26, 1963: 28.

456 Schwartz, Seth. "Black History Month: The Roy Curry Story by Seth Schwartz." 2011. http://www.takingit2thehouse.com/2012/02/black-history-month-the-roy-curry-story-by-seth-schwartz/ (accessed November 20, 2014).

457 Miller, Phil. "Gophers great Stephens makes college football's Hall of Fame." May 18, 2011. http://www.startribune.com/sports/gophers/122108904.html (accessed November 21, 2014).

458 "Sandy Stephens (2009)". Fayette County Sports Hall of Fame. 2010. http://www.fayettecountysportshalloffame.com/stephens.html (accessed November 21, 2014). A native of Uniontown, Pennsylvania, Stephens was inducted into the Fayette County Sports Hall of Fame in 2009: "Stephens was a sports hero of mythic proportions; he was a legend on the playgrounds in Uniontown."

459 *Pittsburgh Courier*. "Stephens Vows to Halt 'No Negro QB' Fiction." January 13, 1962: A29.

460 Schwartz, Seth. "Black History Month: The Roy Curry Story by Seth Schwartz." 2011. http://www.takingit2thehouse.com/2012/02/black-history-month-the-roy-curry-story-by-seth-schwartz/ (accessed November 20, 2014).

461 Nunn Jr., Bill, interview by Andrew Conte. (November 30, 2012).

[462] *Pittsburgh Courier.* "Pro Ban on Tan Quarterbacks Costly." September 11, 1965: 22.

[463] Congress of Racial Equality. "Freedom Summer: Three CORE members murdered in Mississippi." http://www.core-online.org/History/freedom_summer.htm (accessed November 24, 2014). Smith, Stephen. "*Mississippi Burning* murders resonate 50 years later." CBS News. June 20, 2014. http://www.cbsnews.com/news/mississippi-burning-murders-resonate-50-years-later/ (accessed November 24, 2014).

[464] "Teaching With Documents: The Civil Rights Act of 1964 and the Equal Employment Opportunity Commission." National Archives. http://www.archives.gov/education/lessons/civil-rights-act/ (accessed November 24, 2014).

[465] Nunn Jr., Bill. "39th *Courier* All-America Team To Be Feted December 18th." *Pittsburgh Courier*, December 12, 1964: 13.

[466] Nunn Jr., Bill. "*Courier*-Royal Crown Cola December Banquet to Honor All-Americans, National Grid Champs, Coach-Player-Lineman of the Year and Starts of NFL-AFL." *Pittsburgh Courier*, September 26, 1964: 13.

[467] Nunn Jr., Bill. "*Courier*-Royal Crown Cola December Banquet to Honor All-Americans, National Grid Champs, Coach-Player-Lineman of the Year and Starts of NFL-AFL." *Pittsburgh Courier*, September 26, 1964: 13.

[468] *Pittsburgh Courier.* "Courier All-Americans 90 Per Cent Pro Prospects." September 26, 1964: 22.

[469] *Pittsburgh Courier.* "Tan Rookies Furnish 11 of 22 NFL All-Stars; AFL Selects Six." January 2, 1965: 22.

[470] *Pittsburgh Courier.* "Tan Rookies Furnish 11 of 22 NFL All-Stars; AFL Selects Six." January 2, 1965: 22.

[471] Nunn Jr., Bill. "Change of Pace." *Pittsburgh Courier*, December 19, 1964: 23.

[472] Nunn Jr., Bill. "Change of Pace." *Pittsburgh Courier*, December 19, 1964: 23.

[473] *Pittsburgh Courier.* "*Courier* All-Americans 90 Per Cent Pro Prospects." September 26, 1964: 22.

[474] *Pittsburgh Courier.* "*Courier* All-America Fete a Huge Success." *Pittsburgh Courier*, December 26, 1964: 1.

[475] Nunn Jr., Bill. "39th *Courier* All-America Team To Be Feted December 18th." *Pittsburgh Courier*, December 12, 1964: 13. The quotes are taken from the article Nunn wrote about the All-America players in the days before the banquet.

[476] *Pittsburgh Courier*. "*Courier* All-America Fete a Huge Success." December 26, 1964: 1.

[477] *Pittsburgh Courier*. "*Courier* Selectees To Be Hailed Dec. 18." December 5, 1964: 23.

[478] *Pittsburgh Courier*. "*Courier* All-Americans 90 Per Cent Pro Prospects." September 26, 1964: 22.

[479] Smith, Wendell. "Unveiling of Galimore-Farrington Awards To Bring Back Memories of Bears' Stars." *Pittsburgh Courier*, December 19, 1964: 23.

[480] Schalk Johnson, Toki. "Toki Types." *Pittsburgh Courier*, December 26, 1964: 7.

[481] *Pittsburgh Courier*. "*Courier* All-America Fete a Huge Success." December 26, 1964: 1.

[482] *Pittsburgh Courier*. "Galaxy of Stars Ready for All-America Sports Banquet." December 19, 1964: 23.

[483] Mule, Marty. "Dave Dixon, driving force behind Superdome, dies." *The Times-Picayune*, August 8, 2010. Dave Dixon later became a key player in forming the NFL's Saints and convincing local governments to build the Superdome.

[484] Kendle, Jon. "Players boycott AFL All-Star Game." Pro Football Hall of Fame. February 18, 2010. http://www.profootballhof.com/history/2010/2/18/players-boycott-afl-all-star-game/ (accessed December 1, 2014).

[485] MacCambridge, 2004. p. 249.

[486] Smith, Wendell. "New Orleans Still Ranks as Tank Town." *Pittsburgh Courier*, January 23, 1965: 23.

[487] Guido, George. "Former local star Cookie Gilchrest battles new opponent." *Pittsburgh Tribune-Review*, May 6, 2007. A native of Brackenridge, Pa., Gilchrist led Har-Brack High School in Natrona Heights to the 1953 WPIAL championship game.

[488] Kendle, Jon. "Players boycott AFL All-Star Game." Pro Football Hall of Fame. February 18, 2010. http://www.profootballhof.com/history/2010/2/18/players-boycott-afl-all-star-game/ (accessed December 1, 2014).

489 Kendle, Jon. "Players boycott AFL All-Star Game." Pro Football Hall of Fame. February 18, 2010. http://www.profootballhof.com/history/2010/2/18/players-boycott-afl-all-star-game/ (accessed December 1, 2014).

490 Smith, Wendell. "New Orleans Still Ranks as Tank Town." *Pittsburgh Courier*, January 23, 1965: 23.

491 Smith, Wendell. "New Orleans Still Ranks as Tank Town." *Pittsburgh Courier*, January 23, 1965: 23.

492 "Change of Pace." *Pittsburgh Courier*, January 23, 1965: 23.

493 Curry, Earnest. "New Orleans Skyline." *Pittsburgh Courier*, January 23, 1965: 18.

494 Smith, Wendell. "New Orleans Still Ranks as Tank Town." *Pittsburgh Courier*, January 23, 1965: 23.

495 Curry, Ernest (Butch). "New Orleans Must Accept Blame for Negro Walkout." *Pittsburgh Courier*, January 23, 1965: 22.

496 Kendle, Jon. "Players boycott AFL All-Star Game." Pro Football Hall of Fame. February 18, 2010. http://www.profootballhof.com/history/2010/2/18/players-boycott-afl-all-star-game/ (accessed December 1, 2014). In 2010, Jon Kendle, a Pro Football Hall of Fame researcher, put the moment of the AFL boycott into historic perspective: "The boycott was clearly a milestone event that went beyond the world of sports and was more a reflection of American society at the time. It helped shine a spotlight on Congress's ability to enforce the Civil Rights Act of 1964 and proved that if America was to desegregate, the culture needed to change its mindset and adopt a more progressive view of the human race as quickly as possible."

497 Roberts, Ric. "'Steelers Will Use Any Able Quarterback' — Rooney." *Pittsburgh Courier*, December 25, 1965: 11A.

Chapter 7

498 Latterman, Mark A. "Lowell Perry." *The Coffin Corner*, 1994. "A skinny 15-year-old boy and his dad were cheering the Pittsburgh Steelers new rookie star, Lowell Perry as he roared whippet-like around the New York Giants' fabled 1956 defensive line and headed full-throttle for the open field. The boy's cheers turned to tears when Giants' star, Roosevelt Grier crunched Perry from behind and linebacker Bill Svoboda hit him from the side simultaneously, filling the stadium with a sickening 'crack,' which silenced the Steelers' faithful. I will never forget my sadness as the stretcher carried my new hero from the field. Perry's pelvis was fractured, his hip dislocated and he never played pro football again."

[499] "Heinz Hall History." 2014. https://www.pittsburghsymphony.org/pso_home/web/hh-history (accessed December 16, 2014).

[500] Rooney Jr., Art, interview by Andrew Conte. Steelers vice president (September 4, 2013).

[501] Rooney, Masich, & Halaas, 2007. p. 134.

[502] *Pittsburgh Courier.* "Record Throng Thrilled By 2nd Annual All-America Fete." January 15, 1966: 1A.

[503] Rooney, Dan, interview by Andrew Conte. Chairman, Pittsburgh Steelers; U.S. Ambassador to Ireland (May 1, 2012).

[504] Rooney, Masich, & Halaas, 2007. p. 134.

[505] Rooney, Masich, & Halaas, 2007. p. 134.

[506] Rooney, Dan, interview by Andrew Conte. Chairman, Pittsburgh Steelers; U.S. Ambassador to Ireland (May 1, 2012).

[507] The Pick-Roosevelt Hotel, Sixth Street and Penn Avenue. https://www.cardcow.com/174173/pick-roosevelt-hotel-sixth-street-penn-avenue-pittsburgh-pennsylvania/ (accessed December 16, 2014).

[508] Rooney Jr., Art, interview by Andrew Conte. Steelers vice president (September 4, 2013). Art Rooney Jr. talked frankly and with great detail about the moment he met Nunn.

[509] Nunn Jr., Bill, interview by Andrew Conte. (June 9, 2012).

[510] Rooney, Dan, interview by Andrew Conte. Chairman, Pittsburgh Steelers; U.S. Ambassador to Ireland (May 1, 2012).

[511] Draft 1968. http://www.nfl.com/draft/history/fulldraft?season=1968 (accessed December 18, 2014).

[512] Draft Steelers. http://www.nfl.com/draft/history/fulldraft?teamId=3900&type=team (accessed December 18, 2014).

[513] Nunn Jr., Bill, interview by Andrew Conte. (June 9, 2012).

[514] *New Pittsburgh Courier.* "Nunn Resigns at *Courier*; To Work for Steelers." May 9, 1970: 11. My primary sources conflict on when Nunn actually started fulltime with the Steelers. Dan Rooney's autobiography states that he approached Nunn about working for the team in late 1967 and that Nunn started work fulltime in 1969. That agrees with Nunn's narrative in June 2012 when he said he told the Steelers he needed a year to transition from the *Courier*. The newspaper ran its "Nunn Resigns" story in May 1970. Part of the confusion likely stems from this being a fluid time for Nunn and the team.

[515] Rooney, Masich, & Halaas, 2007. pp. 126-128.

516 "University of North Texas." http://www.tshaonline.org/handbook/online/articles/kcu53 (accessed December 18, 2014).

517 Rooney, Masich, & Halaas, 2007. p. 129.

518 *Pittsburgh Press.* "Greene's Asking Price a Big Figure to Tackle." January 19, 1969: 62.

519 Livingston, Pat. "Noll Red Hot at Draft Table." *Pittsburgh Press*, January 29, 1969: 62. The teams participating in BLESTO changed over the years.

520 McHugh, Roy. "Terry Gets Through His Longest Day." *Pittsburgh Press*, January 29, 1969: 62.

521 McHugh, Roy. "Terry Gets Through His Longest Day." *Pittsburgh Press*, January 29, 1969: 62.

522 Livingston, Pat. "Noll Red Hot at Draft Table." *Pittsburgh Press*, January 29, 1969: 62.

523 Martin, Clifford T. "Ark. AM&N Lions are 'Ambitious'." *Pittsburgh Courier*, September 2, 1967: 10.

524 Greenwood, L.C., interview by Andrew Conte. (July 25, 2013). I interviewed Greenwood just a month before he died. The ravages of a lifetime of football were obvious across his body. We met at Greenwood's office on Main Street in the Pittsburgh suburb of Carnegie in a storefront along a no-longer-thriving section of the street. The front windows are filled floor-to-ceiling with a copper-colored one-way glass so that when you're pulling up or walking to the front door, you have a sensation of not knowing whether you're being watched. Greenwood needed several minutes to move from his office near the back of the building to the front door, so I stood there the whole time trying not to look at my reflection in the mirrored glass because I didn't know whether anyone was watching. When he opened the door, Greenwood appeared tall and muscular, but also gray and hobbled at the knees by a violent game. His fingers bent at awkward angles, with the tips of the digits knocked out of line. He graciously talked with me for about an hour. He had written a children's book and wanted help finding a publisher. His agent believed the book might help Greenwood make one last attempt at being enshrined in the Pro Football Hall of Fame. He had been a finalist multiple times but never received enough votes.

525 Nunn Jr., Bill. "43rd All America Team Super Charged." *Pittsburgh Courier*, December 21, 1968: 14.

[526] Greenwood, L.C., interview by Andrew Conte. (July 25, 2013). This section is based entirely on Greenwood's recollection. I did not ask Nunn about the meeting before he died.

[527] *Pittsburgh Press.* "Greene's Asking Price a Big Figure to Tackle." January 19, 1969: 62.

[528] Greene, Joe, interview by Andrew Conte. Steelers player and coach (February 27, 2015).

[529] Nunn Jr., Bill, interview by Andrew Conte. (November 30, 2012).

[530] Nunn Jr., Bill, interview by Andrew Conte. (June 9, 2012).

[531] Nunn Jr., Bill, interview by Andrew Conte. (June 9, 2012).

[532] Roberts, Ric. "Tap McGee, Hinton, Greene, Greenwood." *New Pittsburgh Courier*, September 20, 1969: 28.

[533] "Detroit Lions 13 at Pittsburgh Steelers 16." http://www.pro-football-reference.com/boxscores/196909210pit.htm (accessed December 30, 2014).

[534] Livington, Pat. "Steelers Champs ... At Losing." *Pittsburgh Press*, December 22, 1969: 34.

[535] Abrams, Al. "Honest to Goodness — Steelers Win...." *Pittsburgh Post-Gazette*, January 10, 1970: 6.

[536] *New Pittsburgh Courier.* "All American Fete Thrills Pittsburghers." January 17, 1970: 1.

[537] Roberts, Ric. "Steelers Grab Four Black College Heroes In Draft." *New Pittsburgh Courier*, February 7, 1970: 24.

[538] Sell, Jack. "'Scout' Noll: Terry Mobile in Mobile." *Pittsburgh Post-Gazette*, January 28, 1970.

[539] Nunn Jr., Bill. "All-America Teams Tap 22 'Sparklers'." *New Pittsburgh Courier*, December 20, 1969: 13.

[540] *New Pittsburgh Courier.* "22 Grid Stars, Muhammad Thrill 600 at All-American." January 23, 1971: 15.

[541] Nunn Jr., Bill. "Change of Pace." *New Pittsburgh Courier*, January 30, 1971: 16.

[542] Peters, Jess. "Courier-RC Cola Black All-Americans Honored at Annual Banquet January 8." *New Pittsburgh Courier*, January 2, 1971: 1.

[543] Lewis, Frank, interview by Andrew Conte. (December 10, 2014).

[544] Wulf, Steve. "'All hell broke loose'." *ESPN The Magazine*, January 20, 2014.

545 Lewis, Frank, interview by Andrew Conte. (December 10, 2014).

546 Rooney, Masich, & Halaas, 2007. p. 138.

547 Nunn Jr., Bill, interview by Andrew Conte. (December 5, 2012).

548 Kolb, Jon, interview by Andrew Conte. Retired Steelers left tackle (January 9, 2015).

549 Their shared purpose carried past their playing days too. Kolb worked as a coach for the Steelers after he finished playing, but lost his job with the other assistants when Noll retired in 1991. Joe Greene had no trouble finding another coaching job right away. But Kolb said he will forever remember that Greene called him every day while he was unemployed, to keep up Kolb's spirits and to see who he could call to help Kolb make a connection. "I will never forget Joe Greene calling me," Kolb said.

550 Zinser, Lynn. "Crimson Tide Pioneer Is Often Overlooked." *The New York Times*, July 18, 2004.

551 Nunn Jr., Bill, interview by Andrew Conte. (November 30, 2012).

552 Mitchell, John, interview by Andrew Conte. Steelers, Assistant Head Coach/Defensive Line (March 2, 2015).

553 Amdur, Neil. "Black End Fits In Smoothly at Alabama." *The New York Times*, December 27, 1971: 37.

554 Rooney, Dan, interview by Andrew Conte. Chairman, Pittsburgh Steelers; U.S. Ambassador to Ireland (May 1, 2012).

555 Rooney, Masich, & Halaas, 2007. p. 139.

556 Wexell, Jim. *Tales From Behind the Steel Curtain: The Best Stories of the '79 Steelers*. New York: Sports Publishing, 2004. "That name up there," Nunn said pointing to the draft board where Gilliam still had not been taken by anyone. "That's what's wrong with football."

557 Rooney, Dan, interview by Andrew Conte. Chairman, Pittsburgh Steelers; U.S. Ambassador to Ireland (May 1, 2012).

558 *New Pittsburgh Courier*. "All-Americans, 22 Strong, Thrill Capacity Crowd at Courier Banquet." January 22, 1972: 9.

559 Peters, Jess. "Steelers Draft *Courier* All-America Quarterback." *New Pittsburgh Courier*, February 12, 1972: 15.

560 *Pittsburgh Press*. "Lamonica Gets a Delayed Call From Madden." September 18, 1972: 26.

561 Musick, Phil. "Could '72 Be Year of the Steelers?" *Pittsburgh Press*, September 18, 1972: 25.

562 Immaculate Reception original broadcast, 2012. http://youtu.be/GMuUBZ_DAeM.

563 "The Immaculate Reception." Pro Football Hall of Fame. http://www.profootballhof.com/history/release.aspx?release_id=762 (accessed January 19, 2015).

564 Robinson, Alan. "'Greatest play' turns 40 today." December 23, 2012. http://www.steelers.com/news/article-1/Greatest-play-turns-40-today/1660205f-4849-4bbe-8fe4-357bf1870d5b (accessed January 19, 2015).

CHAPTER 8

565 Stallworth, John, interview by Andrew Conte. Receiver, Pittsburgh Steelers (February 4, 2015).

566 Stallworth, John, interview by Andrew Conte. Receiver, Pittsburgh Steelers (February 4, 2015). "Nunn never said anything to me. He didn't say, 'Oh, that's a much better time. That's great.' He didn't say anything. … I didn't have a whole lot of different feeling about it before and after. I asked the question, 'Was my time better?' He said, 'Well, it was okay.'"

567 *Pittsburgh Courier*. "42nd All-America Team…A Coach's Dream." December 23, 1967: 10.

568 Rooney Jr., Art, interview by Andrew Conte. Steelers vice president (September 4, 2013).

569 Nunn Jr., Bill. "1973 *Courier* All-Americans." *New Pittsburgh Courier*, December 22, 1973: 27.

570 Rooney Jr., Art, interview by Andrew Conte. Steelers vice president (September 4, 2013).

571 Musick, Phil. "Reward for a Long Wait: USC's Lynn Swann." *Pittsburgh Press*, January 30, 1974: 50. "In a year which has produced a skinny crop of collegians, it would probably be the only meaningful one."

572 Musick, Phil. "Reward for a Long Wait: USC's Lynn Swann." *Pittsburgh Press*, January 30, 1974: 50.

573 Rooney, Masich, & Halaas, 2007. p. 151.

574 Musick, Phil. "Reward for a Long Wait: USC's Lynn Swann." *Pittsburgh Press*, January 30, 1974: 50.

575 Rooney, Masich, & Halaas, 2007. p. 152.

[576] Rooney Jr., Art, interview by Andrew Conte. Steelers vice president (September 4, 2013).

[577] Stallworth, John, interview by Andrew Conte. Receiver, Pittsburgh Steelers (February 4, 2015). "I had kind of mixed emotions. I was happy to be drafted. And they let it be known that they took a receiver ahead of me. So I'm thinking, 'Well, I wasn't even their number one choice.' And fourth round? I was kind of hoping for more than the fourth round. But still I had been drafted and I was being given the opportunity to go and to play professional football, and I was excited about that."

[578] Nunn Jr., Bill. "1973 Courier All-Americans." *New Pittsburgh Courier*, December 22, 1973: 27.

[579] Rooney, Masich, & Halaas, 2007. pp. 153-155.

[580] Stallworth, John, interview by Andrew Conte. Receiver, Pittsburgh Steelers (February 4, 2015).

[581] Nunn Jr., Bill. "Change of Pace." *Pittsburgh Courier*, August 3, 1974: 24.

[582] Stallworth, John, interview by Andrew Conte. Receiver, Pittsburgh Steelers (February 4, 2015).

[583] Stallworth, John, interview by Andrew Conte. Receiver, Pittsburgh Steelers (February 4, 2015).

[584] Carter, Ulish. "Gilliam Smashes Records in Denver Tie." *New Pittsburgh Courier*, September 28, 1974: 1.

[585] Nunn Jr. Bill. "Change of Pace." *Pittsburgh Courier*, September 28, 1974: 27.

[586] Carter, Ulish. "Gilliam Under Pressure Every Week." *New Pittsburgh Courier*, October 19, 1974: 25.

[587] *New Pittsburgh Courier*. "Voice of The *Courier*." November 2, 1974: 7.

[588] Nunn Jr. Bill. "Change of Pace." *New Pittsburgh Courier*, October 19, 1974: 26.

[589] Nunn Jr., Bill. "Change of Pace." *New Pittsburgh Courier*, November 2, 1974: 26.

[590] Nunn Jr., Bill. "Change of Pace." *New Pittsburgh Courier*, November 30, 1974: 26.

[591] Rooney, Masich, & Halaas, 2007. p. 157.

[592] Rooney, Masich, & Halaas, 2007. p. 157.

593 Labriola, Bob. "Pittsburgh's going to the Super Bowl." April 3, 2011. http://www.steelers.com/news/article-1/Pittsburghs-going-to-the-Super-Bowl/06d783e2-da00-40ea-a9db-26828b85b554 (accessed February 11, 2015).

594 Nunn Jr. Bill. "The *New Pittsburgh Courier*'s All-America Football Team." *New Pittsburgh Courier*, December 28, 1974: 1.

595 Carter, Ulish. "Payton, Johnson, Casem Honored at *Courier* All-American Banquet." *New Pittsburgh Courier*, January 18, 1975: 22.

596 Carter, Ulish. "Annual All-American Banquet." *New Pittsburgh Courier*, January 25, 1975: 21.

597 Varley, Teresa. "JT Thomas: 'That game was won in the tunnel.'" Steelers.com. November 25, 2014. http://www.steelers.com/news/article-1/JT-Thomas-That-game-was-won-in-the-tunnel/19ff7966-aa39-4b1b-8011-821e991f6cac (accessed February 17, 2015).

598 *Pittsburgh Press*. "Hero Harris Shares Credit." January 13, 1975: 28.

599 Stuart, M.S. "Local Race Leaders Should Organize Now to Forestall Trouble When Negro Soldiers Return." *Pittsburgh Courier*, August 25, 1945: 6.

600 Musick, Phil. "Steelers Have What It Takes, On Cloud IX After Super Win." *Pittsburgh Press*, January 13, 1975: 27.

601 Roberts, Ric. "Five Courier Chosen Aces Among 'Greats'." *Pittsburgh Courier*, September 26, 1964: 22.

602 Stellino, Vito. "Steelers Turn Raiders Greene With Envy." *Pittsburgh Post-Gazette*, January 5, 1976: 12.

603 Rand, Jonathan. *Run it! and Let's Get the Hell Out of Here!: The 100 Best Plays in Pro Football History.* Guilford, CT: The Globe Pequot Press, 2007.

604 Nunn Jr., Bill, interview by Andrew Conte. (June 9, 2012).

605 Nunn Jr. Bill. "Taylor First Black Head?" *New Pittsburgh Courier*, August 14, 1976: 22.

606 Wooten, John, interview by Andrew Conte. NFL player, scout (February 26, 2015).

607 Nunn Jr. Bill. "Change of Pace." *New Pittsburgh Courier*, January 29, 1977: 23.

608 Nunn Jr. Bill. "1978 Black All-Americans." *New Pittsburgh Courier*, December 30, 1978: 1.

[609] Jefferies, Eddie. "Super Bowl Title, Black All Americans Return to Pittsburgh." *New Pittsburgh Courier*, January 27, 1979: 1.

[610] "Super Bowl XIV Rewind." Steelers.com. July 13, 2014. http://www.steelers.com/news/article-1/Super-Bowl-XIV-Rewind/d54350a4-4797-4897-9c82-8e8a2badec5a (accessed February 24, 2015).

[611] Stallworth, John, interview by Andrew Conte. Receiver, Pittsburgh Steelers (February 4, 2015).

[612] Nunn Jr., Bill, interview by Andrew Conte. (November 30, 2012).

[613] Mihoces, Gary. "Spoils Worth the Trip." *The Victoria Advocate*, January 22, 1980: 3B.

[614] Stallworth, John, interview by Andrew Conte. Receiver, Pittsburgh Steelers (February 4, 2015).

[615] Greene, Joe, interview by Andrew Conte. Steelers player and coach (February 27, 2015).

Epilogue

[616] "Players / Coaches with the Most Super Bowl Rings." StatisticBrain.com. http://www.statisticbrain.com/players-coaches-with-the-most-super-bowl-rings/ (accessed March 2, 2015). Dan Rooney, Art Rooney Jr., Chuck Noll, Bill Nunn Jr. and Joe Greene (four as a player, two as staff)

[617] Greene, Joe, interview by Andrew Conte. Steelers player and coach (February 27, 2015).

[618] "History." *New Pittsburgh Courier*. http://newpittsburghcourieronline.com/history/ (accessed March 2, 2015).

[619] Jefferies, Eddie. "*Courier*'s 55th Annual All-America Team." *New Pittsburgh Courier*, February 9, 1980: 9.

[620] Rooney, Halaas, & Masich, 2007. p. 245.

[621] "NFL names minority coaching program after Bill Walsh." January 29, 2009. http://49ers.pressdemocrat.com/nfl_names_minority_coaching_program_after_bill_walsh/ (accessed March 1, 2015).

[622] "Fritz Pollard Alliance Proudly Presents Its 12th Annual Meeting/Awards Reception." Indianapolis, 2015.

[623] Wooten, John, interview by Andrew Conte. NFL player, scout (February 26, 2015).

[624] Wooten, John, interview by Andrew Conte. NFL player, scout (February 26, 2015).

[625] "Mike Tomlin Head Coach." Steelers.com. http://www.steelers.com/team/coaches/mike-tomlin/4bf07eef-17d9-4b67-b634-c20700be0670 (accessed March 2, 2015).

[626] Wooten, John, interview by Andrew Conte. NFL player, scout (February 26, 2015).

[627] Wooten, John, interview by Andrew Conte. NFL player, scout (February 26, 2015).

[628] Colbert, Kevin, interview by Andrew Conte. General Manager, Steelers (February 26, 2015).

[629] Colbert, Kevin, interview by Andrew Conte. General Manager, Steelers (February 26, 2015).

[630] Gorscak, Mark, interview by Andrew Conte. College Scout, Steelers (February 26, 2015).

[631] Meyer, Stephen, interview by Andrew Conte. Scouting Intern, Steelers (February 26, 2015).

[632] Colbert, Kevin, interview by Andrew Conte. General Manager, Steelers (February 26, 2015).

[633] Nunn Jr., Bill, interview by Andrew Conte. (April 9, 2014).

[634] "Grace Memorial Presbyterian Church." http://www.visitpittsburgh.com/listings/Grace-Memorial-Presbyterian-Church/7131/ (accessed February 28, 2015).

[635] Rooney II, Art. Steelers president (May 14, 2014).

[636] Nunn III, Bill. (May 14, 2014).

[637] "Bill Nunn Biography." IMDb.com. http://www.imdb.com/name/nm0638056/bio?ref_=nm_ov_bio_sm (accessed March 3, 2015).

[638] "Nunn-Wooten Scouting Fellowship." NFL Player Engagement. January 18, 2015. https://www.nflplayerengagement.com/next/articles/nunn-wooten-scouting-fellowship/ (accessed March 3, 2015).

[639] Birk, Matt, interview by Andrew Conte. National Football League, Director of Football Development (March 5, 2015).